From...  S0-BFC-556

PORTABLE

Virgin Islands

3rd Edition

by Darwin Porter & Danforth Prince

Here's what critics say about Frommer's:

"Amazingly easy to use. Very portable, very complete."

—*Booklist*

"Detailed, accurate, and easy-to-read information for all price ranges."

—*Glamour Magazine*

WILEY

Wiley Publishing, Inc.

Published by:

WILEY PUBLISHING, INC.

111 River St.
Hoboken, NJ 07030-5774

ISBN-13: 978-0-7645-9664-3
ISBN-10: 0-7645-9664-0

Editor: Kathleen Warnock
Production Editor: Melissa S. Bennett
Photo Editor: Richard Fox
Cartographer: Roberta Stockwell
Production by Wiley Indianapolis Composition Services

For information on our other products and services or to obtain technical
support, please contact our Customer Care Department within the U.S. at
800/762-2974, outside the U.S. at 317/572-3993 or fax 317/572-4002.

Wiley also publishes its books in a variety of electronic formats. Some content that appears in print may not be available in electronic formats.

Manufactured in the United States of America

5   4   3   2   1

Contents

List of Maps

ABOUT THE AUTHOR

As a team of veteran travel writers, **Darwin Porter** and **Danforth Prince** have produced numerous titles for Frommer's, including best-selling guides to Italy, France, the Caribbean, England, and Germany. Porter, a former bureau chief of *The Miami Herald,* is also a Hollywood biographer, his most recent releases entitled *Katharine the Great,* the latter a close-up of the private life of the late Katharine Hepburn, and *Howard Hughes: Hell's Angel.* Prince was formerly employed by the Paris bureau of the *New York Times,* and is today the president of Blood Moon Productions and other media-related firms.

AN INVITATION TO THE READER

In researching this book, we discovered many wonderful places—hotels, restaurants, shops, and more. We're sure you'll find others. Please tell us about them, so we can share the information with your fellow travelers in upcoming editions. If you were disappointed with a recommendation, we'd love to know that, too. Please write to:

Frommer's Portable Virgin Islands, 3rd Edition
Wiley Publishing, Inc. • 111 River St. • Hoboken, NJ 07030-5774

AN ADDITIONAL NOTE

Please be advised that travel information is subject to change at any time—and this is especially true of prices. We therefore suggest that you write or call ahead for confirmation when making your travel plans. The authors, editors, and publisher cannot be held responsible for the experiences of readers while traveling. Your safety is important to us, however, so we encourage you to stay alert and be aware of your surroundings. Keep a close eye on cameras, purses, and wallets, all favorite targets of thieves and pickpockets.

FROMMER'S STAR RATINGS, ICONS & ABBREVIATIONS

Every hotel, restaurant, and attraction listing in this guide has been ranked for quality, value, service, amenities, and special features using a **star-rating system.** In country, state, and regional guides, we also rate towns and regions to help you narrow down your choices and budget your time accordingly. Hotels and restaurants are rated on a scale of zero (recommended) to three stars (exceptional). Attractions, shopping, nightlife, towns, and regions are rated according to the following scale: zero stars (recommended), one star (highly recommended), two stars (very highly recommended), and three stars (must-see).

In addition to the star-rating system, we also use **seven feature icons** that point you to the great deals, in-the-know advice, and unique experiences that separate travelers from tourists. Throughout the book, look for:

Finds	Special finds—those places only insiders know about
Fun Fact	Fun facts—details that make travelers more informed and their trips more fun
Kids	Best bets for kids and advice for the whole family
Moments	Special moments—those experiences that memories are made of
Overrated	Places or experiences not worth your time or money
Tips	Insider tips—great ways to save time and money
Value	Great values—where to get the best deals

The following **abbreviations** are used for credit cards:

AE	American Express	DISC	Discover	V	Visa
DC	Diners Club	MC	MasterCard		

FROMMERS.COM

Now that you have the guidebook to a great trip, visit our website at **www.frommers.com** for travel information on more than 3,000 destinations. With features updated regularly, we give you instant access to the most current trip-planning information available. At Frommers.com, you'll also find the best prices on airfares, accommodations, and car rentals—and you can even book travel online through our travel booking partners. At Frommers.com, you'll also find the following:

- Online updates to our most popular guidebooks
- Vacation sweepstakes and contest giveaways
- Newsletter highlighting the hottest travel trends
- Online travel message boards with featured travel discussions

Planning Your Trip to the Virgin Islands

A little advance planning can go a long way. In this chapter, we give you all the information you need to know before you go, including how to get the lowest rates on flights, lodging, and car rentals. We also help you decide which island(s) to visit and when to go.

1 Choosing the Perfect Island

Peering at the tiny Virgin Islands chain on a world map, you may find it difficult to distinguish the different islands. They vary widely, however, in looks and personality, and so will your vacation, depending on which island or islands you choose. It's important to plan ahead. For example, if you're an avid golfer, you won't want spend a week on a remote British Virgin Island with only a rinky-dink 9-hole course or no course at all. But that same island might be perfect for a young couple contemplating a romantic honeymoon. By providing detailed information about the character of each island in both the U.S. Virgin Islands and the British Virgin Islands, we hope to guide you to your own idea of paradise.

U.S. VS. BRITISH VIRGIN ISLANDS

American and British cultures have left different imprints on the Virgin Islands. The **U.S. Virgin Islands,** except for St. John, offer much of the commercial hustle-and-bustle of the mainland, including supermarkets and fast-food chains. In contrast, the British islands, to the east, are sleepier. Except for a few deluxe hotels (mostly on Virgin Gorda), they recall the way the Caribbean was before the advent of high-rise condos, McDonald's, and fleets of cruise ships.

If you want shopping, a wide selection of restaurants and hotels, and nightlife, head to the U.S. Virgin Islands, particularly **St. Thomas** and **St. Croix.** With a little research and effort, you can

The Virgin Islands

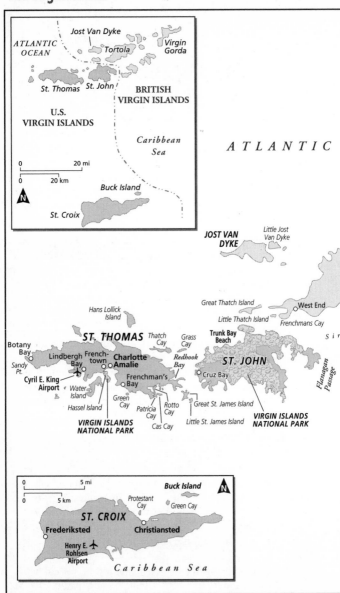

ATLANTIC OCEAN

Jost Van Dyke

Tortola

Virgin Gorda

St. Thomas   St. John

BRITISH VIRGIN ISLANDS

U.S. VIRGIN ISLANDS

Caribbean Sea

0   20 mi
0   20 km

N

Buck Island

St. Croix

ATLANTIC

JOST VAN DYKE

Little Jost Van Dyke

Great Thatch Island

Little Thatch Island

West End

Frenchmans Cay

S i r

Hans Lollick Island

ST. THOMAS

Thatch Cay

Grass Cay

Trunk Bay Beach

Botany Bay

Lindbergh Bay

French-town

Charlotte Amalie

Redhook Bay

ST. JOHN

Sandy Pt.

Cyril E. King Airport

Frenchman's Bay

Cruz Bay

Flanagan Passage

Water Island

Green Cay

Hassel Island

Patricia Cay

Rotto Cay

Great St. James Island

VIRGIN ISLANDS NATIONAL PARK

Cas Cay

Little St. James Island

VIRGIN ISLANDS NATIONAL PARK

0   5 mi
0   5 km

Buck Island

N

Protestant Cay

Green Cay

ST. CROIX

Frederiksted

Christiansted

Henry E. Rohlsen Airport

Caribbean Sea

2

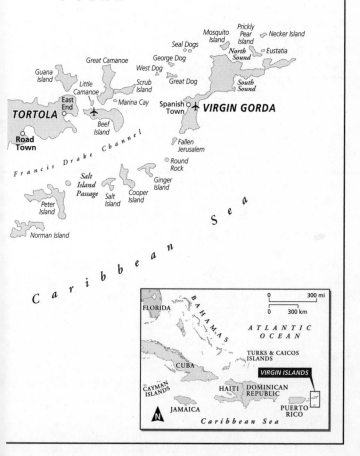

0 — 5 mi
0 — 5 km

■ British Virgin Islands
■ U.S. Virgin Islands

OCEAN

ANEGADA

The Settlement

Prickly
Pear
Island

Mosquito
Island

Necker Island

Seal Dogs

Eustatia

George Dog

*North
Sound*

West Dog

Great Camanoe

Scrub
Island

Great Dog

*South
Sound*

Guana
Island

*Little
Camanoe*

Marina Cay

East
End

Spanish
Town

VIRGIN GORDA

TORTOLA

*Beef
Island*

**Road
Town**

*Fallen
Jerusalem*

F r a n c i s   D r a k e   C h a n n e l

*Round
Rock*

*Salt
Island
Passage*

*Ginger
Island*

*Salt
Island*

*Cooper
Island*

*Peter
Island*

C a r i b b e a n   S e a

Norman Island

0 — 300 mi
0 — 300 km

FLORIDA

B A H A M A S

*ATLANTIC
OCEAN*

TURKS & CAICOS
ISLANDS

CUBA

CAYMAN
ISLANDS

VIRGIN ISLANDS

HAITI

DOMINICAN
REPUBLIC

JAMAICA

PUERTO
RICO

Caribbean Sea

also find peace and quiet on these two islands, most often at outlying resorts. But overall, among the U.S. Virgin Islands, only St. John matches the British Virgins for tranquillity. **St. John** is a rugged mixture of bumpy dirt roads, scattered inhabitants, and a handful of stores and services. It's protected by the U.S. Forest Service, and remains the least developed of the U.S. islands.

The **British Virgin Islands** seem to be lingering in the past, although change is in the air. **Tortola** is the most populated isle, but its shopping, nightlife, and dining are still limited. It's more of a spot for boaters of all stripes—it's considered the cruising capital of the Caribbean. To the east, **Virgin Gorda** claims most of the B.V.I.'s deluxe hotels. There are also attractive accommodations and restaurants on the smaller islands.

If you'd like to meet and mingle with locals, and get to know the islanders and their lifestyle, it's much easier to do so in the sleepy B.V.I. than in the hustle-bustle of St. Thomas or even St. Croix. The only U.S. Virgin Island that has the laid-back quality of the B.V.I. is St. John—except that the "local native" you are likely to meet is often a mainland expat, not a Virgin Islander born and bred.

There are frequent ferry connections between St. Thomas and St. John, but traveling among the other islands is a bit difficult, requiring private boats or airplane flights (see the "Getting Around the Islands," section later in this chapter for more details). The day will surely come when transportation from island to island will be made more convenient and frequent, but that day hasn't arrived yet.

THE MAJOR ISLANDS IN BRIEF

The islands previewed below are the sites of the most shopping, hotels, restaurants, attractions, and nightlife. A few words about islands that aren't mentioned below: For those who want to avoid the masses, the British Virgin Islands have a number of escapist-friendly islands such as Peter Island, Mosquito Island, and Guana Island. These are private hideaways, often with expensive resorts (which are the main reason for going there in the first place). Even if you're staying at a resort on Virgin Gorda or Tortola, you might want to join a boat excursion to visit some of the lesser-known islands (with time devoted to R & R on a nearly deserted beach, of course).

ST. THOMAS

The most developed of the U.S. Virgin Islands, St. Thomas resembles a small city at times. There are peaceful retreats here, but you must seek them out. The harbor at **Charlotte Amalie,** the capital, is one of the largest cruise-ship magnets in the Caribbean. Many locals try to avoid Charlotte Amalie when the greatest concentration of vessels is in port (usually Dec–Apr). Charlotte Amalie offers the widest selection of duty-free shopping in the Caribbean. However, you must browse carefully through the labyrinth of bazaars to find the real bargains.

St. Thomas, like most of the Virgin Islands, gives you plenty of opportunity to get outside and get active, although many visitors come here simply to sit, sun, and maybe go for a swim. **Magens Bay Beach,** with its tranquil surf and sugar-white sand, is one of the most beautiful beaches in the world, but it is likely to be packed, especially on heavy cruise-ship days. More secluded beaches include **Secret Harbour** and **Sapphire Beach** in East End.

St. Thomas has only one golf course, **Mahogany Run,** but it's a real gem. The 3 trickiest holes (13, 14, and 15) are known throughout the golfing world as the "Devil's Triangle."

Yachts and boats anchor at **Ramada Yacht Haven Marina** in Charlotte Amalie and at **Red Hook Marina** on the island's isolated eastern tip, though the serious yachting crowd gathers at Tortola in the British Virgin Islands (see "Tortola," below). Sport fishers angle from the **American Yacht Harbor** at Red Hook. The island also attracts snorkelers and divers—there are many outfitters offering equipment, excursions, and instruction. Kayaking and parasailing are also drawing more beach bums away from the water's edge.

St. Thomas has the most eclectic and sophisticated restaurant scene in the Virgin Islands. Emphasis is on French and Continental fare, but the wide selection also includes options from Mexican, West Indian, and Italian to Asian and American. St. Thomas pays more for its imported (usually European) chefs and secures the freshest of ingredients from mainland or Puerto Rican markets.

There's also a wide variety of accommodations on St. Thomas, from **Bluebeard's Castle** (a perennial favorite) to more modern beachfront complexes in the East End, including the manicured **Elysian Beach Resort.** Apartment and villa rentals abound, and you can also find a handful of old-fashioned B&B–style guesthouses.

If St. Thomas has one drawback, it's that it is no longer as safe a destination as it used to be. Crime has been on the rise, and muggings are frequent. Wandering the island at night, especially on the back streets of Charlotte Amalie, is not recommended.

ST. JOHN

Our favorite of the U.S. Virgin Islands, St. John has only two deluxe hotels, but you'll find charming inns and plenty of campgrounds. The island's primary attraction is the **U.S. Virgin Islands National Park,** which covers more than half the island. Guided walks and safari bus tours are available to help you navigate the park, which is full of pristine beaches, secret coves, flowering trees, and ghostly remains of sugar-cane plantations. An extensive network of trails invites hiking. A third of the park is underwater. **Trunk Bay,** which also boasts the island's finest beach, has an amazing underwater snorkeling trail. Scuba diving is another major attraction on St. John.

St. John has a handful of posh restaurants, as well as a number of colorful, West Indian eateries. Many residents and long-term visitors like to bring ingredients over from St. Thomas, where prices are lower and the selection is broader. Nightlife isn't a major attraction here; it usually consists of sipping rum drinks in a bar in **Cruz Bay,** and maybe listening to a local calypso band. After spending a day outdoors, most visitors on St. John are happy to turn in early.

ST. CROIX

This island is the second-most-visited destination in the U.S. Virgin Islands. Like St. Thomas, St. Croix is highly developed. Cruise-ship passengers flood **Frederiksted** and the capital, **Christiansted,** looking for duty-free goods and a handful of white sand to take home in a plastic bag. Although parts of the island resemble American suburbia, some of St. Croix's true West Indian–style buildings have been preserved, along with many of its rich cultural traditions.

One of the best reasons to take a trip to St. Croix, even if only for a day, is to visit **Buck Island National Park,** just 1½ miles off St. Croix's northeast coast. The park's offshore reef attracts snorkelers and certified divers from around the world. Blue signs posted along the ocean floor guide you through a forest of staghorn coral swarming with flamboyant fish.

St. Croix is the premier golfing destination in the Virgin Islands, mainly because it boasts **Carambola,** the archipelago's most challenging 18-hole course. St. Croix is also a tennis mecca of sorts: The luxurious **Buccaneer Hotel** has some of the best courts in the Virgin Islands and hosts several annual tournaments. Other sports for active vacationers include horseback riding, parasailing, sport fishing, water-skiing, snorkeling, and scuba diving.

The restaurants on St. Croix are not as good as those on St. Thomas, although they claim to be. The highly touted **Top Hat,** for example, prides itself on its Danish dishes, but split-pea soup and *frikadeller* (meatballs with red cabbage) may not be exactly what you're looking for on a hot Caribbean night. Life after dark is mostly confined to a handful of bars in Christiansted.

As for accommodations, St. Croix has only a few real luxury hotels, but there are a lot of small, attractive inns (we highly recommend **Pink Fancy**). And, as on St. Thomas, it's easy to find villas and condos for rent at reasonable weekly rates.

For the most part, life here is laid-back; however, St. Croix is not problem-free. At night, use discretion and avoid the back streets of Christiansted and Frederiksted, on the western coast.

TORTOLA

Tortola is the hub of the British Virgin Islands, but not always the best place for visitors, especially if you're planning to spend more than a couple of days here; we think Virgin Gorda (see below) has better hotels and restaurants. **Road Town,** the capital, with its minor shopping, routine restaurants, and uninspired architecture, requires a couple of hours at the most. Once you leave Road Town, however, you'll find Tortola more alluring. The island's best and most unspoiled beaches, including **Smuggler's Cove** (with its collection of snorkeling reefs), lie at the island's western tip. Tortola's premier beach is **Cane Garden Bay,** a 2.4km (1½-mile) stretch of white sand. Because of the gentle surf, it's one of the safest places for families with small children. For hikers, a highlight of a visit is an exploration of **Sage Mountain National Park,** where trails lead to a 543m (1,780-ft.) peak that offers panoramic views. The park is rich in flora and fauna, from mamey trees to mountain doves.

Although many visitors to the Caribbean look forward to fishing, hiking, horseback riding, snorkeling, and surfing, what makes Tortola exceptional is boating. It is *the* boating center of the British Virgin Islands, which are among the most cherished sailing territories on the planet. The island offers some 100 charter yachts and 300 bareboats, and its marina and shore facilities are the most up-to-date and extensive in the Caribbean Basin.

The crystal-clear waters compensate for the island's lackluster bars and restaurants. You can count on simple, straightforward food; we suggest locally caught fish grilled with perhaps a little lime butter.

VIRGIN GORDA

Our favorite British Virgin Island is Virgin Gorda, the third-largest member of the archipelago, with a permanent population of about 1,000 lucky souls. Many visitors come over just for a day to check out the **Baths,** an astounding collection of gigantic rocks, boulders, and tide pools on the southern tip. Crafted by volcanic pressures millions of years ago, the boulders have eroded into shapes reminiscent of a Henry Moore sculpture. With more than 20 uncrowded beaches, the best known of which are **Spring Beach** and **Trunk Beach,** Virgin Gorda is a sun worshiper's dream come true.

Unlike Tortola, Virgin Gorda has some of the finest hotels in the Virgin Islands, including **Little Dix Bay** and **Biras Creek.** One caveat: You must be willing to pay a high price for the privilege of staying at one of these regal resorts. There are also more reasonably priced places to stay, such as **Olde Yard Inn.** Outside the upscale hotels, restaurants tend to be simple places serving local West Indian cuisine. No one takes nightlife too seriously on Virgin Gorda, so there isn't very much of it.

2 Visitor Information

TOURIST INFORMATION OFFICES

IN CYBERSPACE   You can surf the **U.S.V.I. Division of Tourism's** website at www.usvitourism.vi. The **British Virgin Islands Tourist Board** can be found at www.bvitourism.com.

IN THE U.S.   Before you take off for the U.S. Virgin Islands, you can get information from the **U.S. Virgin Islands Division of Tourism,** 1270 Avenue of the Americas, Suite 2108, New York, NY 10020 (© **800/372-USVI** or 212/332-2222). There are additional offices at the following locations: 245 Peachtree Center Ave., Suite MB05, Atlanta, GA 30303 (© **404/688-0906**); 500 N. Michigan Ave., Suite 2030, Chicago, IL 60611 (© **312/670-8784**); 444 N. Capital St. NW, Suite 298, Washington, DC 20001 (© **202/624-3590**); 2655 Le Jeune Rd., Suite 907, Coral Gables, FL 33134 (© **305/442-7200**); and 3460 Wilshire Blvd., Suite 412, Los Angeles, CA 90010 (© **213/739-0138**).

For details on the British Virgin Islands, get in touch with the **British Virgin Islands Tourist Board,** 1270 Broadway, Suite 705, New York, NY 10001 (© **800/835-8530** or 212/696-0400). Additional locations are at 3450 Wilshire Blvd., Suite 1202, Los Angeles, CA 90010 (© **213/736-8931**); and 3390 Peachtree Rd. NE, Suite 1000, Atlanta, GA 30326 (© **404/260-8018**).

IN CANADA You can pick up information about the U.S. Virgin Islands from the **U.S.V.I. Government Tourist** office at 3300 Bloor St. W., Suite 3120, Toronto, ON M8X 2X3 (© **416/233-1414**). The B.V.I. Tourist Board has no offices in Canada.

IN THE U.K. Information is available at the **B.V.I. Information Office,** 55 Newman St., London W1P 3PG (© **020/7355-9585**). For the U.S. Virgin Islands, information is available at the **U.S.V.I. Division of Tourism,** Clove Hitch Quay, Plantation Wharf, York Place, London SW11 3TW (© **0171/971-5262**).

3 Entry Requirements & Customs

ENTRY REQUIREMENTS

For information on how to get a passport, go to "Passports" in the "Fast Facts" section, later in this chapter—the websites listed provide downloadable passport applications as well as the current fees for processing passport applications. For an up-to-date country-by-country listing of passport requirements around the world, go to the "Foreign Entry Requirement" Web page of the U.S. State Department at **www.travel.state.gov/foreignentryreqs.html**.

CUSTOMS

The U.S. Virgin Islands are duty-free ports, which means that many goods imported to the islands are not subject to import taxes and therefore can be sold at a discount. Shoppers can take advantage of the duty-free bargains, but only up to a limit prescribed by their government. On leaving the U.S.V.I., Americans must clear Customs. Customs procedures for Canadian, Australian, British, and other travelers to the U.S.V.I. are the same as on the U.S. mainland.

In the British Virgin Islands (which aren't duty-free ports), there is a Customs review upon entry.

Customs restrictions on what you can bring to both the B.V.I. and U.S.V.I. are rather flexible. Usually you are waved through Immigration and Customs after only a question or two, especially if you appear to be a vacationer. You're allowed to bring in a "reasonable" amount of duty-free goods for personal use; the Customs agent has the right to determine what constitutes a reasonable amount. (One or two bottles of perfume—yes. Three dozen? No.) You can bring 2 liters of alcohol and 2 cartons of cigarettes into both B.V.I. and U.S.V.I., but few visitors do, especially in the U.S.V.I., where discounted liquor is sold. In general, it's a question of what you take out of the Virgin Islands duty-free—not what you bring in. The importation of firearms or dangerous materials is forbidden.

BRINGING IT ALL HOME

FOR U.S. RESIDENTS   The U.S. government allows citizens a total of $1,200 worth of duty-free imports from the U.S.V.I. every 30 days. The duty-free exemption for purchases made in the British Virgin Islands is $600. Purchases made in the U.S. Virgin Islands over the duty-free exemption are taxed at a flat rate of 5% (10% in the British Virgin Islands).

Family members traveling together can make joint declarations. For a husband and wife with two children, the exemption in the U.S. Virgin Islands is $4,800.

Unsolicited gifts worth up to $200 per day can be sent from the U.S. Virgin Islands to friends and relatives, and they do not have to be declared as part of your $1,200 duty-free allowance. Gifts mailed from the British Virgin Islands cannot exceed $50 per day.

U.S. citizens can bring back 5 liters of liquor duty-free, plus an extra liter of rum (including Cruzan rum) if one of the bottles is produced in the Virgin Islands. Goods made on the island are also duty-free, including perfume, jewelry, clothing, and original paintings; however, if the price of an item exceeds $25, you must be able to show a certificate of origin.

Be sure to collect receipts for all purchases in the Virgin Islands, and beware of merchants offering to give you a false receipt—he or she might be an informer to U.S. Customs. Also, keep in mind that any gifts received during your stay must be declared.

For additional information on what you can bring back, download the invaluable free pamphlet *Know Before You Go* online at **www.cbp.gov**. (Click on "Travel," then "Know Before You Go.") Or contact the **U.S. Customs & Border Protection (CBP),** 1300 Pennsylvania Ave., NW, Washington, DC 20229 (© **877/287-8867**). If you need a refresher on U.S.V.I. requirements once you're there, call © **340/774-4554** in St. Thomas.

FOR CANADIAN RESIDENTS   For a summary of Canadian rules, write for the booklet *I Declare,* issued by the **Canada Border Services Agency** (© **800/461-9999** in Canada, or 204/983-3500; www.cbsa-asfc.gc.ca). Canada allows its citizens a C$750 exemption, and you're allowed to bring back duty-free one carton of cigarettes, one can of tobacco, 40 imperial ounces of liquor, and 50 cigars. You're also allowed to mail gifts to Canada valued at less than C$60 a day, provided they're unsolicited and don't contain alcohol or tobacco (write on the package "Unsolicited gift, under C$60 value"). All valuables should be declared on the Y-38 form before departure from Canada, including serial numbers of valuables you already own, such as expensive foreign cameras. *Note:* The C$750 exemption can only be used once a year and only after an absence of 7 days.

FOR U.K. RESIDENTS   U.K. citizens returning from a non-E.U. country have a customs allowance of: 200 cigarettes; 50 cigars; 250 grams of smoking tobacco; 2 liters of still table wine; 1 liter of spirits or strong liqueurs (over 22% volume); 2 liters of fortified wine, sparkling wine, or other liqueurs; 60cc (ml) perfume; 250cc (ml) of toilet water; and £145 worth of all other goods, including gifts and souvenirs. People under 17 cannot have the tobacco or alcohol allowance. For more information, contact **HM Customs & Excise** at ℭ **0845/010-9000** (from outside the U.K., 020/8929-0152), or consult their website at www.hmce.gov.uk.

FOR AUSTRALIAN RESIDENTS   The duty-free allowance in Australia is A$400 or, for those under 18, A$200. Citizens can bring in 250 cigarettes or 250 grams of loose tobacco, and 1,125 milliliters of alcohol. If you're returning with valuables you already own, such as foreign-made cameras, you should file form B263. A helpful brochure available from Australian consulates or Customs offices is *Know Before You Go*. For more information, call the **Australian Customs Service** at ℭ **1300/363-263,** or log on to www.customs.gov.au.

4 Money

Both the U.S. Virgin Islands and the British Virgin Islands use the **U.S. dollar** as the form of currency.

British and Canadian travelers will have to convert their currency into U.S. dollars. Conversions between the U.S. dollar and other currencies fluctuate, and the differences could affect the relative costs of your trip. Be sure to check the latest conversion rates before you leave. One U.S. dollar was worth about .76 euros at the time of this writing. (That means that 1 euro was worth approximately US$1.30.) At press time, 1 British pound was approximately US$1.90 or approximately 1.45 euros. At press time, 1 Canadian dollar was approximately 84 U.S. cents, or about 63 euro cents.

ATMS

The easiest and best way to get cash away from home is from an ATM (automated teller machine). The **Cirrus** (ℭ **800/424-7787;** www.mastercard.com) and **PLUS** (ℭ **800/843-7587;** www.visa.com) networks span the globe; look at the back of your bank card to see which network you're on, then call or check online for ATM locations at your destination. Be sure you know your personal identification number (PIN) before you leave home and be sure to find out your daily withdrawal limit before you depart. Also keep in mind that many banks impose a fee every time a card is used at a different bank's ATM, and that fee can be higher for international transactions (up to $5 or more) than for domestic ones (where they're rarely more than $1.50). On top of this, the bank from which you withdraw cash may charge its own fee. To compare banks' ATM fees within the U.S., use **www.bankrate.com**. For international withdrawal fees, ask your bank.

You can also get cash advances on your credit card at an ATM (though the interest rate for advances is usually much higher than for regular purchases). Keep in mind that credit card companies try to protect themselves from theft by limiting the funds you can withdraw outside your home country, so call your credit card company before you leave. Keep in mind that you'll pay interest from the moment of your withdrawal, even if you pay your monthly bills on time.

ATMs are most prevalent in Charlotte Amalie on St. Thomas, and in Christiansted on St. Croix. They are also available in Cruz Bay on St. John and in the British Virgin Islands on Tortola and Virgin Gorda. The other islands do not have ATMs.

TRAVELER'S CHECKS

Traveler's checks are something of an anachronism from the days before ATMs. These days, traveler's checks are less necessary because most cities have 24-hour ATMs that allow you to withdraw small amounts of cash as needed. However, keep in mind that you will likely be charged an ATM withdrawal fee if the bank is not your own, so if you're withdrawing money every day, you might be better off with traveler's checks—provided that you don't mind showing identification every time you want to cash one.

You can get traveler's checks at almost any bank. **American Express** offers denominations of $20, $50, $100, $500, and (for cardholders only) $1,000. You'll pay a service charge ranging from 1% to 4%. You can also get American Express traveler's checks over the phone by calling © **800/221-7282;** Amex gold and platinum cardholders who use this number are exempt from the 1% fee.

Visa offers traveler's checks at Citibank locations nationwide, as well as at several other banks. The service charge ranges between 1.5% and 2%; checks come in denominations of $20, $50, $100,

$500, and $1,000. Call ✆ **800/732-1322** for information. AAA members can obtain Visa checks without a fee at most AAA offices or by calling ✆ **866/339-3378. MasterCard** also offers traveler's checks. Call ✆ **800/223-9920** for a location near you.

If you choose to carry traveler's checks, be sure to keep a record of their serial numbers separate from your checks in the event that they are stolen or lost. You'll get a refund faster if you know the numbers.

CREDIT CARDS

Credit cards are a safe way to carry money: They also provide a convenient record of all your expenses, and they generally offer relatively good exchange rates. You can also withdraw cash advances from your credit cards at banks or ATMs, if you know your PIN. Keep in mind that when you use your credit card abroad, most banks assess a 2% fee above the 1% fee charged by Visa or MasterCard or American Express for currency conversion on credit charges. But credit cards still may be the smart way to go when you factor in things like exorbitant ATM fees and higher traveler's check exchange rates (and service fees).

5 When to Go

CLIMATE

Sunshine is practically an everyday affair in the Virgin Islands. Temperatures climb into the 80s (high 20s Celsius) during the day, and drop into the 70s (low 20s Celsius) at night. Winter is generally the dry season in the islands, but rainfall can occur at any time of the year. You don't have to worry too much, though—tropical showers usually come and go so quickly you won't even really notice. If you're out exploring for the day, you may want to bring rain gear.

Average Temperatures & Rainfall (in.) for St. Thomas

	Jan	Feb	Mar	Apr	May	June	July	Aug	Sept	Oct	Nov	Dec
Temp (°F)	77	77	77	79	79	82	82	83	82	83	81	77
Temp (°C)	25	25	25	26	26	28	28	28	28	28	27	25
Precip.	1.9	1	1	8.3	9.3	1.6	2.3	3.6	2.0	4.4	7.8	2.5

HURRICANES The hurricane season, the dark side of the Caribbean's beautiful weather, officially lasts from June to November. The Virgin Islands chain lies in the main pathway of many a hurricane raging through the Caribbean, and the islands are often hit. If you're planning a vacation in hurricane season, stay abreast of weather conditions. It may pay to get trip-cancellation insurance (p. 15) because of the possibility of hurricanes.

Islanders don't stand around waiting for a hurricane to strike. Satellite forecasts generally give adequate warning to both residents and visitors. And of course, there's always prayer: Islanders have a legal holiday in the third week of July called Supplication Day, when they ask to be spared from devastating storms. In late October, locals celebrate the end of the season on Hurricane Thanksgiving Day.

THE HIGH SEASON & THE OFF SEASON

High season (or winter season) in the Virgin Islands, when hotel rates are at their peak, runs roughly from mid-December to mid-April. However, package and resort rates are sometimes lower in January, as a tourist slump usually occurs right after the Christmas holidays. February is the busiest month. If you're planning on visiting during the winter months, make reservations as far in advance as possible.

Off season begins when North America starts to warm up, and vacationers, assuming that temperatures in the Virgin Islands are soaring into the 100s (30s Celsius), head for less tropical local beaches. However, it's actually quite balmy year-round in the Virgin Islands—thanks to the fabled trade winds—with temperatures varying little more than 5° between winter and summer.

There are many advantages to off-season travel. First, from mid-April to mid-December, hotel rates are slashed a startling 25% to 50%. Second, you're less likely to encounter crowds at swimming pools, beaches, resorts, restaurants, and shops. Especially in St. Thomas and St. Croix, a slower pace prevails in the off season, and you'll have a better chance to appreciate the local culture and cuisine. Of course, there are disadvantages to off-season travel, too: Many hotels use the slower months for construction and/or restoration, fewer facilities are likely to be open, and some hotels and restaurants may close completely when business is really slow.

Additionally, if you're traveling alone and planning a trip during the off season, ask for the hotel's occupancy rate—you may want crowds. The social scene in both the B.V.I. and the U.S.V.I. is intense from mid-December to mid-April. After that, it slumbers a bit. If you seek escape from the world and its masses, summer is the way to go, especially if you aren't depending on meeting others.

HOLIDAYS

In addition to the standard legal holidays observed in the United States, **U.S. Virgin Islanders** also observe the following holidays: Three Kings' Day (Jan 6); Transfer Day, commemorating the transfer of the Danish Virgin Islands to the Americans (Mar 31); Organic Act Day, honoring the legislation that granted voting rights to the islanders (June 20); Emancipation Day, celebrating the freeing of the slaves by the Danish in 1848 (July 3); Hurricane Supplication Day (July 25); Hurricane Thanksgiving Day (Oct 17); Liberty Day (Nov 1); and Christmas Second Day (Dec 26). The islands also celebrate 2 carnival days on the last Friday and Saturday in April: Children's Carnival Parade and the Grand Carnival Parade.

In the **British Virgin Islands,** holidays include the following: New Year's Day; Commonwealth Day (Mar 12); Good Friday; Easter Monday; Whitmonday (sometime in July); Territory Day Sunday (usually July 1); Festival Monday and Tuesday (during the first week of Aug); St. Ursula's Day (Oct 21); Birthday of the Heir to the Throne (Nov 14); Christmas Day; and Boxing Day (Dec 26).

6 Travel Insurance

Check your existing insurance policies and credit card coverage before you buy travel insurance. You may already be covered for lost luggage, canceled tickets or medical expenses. The cost of travel insurance varies widely, depending on the cost and length of your trip, your age and health, and the type of trip you're taking, but expect to pay between 5% and 8% of the vacation itself.

TRIP-CANCELLATION INSURANCE Trip-cancellation insurance helps you get your money back if you have to back out of a trip, if you have to go home early, or if your travel supplier goes bankrupt. Allowed reasons for cancellation can range from sickness to natural disasters to the State Department declaring your destination unsafe for travel. (Insurers usually won't cover vague fears, though, as many travelers discovered who tried to cancel their trips in Oct 2001 because they were wary of flying.) In this unstable world, trip-cancellation insurance is a good buy if you're getting tickets well in advance—who knows what the state of the world, or of your airline, will be in 9 months? Trip-cancellation insurance also makes sense because the Virgin Islands are so prone to hurricanes. Insurance policy details vary, so read the fine print—and especially make sure that your airline or cruise line is on the list of carriers covered in case of bankruptcy. A good resource is **"Travel Guard Alerts,"** a list of companies considered high-risk by Travel Guard International (see website below). Protect yourself further by paying for the insurance with a credit card—by law, consumers can get their money back on goods and services not received if they report the loss within 60 days after the charge is listed on their credit card statement.

Note: Many tour operators, particularly those offering trips to remote or high-risk areas, include insurance in the cost of the trip or can arrange insurance policies through a partnering provider, a convenient and often cost-effective way for the traveler to obtain insurance. Make sure the tour company is a reputable one, however: Some experts suggest you avoid buying insurance from the tour or cruise company you're traveling with, saying it's better to buy from a "third party" insurer than to put all your money in one place.

For more information, contact one of the following insurers: **Access America** (© 866/807-3982; www.accessamerica.com); **Travel Guard International** (© 800/826-4919; www.travelguard.com); **Travel Insured International** (© 800/243-3174; www.travel insured.com); and **Travelex Insurance Services** (© 888/457-4602; www.travelex-insurance.com).

MEDICAL INSURANCE Most health insurance policies cover you if you get sick away from home—but check, particularly if you're insured by an HMO. With the exception of certain HMOs and Medicare/Medicaid, your medical insurance should cover medical treatment—even hospital care—overseas. However, most out-of-country hospitals make you pay your bills upfront, and send you a refund after you've returned home and filed the necessary paperwork. As a safety net, you may want to buy travel medical insurance, particularly if you're traveling to a remote or high-risk area where emergency evacuation is a possible scenario. If you require additional medical insurance, try **MEDEX Assistance** (© 410/453-6300; www.medexassist.com) or **Travel Assistance International** (© 800/821-2828;** www.travelassistance.com; for general information on services, call the company's Worldwide Assistance Services, Inc., at © 800/777-8710).

LOST-LUGGAGE INSURANCE On domestic flights, checked baggage is covered up to $2,500 per ticketed passenger. On international flights (including U.S. portions of international trips), coverage is limited to about $9.07 per pound, up to approximately $635 per checked bag. If you plan to check items more valuable than the standard liability, see if your valuables are covered by your homeowner's policy, get baggage insurance as part of your comprehensive travel-insurance package, or buy Travel Guard's "BagTrak" product. Don't buy insurance at the airport, as it's usually overpriced. Be sure to take any valuables or irreplaceable items with you in your carry-on luggage, as many valuables (including books, money, and electronics) aren't covered by airline policies.

If your luggage is lost, immediately file a lost-luggage claim at the airport, detailing the luggage contents. For most airlines, you must report delayed, damaged, or lost baggage within 4 hours of arrival. The airlines are required to deliver luggage, once found, directly to your house or destination free.

7 Health & Safety

GENERAL AVAILABILITY OF HEALTH CARE

Finding a good doctor in the Virgin Islands is not a problem. See "Fast Facts," later in this chapter, and also in individual island chapters for recommendations. If you do get sick, you may want to ask the concierge at your hotel to recommend a local doctor—even his or her own physician. This will probably yield a better recommendation than any toll-free number would.

BEFORE YOU GO

Pack **prescription medications** in carry-on luggage. Carry written prescriptions (in case you lose your pills or run out) in generic, not brand-name form, and dispense prescription medications from their original labeled vials. If you wear **contact lenses or glasses,** pack an extra pair in case you lose one.

If you suffer from a chronic illness, consult your doctor before your departure. For conditions like epilepsy, diabetes, or heart problems, wear a **Medic Alert Identification Tag** (© 888/633-4298; www.medicalert.org), which will immediately alert doctors to your condition and give them access to your records through Medic Alert's 24-hour hot line.

Contact the **International Association for Medical Assistance to Travelers (IAMAT)** (© 716/754-4883 or 416/652-0137; www.iamat.org) for tips on travel and health concerns in the countries you're visiting. The United States **Centers for Disease Control and Prevention** (© 800/311-3435; www.cdc.gov) provides up-to-date information on necessary vaccines and health hazards by region or country, and offers food safety tips.

COMMON AILMENTS

If you experience **diarrhea,** moderate your eating habits, and drink only bottled water until you recover. If symptoms persist, you should consult a doctor. The best way to prevent **seasickness** is with the scopolamine patch by Transderm Scop, a prescription medication.

Either Bonine or Dramamine is a good over-the-counter medication, although each causes drowsiness. Smooth Sailing is a ginger drink that works quite well to settle your stomach. We find that a ginger pill taken with a meal and followed by Dramamine an hour before boarding a boat also does the job.

The Virgin Islands sun can be brutal. To protect yourself, consider wearing sunglasses and a hat, and use **sunscreen** (SPF 15 and higher) liberally. Limit your time on the beach for the first few days. If you do overexpose yourself, stay out of the sun until you recover. If your sunburn is followed by fever, chills, a headache, or feelings of nausea or dizziness, see a doctor.

Mosquitoes do exist in the Virgin Islands, but they aren't the malaria-carrying mosquitoes that you might find elsewhere in the Caribbean. They're still a nuisance, though. **Sand flies,** which appear mainly in the evening, are a bigger annoyance. Screens can't keep these critters out, so carry your bug repellent.

STAYING SAFE
See individual island chapters for information on safety.

8 Specialized Travel Resources

TRAVELERS WITH DISABILITIES
Some resorts on St. Thomas and St. Croix have made inroads in catering to persons with disabilities; St. John and all of the British Islands lag far behind. As of this writing, about a third of the major resorts (and none of the cheaper guesthouses or villas) in St. Thomas or St. Croix have facilities to accommodate vacationers who have disabilities. If you're planning a vacation in the Virgin Islands, you should contact a travel agent or call the hotel of your choice (an even better option) to discuss your requirements, see if a particular resort is prepared to cater to your needs, and obtain specific information.

For U.S. citizens, the U.S. National Park Service offers a **Golden Access Passport** that gives free lifetime entrance to all properties administered by the N.P.S.—national parks, monuments, historic sites, recreation areas, and national wildlife refuges—for persons who are visually impaired or permanently disabled, regardless of age. You may pick up a Golden Access Passport at any NPS entrance fee area by showing proof of medically determined disability and eligibility for receiving benefits under federal law. Besides free entry, the Golden Access Passport also offers a 50% discount on federal-use fees charged for such facilities as camping, swimming, parking, boat launching, and tours. For more information, go to www.nps.gov/fees_passes.htm or call © **888/467-2757.**

Many travel agencies offer customized tours and itineraries. **Flying Wheels Travel** (© **507/451-5005;** www.flyingwheelstravel. com) offers escorted tours and cruises that emphasize sports and private tours in minivans with lifts. **Access-Able Travel Source** (© **303/232-2979;** www.access-able.com) offers extensive access information and advice for traveling around the world with disabilities. **Accessible Journeys** (© **800/846-4537** or 610/521-0339; www. disabilitytravel.com) caters specifically to slow walkers and wheelchair travelers and their families and friends.

Avis Rent a Car has an "Avis Access" program that offers such services as a 24-hour toll-free number (© **888/879-4273**) for customers with special travel needs; car features such as swivel seats, spinner knobs, and hand controls; and accessible bus service.

Organizations that offer assistance to disabled travelers include **MossRehab** (www.mossresourcenet.org), which provides a library of accessible-travel resources online; **SATH** (Society for Accessible Travel & Hospitality) (© **212/447-7284;** www.sath.org; annual membership fees: $45 adults, $30 seniors and students), which offers a wealth of travel resources for all types of disabilities and informed recommendations on destinations, access guides, travel agents, tour operators, vehicle rentals, and companion services; and the **American Foundation for the Blind (AFB)** (© **800/232-5463;** www.afb.org), a referral resource for the blind or visually impaired that includes information on traveling with Seeing Eye dogs.

For more information specifically targeted to travelers with disabilities, the community website **iCan** (www.icanonline.net/ channels/travel/index.cfm) has destination guides and several regular columns on accessible travel. Also check out the quarterly magazine **Emerging Horizons** ($15 per year, $20 outside the U.S.; www.emerginghorizons.com); and *Open World* magazine, published by SATH (see above; subscription: $13 per year, $21 outside the U.S.).

SENIOR TRAVEL

Mention the fact that you're a senior when you make your travel reservations. Although all of the major U.S. airlines except America West have canceled their senior discount and coupon book programs, many hotels still offer discounts for seniors.

Members of **AARP** (formerly the American Association of Retired Persons), 601 E St. NW, Washington, DC 20049 (© **888/687-2277;**

www.aarp.org), get discounts on hotels, airfares, and car rentals. AARP offers members a wide range of benefits, including *AARP: The Magazine* and a newsletter (both included in the $13 per year membership fee). Anyone over 50 can join.

The **U.S. National Park Service** offers a **Golden Age Passport** that gives seniors 62 years or older lifetime entrance to all properties administered by the National Park Service—national parks, monuments, historic sites, recreation areas, and national wildlife refuges—for a one-time processing fee of $10, which must be purchased in person at any NPS facility that charges an entrance fee. Besides free entry, a Golden Age Passport also offers a 50% discount on federal-use fees charged for such facilities as camping, swimming, parking, boat launching, and tours. For more information, go to www.nps.gov/fees_passes.htm or call © **888/467-2757.**

Many reliable agencies target the 50-plus market. One company that sometimes offers trips to the U.S.V.I. is **Elderhostel** (© 877/ 426-8056; www.elderhostel.org), which arranges study programs for those ages 55 and over (and a spouse or companion of any age). Many courses include airfare, accommodations in university dormitories or modest inns, meals, and tuition. **ElderTreks** (© 800/ 741-7956; www.eldertreks.com) offers small-group tours to off-the-beaten-path or adventure-travel locations, restricted to travelers 50 and older. **INTRAV** (© 800/456-8100; www.intrav.com) is a high-end tour operator that caters to the mature, discerning traveler, not specifically seniors, with trips around the world that include guided safaris, polar expeditions, private-jet adventures, and small-boat cruises down jungle rivers.

Recommended publications offering travel resources and discounts for seniors include: the quarterly magazine *Travel 50 & Beyond* (www.travel50andbeyond.com); *Travel Unlimited: Uncommon Adventures for the Mature Traveler* (Avalon); *101 Tips for Mature Travelers,* available from Grand Circle Travel (© **800/221-2610** or 617/350-7500; www.gct.com); and *Unbelievably Good Deals and Great Adventures That You Absolutely Can't Get Unless You're Over 50* (McGraw-Hill), by Joann Rattner Heilman.

MARRYING IN THE U.S. VIRGIN ISLANDS

No blood tests or physical examinations are necessary, but there is a $25 license fee, a $25 notarized application, and an 8-day waiting period, which is sometimes waived, depending on circumstances.

Frommers.com: The Complete Travel Resource

For an excellent travel-planning resource, we highly recommend **Frommers.com** (www.frommers.com), voted Best Travel Site by *PC Magazine*. We're a little biased, of course, but we guarantee that you'll find the travel tips, reviews, monthly vacation giveaways, bookstore, and online-booking capabilities thoroughly indispensable. Among the special features are our popular **Destinations** section, where you'll get expert travel tips, hotel and dining recommendations, and advice on the sights to see for more than 3,500 destinations around the globe; the **Frommers.com Newsletter,** with the latest deals, travel trends, and money-saving secrets; our **Community** area featuring **Message Boards,** where Frommer's readers post queries and share advice (sometimes even our authors show up to answer questions); and our **Photo Center,** where you can post and share vacation tips. When your research is done, the **Online Reservations System** (www.frommers.com/book_a_trip) takes you to Frommer's preferred online partners for booking your vacation at affordable prices.

Civil ceremonies before a judge of the territorial court cost $200 each; religious ceremonies performed by clergy are equally valid. Fees and schedules for church weddings must be negotiated directly with the officiant. More information is available from the **U.S. Virgin Islands Division of Tourism,** 1270 Avenue of the Americas, New York, NY 10020 (© **800/372-USVI** or 212/332-2222; www.usvitourism.vi). The guide *Getting Married in the U.S. Virgin Islands* is distributed by U.S.V.I. tourism offices; it gives information on all three islands, including wedding planners, places of worship, florists, and limousine services. It also provides a listing of island accommodations that offer in-house wedding services.

Couples can apply for a marriage license for St. Thomas or St. John by contacting the **Territorial Court of the Virgin Islands,** P.O. Box 70, St. Thomas, U.S.V.I. 00804 (© **340/774-0640**). For weddings on St. Croix, contact the **Territorial Court of the Virgin Islands,** Family Division, P.O. Box 929, Christiansted, St. Croix, U.S.V.I. 00821 (© **340/773-1130**).

MARRYING IN THE BRITISH VIRGIN ISLANDS

There's no requirement of island residency, but a couple must apply for a license at the attorney general's office, and stay in the B.V.I. for at least 3 days while the paperwork is processed. You'll need to present a passport or original birth certificate and photo identification, plus certified proof of your single marital status, including any divorce or death certificates pertaining to former spouses. Two witnesses must accompany the couple. The license fee is $110. Local registrars will perform marriages, or you can choose your own officiant. For information and an application for a license, contact the **Registrar's Office,** P.O. Box 418, Road Town, Tortola, B.V.I. (*©* **284/494-3701** or 284/494-3492).

9 Getting There

The bigger islands, like St. Thomas, have regularly scheduled air service on North American carriers, and the smaller islands are tied into this network through their own carriers.

If you're coming from the United Kingdom, you'll likely fly first to Miami then take American Airlines or some other carrier on to your final destination. Although there are special deals, round-trip fares from New York to St. Thomas range from $269 to $1,896 per person, from Miami to St. Thomas $397 to $1,186 round-trip.

For more information on how to reach each island by plane, refer to the "Getting There" sections in the individual island chapters. For information on getting around between the islands, see p. 24.

GETTING THROUGH THE AIRPORT

With the federalization of airport security, security procedures at U.S. airports are more stable and consistent than ever. Generally, you'll be fine if you arrive **1 hour** before a domestic flight and **2 hours** before an international flight; if you show up late, tell an airline employee and she'll probably whisk you to the front of the line.

Bring a **current, government-issued photo ID** such as a driver's license or passport. Keep your ID at the ready to show at check-in, the security checkpoint, and sometimes even the gate. (Children under 18 do not need government-issued photo IDs for domestic flights, but they do for international flights to most countries.)

In 2003, the TSA phased out **gate check-in** at all U.S. airports. And **e-tickets** have made paper tickets nearly obsolete. Passengers with e-tickets can beat the ticket-counter lines by using airport **electronic kiosks** or even **online check-in** from your home computer. Online check-in involves logging on to your airline's website, accessing your reservation, and printing out your boarding pass—and the airline may even offer you bonus miles to do so! If you're using a kiosk at the airport, bring the credit card you used to book the ticket or your frequent-flier card. Print out your boarding pass from the kiosk and simply proceed to the security checkpoint with your pass and a photo ID. If you're checking bags or looking to snag an exit-row seat, you will be able to do so using most airline kiosks. Even the smaller airlines are employing the kiosk system, but always call your airline to make sure these alternatives are available. **Curbside check-in** is also a good way to avoid lines, although a few airlines still ban curbside check-in; call before you go.

Security checkpoint lines can still be quite long. If you have trouble standing for long periods of time, tell an airline employee; the airline will provide a wheelchair. Speed up security by **not wearing metal objects** such as big belt buckles. If you've got metallic body parts, a note from your doctor can prevent a long chat with the security screeners. Only **ticketed passengers** are allowed past security, except for folks escorting disabled passengers or children.

Federalization has stabilized **what you can carry on** and **what you can't.** The general rule is that sharp things are out, nail clippers are okay, and food and beverages must be passed through the X-ray machine—but that screeners can't make you drink from your coffee cup. Bring food in your carry-on rather than checking it, as explosive-detection machines used on checked luggage have been known to mistake food (especially chocolate, for some reason) for bombs.

Tips Travel in the Age of Bankruptcy

Airlines go bankrupt, so protect yourself by **buying your tickets with a credit card,** as the Fair Credit Billing Act guarantees that you can get your money back from the credit card company if a travel supplier goes under (and if you request the refund within 60 days of the bankruptcy.) **Travel insurance** can also help, but make sure it covers against "carrier default" for your specific travel provider. And be aware that if a U.S. airline goes bust mid-trip, a 2001 federal law requires other carriers to take you to your destination (albeit on a space-available basis) for a fee of no more than $25, provided you rebook within 60 days of the cancellation.

Travelers in the U.S. are allowed one carry-on bag, plus a "personal item" such as a purse, briefcase, or laptop bag. Carry-on hoarders can stuff all sorts of things into a laptop bag; as long as it has a laptop in it, it's still considered a personal item. The Transportation Security Administration (TSA) has issued a list of restricted items; check its website (www.tsa.gov) for details.

Airport screeners may decide that your checked luggage needs to be searched by hand. You can now purchase luggage locks that allow screeners to open and re-lock a checked bag if hand-searching is necessary. Look for Travel Sentry certified locks at luggage or travel shops and Brookstone stores (you can buy them online at www.brookstone.com). These locks, approved by the TSA, can be opened by luggage inspectors with a special code or key. For more information on the locks, visit www.travelsentry.org. If you use something other than TSA-approved locks, your lock will be cut off your suitcase if a TSA agent needs to hand-search your luggage.

10 Getting Around the Islands

Be sure to check out the "Getting Around" sections in the individual island chapters.

BY PLANE

Travelers can fly between St. Thomas and St. Croix, and between St. Thomas and Virgin Gorda. St. John doesn't have an airport; passengers usually land first at St. Thomas, then travel to St. John by boat. **Seaborne** (© **340/773-6442;** www.seaborneairlines.com) makes the trips between St. Thomas and St. Croix. To travel between St. Thomas and Virgin Gorda by plane, contact **St. Thomas Air** (© **800/522-3084**). Fares average about $100 for these trips.

BY BOAT

Ferry service is a vital link between St. Thomas and St. John; private water taxis also operate on this route. Launch services link Red Hook, on the East End of St. Thomas, with both Charlotte Amalie in St. Thomas and Cruz Bay in St. John.

In the B.V.I., ferries and private boats link Road Town, Tortola, with the island's West End; there's also service to and from Virgin Gorda and some of the smaller islands, such as Anegada and Jost Van Dyke. However, on some of the really remote islands, boat service may only be once a week. Many of the private islands, such as Peter Island, provide launches from Tortola.

You can travel by public ferry from Charlotte Amalie, on St. Thomas, to West End and Road Town on Tortola, a 45-minute voyage. Boats making this run include **Native Son** (© 284/495-4617) and **Smith's Ferry Service** (© 284/495-4495). **Inter-Island Boat Services** (© 284/495-4166) specializes in a somewhat obscure routing—from St. John to the West End on Tortola.

For details on specific ferry connections, including sample fares, see the "Getting Around" sections of the individual island chapters.

BY CAR

A rented car is often the best way to get around the Virgin Islands. Just remember the most important rule: In both the U.S. and the British Virgin Islands, *you must drive on the left.*

All the major car-rental companies are represented in the U.S. Virgin Islands, including **Avis** (© 800/331-1212; www.avis.com), **Budget** (© 800/472-3325; www.budget.com), and **Hertz** (© 800/654-3131; www.hertz.com); many local agencies also compete in the car-rental market (see the "Getting Around" sections in individual island chapters). On St. Thomas and St. Croix, you can pick up most rental cars at the airport. On St. John there are car-rental stands at the ferry dock. Cars are sometimes in short supply during the high season, so reserve as far in advance as possible.

Parking lots in the U.S. Virgin Islands can be found in Charlotte Amalie, on St. Thomas, and in Christiansted, on St. Croix (in Frederiksted, you can generally park on the street). Most hotels, except those in the center of Charlotte Amalie, have free parking lots.

In the British Virgin Islands, many visitors don't even bother renting a car, mainly because taxi service is adequate, but also because they'll have to drive on the left along roads that can be hairy when they exist at all—some of the roads are like roller-coaster rides. To rent a car on the B.V.I., you must purchase a local driver's license for $10 from police headquarters or at the car-rental desk, and you must be at least 25 years old. Major U.S. companies are represented in these islands, and there are many local companies as well. Vehicles come in a wide range of styles and prices, including jeeps, Land Rovers, minimokes, and even six- to eight-passenger Suzukis. Weekly rates are usually slightly cheaper.

GASOLINE   There are plenty of service stations on St. Thomas, especially on the outskirts of Charlotte Amalie and at strategic points in the north and in the more congested East End. On St. Croix, most gas stations are in Christiansted, but there are also some along the major roads and at Frederiksted. On St. John, make sure your tank is filled up at Cruz Bay before heading out on a tour of the island.

Gas stations are not as plentiful on the British Virgin Islands. Road Town, the capital of Tortola, has the most; fill up here before touring the island. Virgin Gorda has a limited but sufficient number of gas stations. Chances are you won't be using a car on the other, smaller British Virgin Islands. At press time, gas prices range from $2.15 to $2.39 a gallon. This is most definitely subject to change.

BREAKDOWNS   All the major islands, including St. Thomas, St. John, St. Croix, Tortola, and Virgin Gorda, have garages that will tow vehicles. Always call the rental company first if you have a breakdown. If your car requires extensive repairs because of a mechanical failure, a new one will be sent to replace it.

BY TAXI

Taxis are the main mode of transport on all the Virgin Islands. On **St. Thomas,** taxi vans carry up to a dozen passengers to multiple destinations, and smaller private taxis are available. Rates are posted at the airport, where you'll find plenty of taxis on arrival. On **St. John,** private taxis and vans for three or more passengers are available. On **St. Croix,** taxis congregate at the airport, in Christiansted, and in Frederiksted, where the cruise ships arrive. Many hotels often have a "fleet" of taxis available for guests. Taxis are unmetered, and you should negotiate the rate before taking off.

On the **British Virgin Islands,** taxis are sometimes the only way to get around. Service is available on Tortola, Virgin Gorda, and Anegada, and rates are fixed by the local government.

BY BUS

The only islands with really recommendable bus service are **St. Thomas** and **St. Croix.** On St. Thomas, buses leave from Charlotte Amalie and circle the island; on St. Croix, air-conditioned buses run from Christiansted to Frederiksted. Bus service elsewhere is highly erratic; it's mostly used by locals going to and from work.

BY BICYCLE

Much of the hilly terrain of the Virgin Islands does not lend itself to cycling. St. John, however, is a decent place for bike rides, and St. Croix is ideal. For specific information on bicycle rentals, see the "Getting Around" sections of the individual island chapters.

FAST FACTS: The Virgin Islands

American Express See "Fast Facts," in individual island chapters for American Express locations.

Area Code The area code for the U.S.V.I. is **340**; in the B.V.I., it's **284**. You can dial direct from North America.

Currency U.S. currency is used in both the U.S. and the British Virgin Islands.

Driving Rules In both the U.S.V.I. and the B.V.I., you must drive on the left. See "Getting Around the Islands," above, for more details.

Electricity The electrical current in the Virgin Islands is the same as on the U.S. mainland: 110 volts AC, 60 cycles.

Embassies & Consulates There are no embassies or consulates in the Virgin Islands. If you have a passport issue, go to the local police station, which in all islands is located at the center of government agencies. Relay your problem to whomever is at reception, and you'll be given advice about which agencies can help you.

Emergencies Call ⓒ **911**.

Etiquette & Customs Unlike in some parts of the Caribbean, nudity is frowned upon throughout the U.S.V.I. and B.V.I. and is punishable by law. However, even though it's an offense, standards are more relaxed in the U.S.V.I.

Hitchhiking In the British Virgin Islands, travel by thumb is illegal; in the U.S. Virgin Islands, it isn't illegal, but it isn't widely practiced. We don't recommend it anywhere.

Internet Access There is limited Internet access on the major islands in the Virgin Islands chain, including St. Thomas (the best), St. Croix, St. John, Tortola, and Virgin Gorda. On some of the more remote islands, you may be completely out of luck. Many visitors log on at their hotel. Costs in general are about $2 to $5 per half-hour.

Liquor Laws You must be 21 years of age or older to purchase liquor at a store or in a restaurant.

Newspapers & Magazines Daily U.S. newspapers are flown into St. Thomas, St. Croix, Tortola, and Virgin Gorda. For local papers, see individual island chapters.

Passports **For Residents of the United States:** Whether you're applying in person or by mail, you can download passport applications from the U.S. State Department website at **www.travel.state.gov** (click on "Applications and Forms" under "Passports" on the homepage). To find your regional passport office, either check the U.S. State Department website or call the **National Passport Information Center** toll-free number (℃ **877/487-2778**) for automated information.

For Residents of Canada: Passport applications are available at travel agencies throughout Canada or from the central **Passport Office,** Department of Foreign Affairs and International Trade, Ottawa, ON K1A 0G3 (℃ **800/567-6868;** www.ppt.gc.ca).

For Residents of the United Kingdom: To pick up an application for a standard 10-year passport (5-year passport for children under 16), visit your nearest passport office, major post office, or travel agency or contact the **United Kingdom Passport Service** at ℃ **0870/521-0410** or search its website at www.ukpa.gov.uk.

For Residents of Ireland: Apply for a 10-year passport at the **Passport Office,** Setanta Centre, Molesworth Street, Dublin 2 (℃ **01/671-1633;** www.irlgov.ie/iveagh). Those under age 18 and over 65 must apply for a €12 3-year passport. You can also apply at 1A South Mall, Cork (℃ **021/272-525**) or at most main post offices.

For Residents of Australia: You can pick up an application from your local post office or any branch of Passports Australia, but you must schedule an interview at the passport office to present your application materials. Call the **Australian Passport Information Service** at ℃ **131-232,** or visit the government website at www.passports.gov.au.

For Residents of New Zealand: You can pick up a passport application at any New Zealand Passports Office or download it from their website. Contact the **Passports Office** at ℃ **0800/ 225-050** in New Zealand or 04/474-8100, or log on to www.passports.govt.nz.

Pets To bring your pet to the U.S.V.I., you must have a health certificate from a mainland veterinarian and show proof of vaccination against rabies. Very few hotels allow animals, so check in advance. If you're strolling with your dog through the national park on St. John, you must keep it on a leash. Pets are not allowed at campgrounds, picnic areas, or on public beaches. Both St. Croix and St. Thomas have veterinarians listed in the Yellow Pages.

Your dog or cat is permitted entry into the B.V.I. without quarantine if accompanied by an Animal Health Certificate issued by the Veterinary Authority in your country of origin. This certificate has a number of requirements, including a guarantee of vaccination against rabies.

Police Dial ℭ **911** for emergencies. See individual island chapters for more detailed information.

Radio & TV St. Thomas, St. John, and St. Croix all receive cable and commercial TV stations. Radio weather reports can be heard at 8:30am and 7:30pm on 99.5 FM.

The B.V.I. has two local FM stations with nonstop music, including Z-HIT (94.3) and Z-WAVE (97.3). There's one local TV station and one cable station.

Taxes See individual island chapters for information.

Time Zone The Virgin Islands are on Atlantic Standard Time, which is 1 hour ahead of Eastern Standard Time. However, the islands do not observe daylight saving time, so in the summer, the Virgin Islands and the East Coast of the U.S. are on the same time. In winter, when it's 6am in Charlotte Amalie, it's 5am in Miami; during daylight saving time it's 6am in both places.

Visas U.S. and Canadian citizens do not need a visa to enter the U.S. Virgin Islands. Visitors from other nations should have a U.S. visa; those visitors may also be asked to produce an onward ticket. In the British Virgin Islands, visitors who stay for less than 6 months don't need a visa if they possess a return or onward ticket.

Useful Phone Numbers

U.S. Dept. of State Travel Advisory: ℭ 202/647-5225 (manned 24 hr.)

U.S. Passport Agency: ℭ 202/647-0518

U.S. Centers for Disease Control International Traveler's Hotline: ℭ 404/332-4559

Water Most visitors drink the local tap water with no harmful aftereffects. Those with more delicate stomachs might want to stick to bottled water.

St. Thomas

St. Thomas, the busiest cruise-ship harbor in the West Indies, is not the largest of the U.S. Virgins—St. Croix, 40 miles south, holds that distinction. But bustling Charlotte Amalie, at the heart of the island, is the capital of the U.S.V.I., and it remains the shopping hub of the Caribbean. The beaches on this island are renowned for their white sand and calm, turquoise waters, including the very best of them all, Magens Bay. *National Geographic* rated the island as one of the top destinations in the world for sailing, scuba diving, and fishing.

Charlotte Amalie, with its white houses and bright red roofs glistening in the sun, is one of the most beautiful towns in the Caribbean. It's most famous for shopping, but the town is also filled with historic sights, like Fort Christian, an intriguing 17th-century building constructed by the Danes. The town's architecture reflects the island's culturally diverse past: You'll pass Dutch doors, Danish red-tile roofs, French iron grillwork, and Spanish-style patios.

Because of St. Thomas's thriving commercial activity—as well as its lingering drug and crime problems—the island is often referred to as the most "unvirgin" of the Virgin Islands. Charlotte Amalie's Main Street is like a 3- to 4-block-long shopping center. Although this area tends to be overcrowded, the island's beaches, major hotels, most restaurants, and entertainment facilities are, for the most part, removed from the cruise-ship chaos. And you can always find seclusion at a hotel in more remote sections of the island. Hotels on the north side of St. Thomas look out at the Atlantic; those on the south side front the calmer Caribbean Sea.

St. Thomas has much to recommend it—not only perfect sandy beaches but also the best dining in the islands and a string of the most upmarket resorts. But no one ever said St. Thomas was the friendliest of the Virgin Islands. It is, in fact, the unfriendliest—a rather impersonal place overrun with cruise-ship passengers and locals who cast a rather cynical eye toward tourists. It can even be dangerous at night, especially on the back streets of Charlotte Amalie.

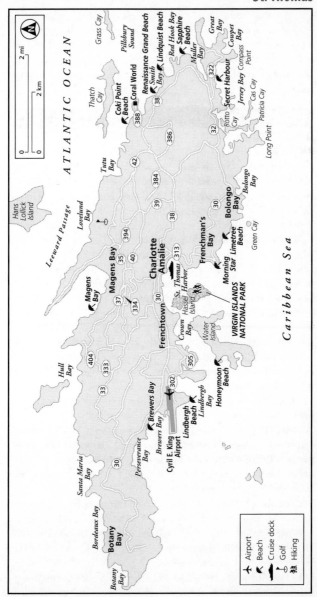

ATLANTIC OCEAN

Grass Cay

Pillsbury Sound

Thatch Cay

Great Bay

Coupet Bay

Compass Point

Jersey Bay

Cas Cay

Patricia Cay

Long Point

Renaissance Grand Beach

Lindquist Beach

Sapphire Beach

Red Hook Bay

Muller Bay

Secret Harbour

Coral World

Smith Bay

Coki Point Beach

322

32

388

386

38

Bolongo Bay

Bolongo

30

Green Cay

Caribbean Sea

42

384

39

38

Tutu Bay

Hans Lollick Island

Leeward Passage

Loveland Bay

394

35

40

Magens Bay

Charlotte Amalie

313

Frenchman's Bay

Limetree Beach

Morning Star Beach

Magens Bay

37

334

30

Frenchtown

St. Thomas Harbor

Hassel Island

VIRGIN ISLANDS NATIONAL PARK

Crown Bay

Water Island

404

333

305

Hull Bay

Brewers Bay

302

Cyril E. King Airport

Lindbergh Beach

Lindbergh Bay

Honeymoon Beach

Santa Maria Bay

Perseverance Bay

33

30

Bordeaux Bay

Botany Bay

2 mi

2 km

0

0

Airport
Beach
Cruise dock
Golf
Hiking

If you want to escape the hordes, don't come here, as the rush-hour traffic in and out of Charlotte Amalie will reveal. If you're seeking something laid-back, with friendlier people, take the ferry over to St. John (see chapter 3), and you'll enter a world that's more evocative of the sleepier 1950s. St. Thomas is for those who want action.

1 Orientation

ARRIVING

BY PLANE

If you're flying to St. Thomas, you will land at the **Cyril E. King Airport** (© **340/774-5100**), west of Charlotte Amalie on Route 30. From here, you can grab a taxi to your hotel or villa. Chances are you will be staying east of Charlotte Amalie, so keep in mind that getting through town may involve long delays and traffic jams.

Nonstop flights to the U.S. Virgin Islands from New York City take 3¾ hours. Flight time from Miami is about 2½ hours. Flight time between St. Thomas and St. Croix is only 20 minutes. Flying to San Juan from mainland cities and connecting to St. Thomas may cost less than regular nonstop fares.

American Airlines (© **800/433-7300** in the U.S.; www.aa.com) offers frequent service to St. Thomas and St. Croix from the U.S. mainland, with two daily flights from New York to St. Thomas in high season. Passengers flying from other parts of the world are usually routed to St. Thomas through Miami or San Juan, both of which offer nonstop service (often several times a day) to St. Thomas. (American Eagle has nine nonstop flights daily from San Juan to St. Thomas.)

Delta (© **800/241-4141** in the U.S.; www.delta.com) offers two daily nonstop flights between Atlanta and St. Thomas in winter. **US Airways** (© **800/428-4322** in the U.S.; www.usairways.com) has one nonstop daily flight from Philadelphia to St. Thomas, and an additional flight on Saturday.

Cape Air (© **800/352-0714** in the U.S.; www.flycapeair.com) has service between St. Thomas and Puerto Rico. This Massachusetts-based airline offers seven flights daily. Cape Air has expanded its service to include flights from San Juan to St. Croix and flights between St. Croix and St. Thomas.

United Airlines (© **800/538-2929** in the U.S.; www.united.com) has nonstop service on Saturday and Sunday to St. Thomas from Chicago and Washington, D.C.

Continental Airlines (© **800/231-0856** in the U.S.; www.
continental.com) has daily flights from Newark International Airport, in New Jersey, to St. Thomas.

Launched in 2004, **Caribbean Sun Airlines** (© **866/864-6272**)
flies from San Juan to both St. Thomas and St. Croix.

A final hint: Bargain-seekers should ask their airline representative to connect them with the tour desk, which can often arrange discounted hotel rates if a hotel reservation is booked simultaneously with airline tickets.

BY BOAT

Charlotte Amalie is the busiest cruise-ship port in the Caribbean.

If you're in the British Virgin Islands, you can take a boat to Charlotte Amalie from Tortola. Trip time is only 45 minutes between these two capitals, and a one-way ticket is $23 ($44 round-trip). The major carriers to and from Tortola are **Smith's Ferry** (© **340/775-7292**) and **Native Son** (© **340/774-8685**), which are both based in Charlotte Amalie. Boats arrive and depart from Tortola's West End.

St. Thomas is also linked by boat to St. John, about 3 to 5 miles away. Ferries depart from Red Hook Marina on the East End of St. Thomas and arrive at Cruz Bay on St. John. Trip time is about 15 to 20 minutes; the cost is $3 one-way for adults ($2 for kids 2–11). For ferry schedules, call **Transportation Services** at © **340/776-6282.**

It's also possible to take a ferry service from Puerto Rico to St. Thomas, with a stop in St. John. The service, however, is only available on Saturdays—maybe more often if demand increases. Trip time between Fajardo and Charlotte Amalie (St. Thomas) is about 1¾ hours, with the departure at 8am and the return at 4pm. The cost is $55 one-way, $75 round-trip. For more information, call **Transportation Services** at © **340/776-6282.**

VISITOR INFORMATION

At Tolbod Gade 1, across from Emancipation Park, on the waterfront in downtown Charlotte Amalie, the **visitor center** (© **340/774-8784**) is open Monday to Friday 8am to 5pm and Saturday 9am to noon. There's also an information desk at the cruise-ship terminal.

ISLAND LAYOUT
CHARLOTTE AMALIE

Charlotte Amalie, the capital of St. Thomas, is the only town on the island. Its seaside promenade is called **Waterfront Highway,** or simply, **the Waterfront.** From here, you can take any of the streets or alleyways into town to **Main Street** (also called Dronningens Gade).

Principal links between Main Street and the Waterfront include **Raadets Gade, Tolbod Gade, Store Tvaer Gade,** and **Strand Gade.**

Main Street is home to all of the major shops. The western end (near the intersection with Strand Gade) is known as **Market Square.** Once the site of the biggest slave market auctions in the Caribbean Basin, today it's an open-air cluster of stalls where native farmers and gardeners gather daily (except Sun) to peddle their produce. Go early in the morning to see the market at its best.

Running parallel to and north of Main Street is **Back Street** (also known as Vimmelskaft Gade), which is lined with many stores, including some less expensive choices. *Beware:* It can be dangerous to walk along Back Street at night, but it's reasonably safe for daytime shopping.

WEST OF CHARLOTTE AMALIE

The most important of the outlying neighborhoods to the west of Charlotte Amalie is **Frenchtown.** Some of the older islanders still speak a distinctive Norman-French dialect here. Because the heart of Charlotte Amalie is dangerous at night, Frenchtown, with its finer restaurants and interesting bars, has become the place to go after dark. To reach Frenchtown, take Veterans Drive west of town along the Waterfront, turning left (shortly after passing the Windward Passage Hotel on your right) at the sign pointing to the Villa Olga.

The middle-grade hotels to the immediate west of Charlotte Amalie attract visitors who are seeking more moderate rates than those charged at the megaresorts along the gold-plated South Coast. The disadvantage is that you may have to depend on public transportation to reach the sands. The biggest attraction is that you're on the very doorstep of Charlotte Amalie, with all its amusements.

EAST OF CHARLOTTE AMALIE

Traveling east from Charlotte Amalie, along a traffic-clogged highway, St. Thomas Harbor will be on your right. Two of St. Thomas's most famous hotels are located on two hills here: The Inn at Blackbeard's Castle, and Bluebeard's Castle Hotel. If you stay in this area, you'll be in a tranquil setting just a short car or taxi ride from the bustle of Charlotte Amalie. The major disadvantage is that you must reach the sands by some form of transportation; if you want to run out of your hotel room door onto the beach, look elsewhere.

THE SOUTH COAST

This fabled strip, with its good sandy beaches, has put St. Thomas on the tourist map. If you don't mind paying the big bucks, you can stay here in grand style. Many prefer the resorts on the South Coast because they want to be removed from the hustle and bustle of Charlotte Amalie, especially during the day, when it's overrun by cruise-ship passengers and others. Cars, buses, hotel shuttles, and taxis can deliver you to Charlotte Amalie for shopping if you wish.

THE EAST END

The East End is reached by traversing a long, difficult, traffic-clogged road. Once you're here, you can enjoy sea, sand, and sun with little to disturb you (the East End offers even more isolation than the South Coast). This is the site of great beaches such as Sapphire Beach and Lindquist Beach. This section of bays and golden sands offers some ritzy, expensive properties that compete with the megaresorts of the South Coast, but smaller, less-expensive gems also exist. The little settlement at **Red Hook** is a bustling community with raffish charm and lots of loud bars and affordable eateries. It is also the departure point for ferries to St. John.

THE NORTH COAST

The fabled beach at **Magens Bay,** celebrated as one of the finest strips of sand in the Caribbean, put the lush North Coast on the tourist map. Be aware, though, that the beach is often overrun with visitors, especially when cruise-ship arrivals are heavy. The North Coast has few buildings and not much traffic, making it a destination for those who'd like to dine in a less heavily visited area of the island. The vistas here are among the most panoramic on the island, though traveling the roads is like a ride on a roller coaster—the roads have no shoulders and are especially scary for those not familiar with driving on the left. A lot of the northwest coast, especially at Botany Bay, Bordeaux Bay, and Santa Maria Bay, isn't linked to any roads.

2 Getting Around

BY TAXI

Taxis are unmetered, but fares are controlled and widely posted; however, we recommend you negotiate a fare with the driver before you get into the car. A typical fare from Charlotte Amalie to Sapphire Beach is $9 per person. Surcharges, one-third of the price of the excursion, are added after midnight. You'll pay $2 to $4 per bag for luggage. For 24-hour radio-dispatch taxi service, call © **340/774-7457.** If you want to hire a taxi and a driver (who just may be a great tour guide) for a day, expect to pay about $25 per person for 2 hours of sightseeing in a shared car, or $50 per hour for two to four people.

Taxi vans transport 8 to 12 passengers to multiple destinations on the island. It's cheaper to take a van instead of a taxi if you're going between your hotel and the airport. The cost for luggage ranges from $1 to $2 per bag. Call ℂ **340/774-7457** to order a taxi van.

BY BUS

Buses, called **Vitrans,** leave from street-side stops in the center of Charlotte Amalie, fanning out east and west along all of the most important highways. They run between 5:30am and 8pm daily, but waits can be very long and this is a difficult way to get about. A ride within Charlotte Amalie is 75¢; a ride to anywhere else is $1. For schedule and bus-stop information, call ℂ **340/774-5678.**

BY CAR

St. Thomas has many leading North American **car-rental firms** at the airport, and competition is stiff. Before you go, compare the rates of the "big three": **Avis** (ℂ **800/331-1084** or 340/774-1468; www.avis.com), **Budget** (ℂ **800/472-3325** or 340/776-5774; www.budgetrentacar.com), and **Hertz** (ℂ **800/654-3131** or 340/774-1879; www.hertz.com). You can often save money by renting from a local agency, although vehicles sometimes aren't as well maintained. Try **Dependable Car Rental,** 3901 B Altona, Welgunst, behind the Bank of Nova Scotia and the Medical Arts Complex (ℂ **800/522-3076** or 340/774-2253), which will pick up renters at the airport or their hotel; or the aptly named **Discount Car Rental,** 14 Harwood Hwy., outside the airport on the main highway (ℂ **340/776-4858**), which grants drivers a 12% discount on rivals' rates. There is no tax on car rentals in the Virgin Islands.

DRIVING RULES   Always *drive on the left.* The speed limit is 20 mph in town, 35 mph outside town. Take extra caution when driving in St. Thomas, especially at night. Many roads are narrow, curvy, and poorly lit.

FAST FACTS: St. Thomas

American Express Service is provided by **Caribbean Travel Agency/Tropic Tours,** 14AB The Guardian Building, Havensight, Charlotte Amalie (ℂ **340/774-1855**).

Banks Several U.S. banks are in St. Thomas, including **First Bank,** 11A Curaçao Gade, Charlotte Amalie (ℂ **340/776-2222**). Most island banks are open Monday to Thursday 8:30am to

3pm, and Friday 8:30am to 4pm. The banks are your only option if you need to exchange currency. There are over 50 ATMs on the island.

Bookstores **Dockside Bookshop,** Havensight Mall, Charlotte Amalie (℄ **340/774-4937**), where the cruise ships dock, sells books, cards, maps, and board games.

Business Hours Typical business and store hours are Monday to Friday 9am to 5pm and Saturday 9am to 1pm. Some shops open Sunday for cruise-ship arrivals. Bars are usually open daily 11am to midnight or 1am, although some hot spots stay open later.

Cameras & Film Try **Blazing Photos,** Havensight Mall, Charlotte Amalie (℄ **340/776-5547**), near the cruise-ship dock. There's a branch at **Nisky Shopping Center,** Frenchtown (℄ **340/774-1005**).

Dentists The **Smile Center** (℄ **340/775-9110**) is a member of the American Dental Association and is linked with various specialists. Call for information or an appointment.

Doctors **Roy L. Schneider Community Hospital,** 9784 Sugar Estate, Charlotte Amalie (℄ **340/776-8311**), provides services for locals and visitors. Also see "Hospitals," below.

Drugstores Go to **Drug Farm,** 2–4 Ninth St., Charlotte Amalie (℄ **340/776-7098**), or **Havensight Pharmacy,** Havensight Mall, Building 4, Charlotte Amalie (℄ **340/776-1235**).

Emergencies For the police, call ℄ **911;** ambulance, **911;** fire, **921.**

Hospitals The **St. Thomas Hospital** is at 9048 Sugar Estate (℄ **340/776-8311**), Charlotte Amalie.

Internet Access The best place to go is **Little Switzerland,** 5 Main St./Dronningens Gade, Charlotte Amalie (℄ **340/ 776-2010,** ext. 3115). If you order coffee, beer, or other drinks, you can use the computer for free.

Laundry & Dry Cleaning The major hotels provide laundry service, but it's more expensive than a laundromat. For dry cleaning, go to **One-Hour Martinizing,** Barbel Plaza (℄ **340/ 774-5452**), in Charlotte Amalie. A good full-service laundromat is **4-Star Laundromat,** 68 Kronprindsens Gade (℄ **340/ 774-8689**), also in Charlotte Amalie.

Mail Postage rates are the same as on the U.S. mainland: 23¢ for a postcard and 37¢ for a letter to U.S. addresses. For international mail, a first-class letter of up to ½ ounce costs 80¢ (60¢ to Canada or Mexico); a first-class postcard costs 70¢ (50¢ to Canada or Mexico); and a preprinted postal aerogramme costs 70¢.

Newspapers & Magazines Copies of U.S. mainland newspapers, such as the *New York Times, USA Today,* and the *Miami Herald,* arrive daily in St. Thomas and are sold at hotels and newsstands. The latest copies of *Time* and *Newsweek* are also for sale. *St. Thomas Daily News* covers local, national, and international events. *Virgin Islands Playground* and *St. Thomas This Week,* both of which are packed with visitor information, are distributed free all over the island.

Police The main police headquarters is at the **Alexander A. Farrelly Justice Center,** 8172 Sub Base, Charlotte Amalie (© **340/774-2211**).

Post Office The main post office is at 9846 Estate Thomas, Charlotte Amalie (© **340/774-1950**), and is open Monday to Friday 7:30am to 5pm and Saturday 7:30am to noon.

Restrooms You'll find public toilets at beaches and at the airport, but they are limited in town. Most visitors use the facilities of a bar or restaurant.

Safety St. Thomas has an unusually high crime rate, particularly in Charlotte Amalie. Don't wander around at night, particularly on Back Street. Single women should avoid visiting Charlotte Amalie's bars alone at night. Guard your valuables. Store them in hotel safes if possible, and make sure you keep your doors and windows shut at night.

Taxes The only local tax is an 8% surcharge added to all hotel rates.

Telephone & Fax All island phone numbers have seven digits. It is not necessary to use the 340 area code when dialing within St. Thomas. Numbers for all three islands, including St. John and St. Croix, are found in the U.S. Virgin Islands phone book. Hotels will send faxes and telexes for you, usually for a small service charge. Make long distance, international, and collect calls as you would on the U.S. mainland. To reach **Sprint** dial © **800/999-9000,** and to reach **MCI** dial © **800/950-5555.**

Tipping Tip as you would on the U.S. mainland—15% or so on a restaurant check, and a few dollars a day for housekeeping services in a hotel.

Transit Information Call ☎ **340/774-7457** to order a taxi 24 hours a day. Call ☎ **340/774-5100** for airport information and ☎ **340/776-6282** for information about ferry departures for St. John.

Weather For emergency (hurricane and disaster) weather reports, call **Vietema** at ☎ **340/774-2244.**

3 Where to Stay

Nearly every beach on St. Thomas has its own hotel, and the island has more quaint inns than any other place in the Caribbean. The choice of hotels divides almost evenly between places to stay in Charlotte Amalie, and grand resorts along the East End that front the fabulous beaches. There are advantages and disadvantages to both, and your choice of where to stay becomes a matter of personal taste.

If you're in St. Thomas for shopping and you want to be near the best stores, the widest choice of restaurants and bars, and nearly all the historic attractions, chances are you'll elect to stay in Charlotte Amalie. And if you want budget accommodations, or a choice of moderately priced inns, you'll need to be in or near Charlotte Amalie. The downside to staying here is that you'll have to take a shuttle over to a good beach, a ride of no more than 10 to 15 minutes from most Charlotte Amalie properties. If you want the isolation of a resort along with proximity to Charlotte Amalie, with its attractions and its shops, you can book into the Marriott property directly to the east of Charlotte Amalie at Flamboyant Point.

If your dream is to arrive in St. Thomas and anchor yourself directly on a beach, then the East End is your best bet. All the properties here are grand, luxurious resorts with many attractions, including watersports and nightlife. The downside is that if you don't want to take expensive transportation, or drive along narrow, dark, and unfamiliar roads at night, you'll be resort-bound for the evening, as commutes to some of the island's best restaurants are difficult at night. You'll also have to spend time and money if you want to get into Charlotte Amalie for shopping. Almost without exception, the East End beachfront resorts are very expensive. In spite of the high costs, these hotels attract customers who want the decadent resort life that is impossible to find at the smaller inns of Charlotte Amalie.

Remember that hotels in the Virgin Islands slash their prices in summer by 20% to 60%. Unless otherwise noted, the rates listed below *do not* include the 8% government tax.

IN CHARLOTTE AMALIE
MODERATE

Hotel 1829 This is one of the leading small hotels in the Caribbean. It far exceeds the more commercialized Bluebeard's Castle in charm and authenticity. Now a national historic site, the inn has serious island appeal. The building was designed by an Italian architect in a Spanish motif, with French grillwork, Danish bricks, and sturdy Dutch doors. Danish and African workers completed the structure in 1829 (hence the name), and the likes of Edna St. Vincent Millay and Mikhail Baryshnikov have visited. This place stands right in the heart of town, on a hillside 3 minutes from Government House. It's a bit of a climb to the top of this multi-tiered structure—there are many steps but no elevator. The hotel has a shuttle to Magens Bay Beach as well as to the restaurant at the Inn at Blackbeard's Castle.

The rooms are well-designed and attractive, and most face the water. All have old island decor, such as wood beams and stone walls, and a small tiled bathroom. The upper rooms are situated amid a cascade of bougainvillea, overlooking a central courtyard with a miniature pool. The smallest units, in the former slave quarters, are the least comfortable. Some guest rooms are four flights up, so be warned if you have a problem with stairs. We always opt for one of the front bedrooms, as they're the most scenic and spacious.

Kongens Gade (P.O. Box 1567), Charlotte Amalie, St. Thomas, U.S.V.I. 00804. ℂ 800/524-2002 in the U.S., or 340/776-1829. Fax 340/776-4313. www. hotel1829.com. 15 units. Winter $105–$180 double, from $220 suite; off season $75–$135 double, from $160 suite. Rates include continental breakfast. AE, DISC, MC, V. **Amenities:** Bar; small outdoor pool; laundry service; nonsmoking rooms. *In room:* A/C, TV, fridge, hair dryer, iron.

Villa Santana This unique country villa is an all-suite property. It was built by General Antonio Lopez de Santa Anna of Mexico in the 1850s. It offers a panoramic view of Charlotte Amalie and the St. Thomas harbor. The shopping district in Charlotte Amalie is a 5-minute walk; Magens Bay Beach is a 15-minute drive north.

Guest rooms are at La Mansion, once the general's library; La Terraza, originally the wine cellar; La Cocina de Santa Anna, once the central kitchen for the estate; La Casa de Piedra, once the bedroom of the general's attaché; and La Torre, the old pump house, which has been converted into a modern lookout tower. The Mexican-style

Where to Stay in St. Thomas

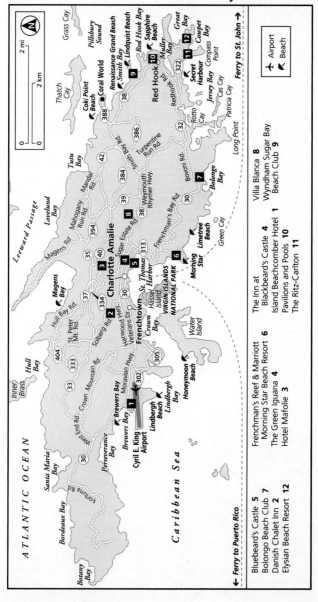

Frenchman's Reef & Marriott
Morning Star Beach Resort **6**

The Green Iguana **4**

Hotel Mafolie **3**

The Inn at
Blackbeard's Castle **4**

Island Beachcomber Hotel **10**

Pavilions and Pools **1**

The Ritz-Carlton **11**

Villa Blanca **8**

Wyndham Sugar Bay
Beach Club **9**

Bluebeard's Castle **5**

Bolongo Beach Club **7**

Danish Chalet Inn **2**

Elysian Beach Resort **12**

← Ferry to Puerto Rico

Ferry to St. John →

✈ Airport

🏖 Beach

41

decor features clay tiles, rattan furniture, and stonework. All rooms have ceiling fans and full kitchens. The property has a sun deck and garden with hibiscus and bougainvillea.

2602 Bjere Gade #2D, Denmark Hill, Charlotte Amalie, St. Thomas, U.S.V.I. 00802. ©/fax 340/776-1311. www.villasantana.com. 6 units. Winter $125–$195 suite for 2; off season $85–$135 suite for 2. AE, MC, V. **Amenities:** Outdoor pool. *In room:* TV, kitchen, beverage maker, iron, no phone.

INEXPENSIVE

Bunker Hill Hotel　We really only recommend this guesthouse if Galleon House or Danish Chalet Inn (see below) are fully booked. Bunker Hill Hotel is not in the safest district, so caution is advised, especially at night. But this clean, centrally located lodge is suitable for anyone who will sacrifice some comfort (you'll have to put up with some street noise) for their budget's sake. Four rooms have balconies, and some offer a view of the lights of Charlotte Amalie and the sea. The furnishings are simple and often threadbare. Rooms are small, and mattresses are well-worn. One room has a microwave and sink, giving it a slight advantage over the others.

7A Commandant Gade, Charlotte Amalie, St. Thomas, U.S.V.I. 00802. © 340/774-8056. Fax 340/774-3172. www.bunkerhillhotel.com. 21 units. Winter $98 double, $129 suite; off season $79 double, $98 suite. Rates include continental breakfast. AE, MC, V. **Amenities:** 2 outdoor pools; deli. *In room:* A/C, TV, fridge (in some).

Galleon House　At the east end of Main Street, about a block from the main shopping area, Galleon House is accessible via a difficult climb, especially in sweltering heat. Nevertheless, its rates are among the most competitive in town, if you don't mind a place operated without state-of-art maintenance and a staff attitude that many readers have complained about. You walk up a long flight of stairs to reach a concrete terrace doubling as the reception area. Each of the small rooms, located in scattered hillside buildings, has a ceiling fan and so-so air-conditioning, plus a cramped bathroom. If you want character, check into the older rooms in the main building. More spacious units with better views lie up the hill in a pair of dull apartment buildings. Breakfast is served on a veranda overlooking the harbor, and Magens Bay Beach is 15 minutes by car or taxi from the hotel. If you check in, say hi to the iguanas for us.

Government Hill (P.O. Box 6577), Charlotte Amalie, St. Thomas, U.S.V.I. 00804. © 800/524-2052 in the U.S., or 340/774-6952. Fax 340/774-6952. www.galleon house.com. 12 units, 11 with bathroom. Winter $79 double without bathroom, $99–$139 double with bathroom; off season $69 double without bathroom, $79–$99 double with bathroom. Extra person $15 each. Rates include full breakfast. AE, MC, V. **Amenities:** Outdoor pool; snorkeling equipment. *In room:* A/C, TV, dataport.

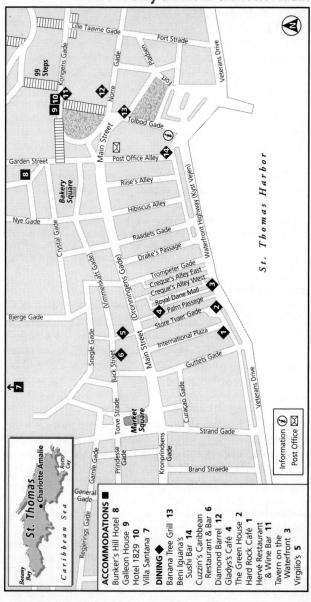

Where to Stay & Dine in Charlotte Amalie

St. Thomas Harbor

St. Thomas
Charlotte Amalie

Botany
Bay

Caribbean Sea

Hassel
Island

Water
Island

Porto
Cay

ACCOMMODATIONS ■
Bunker's Hill Hotel **8**
Galleon House **9**
Hotel 1829 **10**
Villa Santana **7**

DINING ◆
Banana Tree Grill **13**
Beni Iguana's
  Sushi Bar **14**
Cuzzin's Caribbean
  Restaurant & Bar **6**
Diamond Barrel **12**
Gladys's Café **4**
The Green House **2**
Hard Rock Café **1**
Hervé Restaurant
  & Wine Bar **11**
Tavern on the
  Waterfront **3**
Virgilio's **5**

Information ⓘ   Post Office ☒

99 Steps

Bakery Square

Market Square

43

WEST OF CHARLOTTE AMALIE
MODERATE

Island Beachcomber Hotel (Value) (Kids)   This rather standard hostelry near the airport is known for its affordable rates and beautiful location near one of the island's best beaches. Many guests are one-nighters staying over between yacht charters. A beach-party atmosphere prevails, and there's a Tahitian aura to the place, created by tropical foliage, birdcages, bridges, and thatched umbrellas. Rooms are medium in size, with louvered doors and jalousies, excellent lighting, and ceiling fans, plus a patio or porch. All are clean and well maintained, although their furnishings are a bit worn. The standard rooms contain two double beds, while superiors are fitted with a king-size bed. Accommodations face either the garden or the beach; those opening onto the water are grabbed up first.

Lindberg Beach Road, Lindbergh Bay, St. Thomas, U.S.V.I. 00802. © **800/982-9898** in the U.S., or 340/774-5250. Fax 340/774-5615. www.st-thomas.com/islandbeachcomber. 48 units. Winter $135–$148 double; off season $115–$128 double. Children $15 extra. AE, DC, DISC, MC, V. **Amenities:** Restaurant; bar. *In room:* A/C, TV, dataport, fridge, coffeemaker, hair dyer.

INEXPENSIVE

Danish Chalet Inn   High above Charlotte Amalie, on the western edge of the cruise-ship harbor and a 5-minute walk from the harbor front, this trio of buildings sits on a steeply inclined acre of land dotted with tropical shrubs and bougainvillea. The heart and soul of the place is the panoramic terrace, which has a 180-degree view of the cruise ships. The bedrooms are small but neat, clean, and colorful. All are air-conditioned. Much of this hotel's business stems from its willingness to accept 1-night guests (many other small island hotels insist on bookings of several nights). Guests are welcome to use the restaurant and bar at the affiliated property across the street.

4–5 Gamble Nordsidevej (P.O. Box 2875), Charlotte Amalie, St. Thomas, U.S.V.I. 00803. © **877/407-2567** in the U.S., or 340/774-5292. Fax 340/777-5598. www.danishchaletinn.com. 15 units. Year-round $98 double. MC, V. **Amenities:** Limited room service. *In room:* A/C, TV, fridge.

The Green Iguana (★) (Value)   Sitting on Blackbeard's Hill, in the center of Charlotte Amalie, this is one of the best run and most comfortable B&Bs to open in town in many a year. The little inn lies only a 5-minute walk from the center of town, with all its shops, restaurants and bars. Magen Beach is a 10-minute drive over the hill. The midsize bedrooms, decorated in a tropical motif with wicker furnishings, have panoramic views of the harbor, the constantly arriving cruise ships, and the other Virgin Islands. You have a choice of a king-, queen-, or twin-size bed, and each room features a tiled bathroom with shower. The helpful managers live on the property.

37B Blackbeard's Hill, Charlotte Amalie, St. Thomas, U.S.V.I. 00802. ⓒ 800/484-8825 or 340/776-7654. Fax 340/777-4312. www.greeniguana.com. 6 units. Winter $119 double; off season $89 double. Extra person $20. AE, MC, V. **Amenities:** Laundry facilities; nonsmoking rooms. *In room:* A/C, kitchenette, fridge, coffeemaker, iron, safe.

EAST OF CHARLOTTE AMALIE
EXPENSIVE

Bluebeard's Castle Hotel ⚘   This is a popular resort on the side of the bay overlooking Charlotte Amalie (it's not on a beach, but it offers free shuttle service to Magens Bay). It was once the island's number-one hotel, but it was surpassed long ago by newer, more deluxe East End resorts, such as the Ritz-Carlton. The hill surrounding the hotel is heavily built up with everything from offices to time shares. The guest rooms come in a wide variety of shapes and sizes, all pleasantly but blandly decorated; many units have a sitting room. Rooms are priced according to view. Standard rooms have no views, whereas deluxe units have a vista of both harbor and town. Some in-between units open onto the cruise-ship docks. There are shower-tub combos in the bathrooms. Be aware that amenities differ widely in the rooms, so it's wise to ask ahead for what you want.

Bluebeard's Hill (P.O. Box 7480), Charlotte Amalie, St. Thomas, U.S.V.I. 00801. ⓒ 800/438-6493 in the U.S., or 340/774-1600. Fax 340/714-1320. 170 units. Winter $179–$360 double; off season $139–$285 double. AE, DC, DISC, MC, V. **Amenities:** 3 restaurants; bar; outdoor pool; 2 tennis courts; exercise room; laundry service; dry cleaning; nonsmoking rooms. *In room:* A/C, TV, kitchen (in some), coffeemaker (in some), hair dryer, iron (in some).

The Inn at Blackbeard's Castle ⚘   Once a private residence, this is now one of the most charming and atmospheric inns in the Virgin Islands, exceeding in romantic appeal its closest rival, Bluebeard's Castle (see above). Perched high on a hillside above the town, it lies at the site of a 1679 chiseled stone tower that the Danish governor ordered erected. The tower served as a lookout for unfriendly ships, and legend says that Blackbeard himself lived in the tower half a century later. Most of the well-furnished bedrooms and all of the suites are spacious. Travelers on a budget might choose the garden rooms; they're the smallest, and have no balconies, but are near a private pool area. Accommodations are decorated with tile floors or dark wood, with much use made of Caribbean mahogany furnishings. The nearest beach is a 10-minute shuttle ride away.

Blackbeard's Hill (P.O. Box 6227), Charlotte Amalie, St. Thomas, U.S.V.I. 00801. © **800/344-5771** in the U.S., or 340/776-1234. Fax 340/776-4321. www.blackbeards castle.com. 13 units. Winter $110 garden room, $165–$195 balcony or junior suite; off season $90 garden room, $130–$165 balcony or junior suite. AE, DISC, MC, V. **Amenities:** Restaurant; bar; 3 outdoor pools; nonsmoking rooms. In room: A/C, TV, fridge, safe.

MODERATE

Villa Blanca 🦀 *Value* Small, intimate, and charming, this hotel lies 1½ miles east of Charlotte Amalie on 3 secluded acres of hilltop land. Views are among the most panoramic on the island, looking out over the harbor and the green rolling hills. The hotel's main building served as the private home of its present owner, Blanca Terrasa Smith, between 1973 and 1985. After the death of her husband, Mrs. Smith added a 12-room annex in the garden and opened her grounds to paying guests. Today, a homey and caring ambience prevails. Each room contains tile floors, a ceiling fan and/or air-conditioning, a well-equipped kitchenette, a good bed with a firm mattress, and a private balcony or terrace with sweeping views either eastward to St. John or westward to Puerto Rico and the harbor of Charlotte Amalie. No meals are served. On the premises are a freshwater pool and a large covered patio where you can enjoy the sunset. The closest beach is Morningstar Bay, about 4 miles away.

4 Raphune Hill, Rte. 38, Charlotte Amalie, St. Thomas, U.S.V.I. 00801. © **800/ 231-0034** in the U.S., or 340/776-0749. Fax 340/779-2661. www.villablancahotel. com. 14 units. Winter $125–$145 double; off season $85–$115 double. Rates include continental breakfast. AE, DISC, MC, V. **Amenities:** Outdoor pool; nonsmoking rooms; sport-fishing. In room: A/C, TV, kitchenette, beverage maker, hair dryer.

INEXPENSIVE

Hotel Mafolie 🦀 *Finds* A unique gem among bland cookie-cutter hotels, this stunning guesthouse is perched 800 feet above Charlotte Amalie's harbor. Its proprietor, Michael Sigler, and his wife Helga, provide very friendly service at the hotel, while their daughter Natasha and son-in-law AJ take care of the superb restaurant. Mike said to us, "We insist on giving good service, that's just how a family works." All rooms are different, decorated by Helga with that personal touch that you miss at a chain. Rooms have good tiled bathrooms with tub/shower combos. The restaurant draws customers from the upscale Ritz and Marriott nearby.

7091 Estate Mafolie, Mafolie Hill, Charlotte Amalie, St. Thomas, U.S.V.I. 00802. © **800/225-7035** or 340/774-2790. Fax 340/774-4091. www.mafolie.com. 22 units. Winter $105-$115 double, $145 junior suite; off season $85–$95 double, $115 junior suite. Rates include continental breakfast. Children ages 12 and under stay free in parent's room; extra person $15 each. AE, MC, V. **Amenities:** Restaurant; bar; outdoor pool, shuttle to beach. In room: A/C, TV, fridge.

THE SOUTH COAST
VERY EXPENSIVE
Frenchman's Reef & Marriott Morning Star Beach Resort

★★★ Three miles east of Charlotte Amalie on the south shore, this is the largest hotel in the U.S. Virgin Islands, but since the opening of the Ritz-Carlton, it is no longer the plushest or most glamorous. In 2005, the two separate parts of this resort, Frenchman's Reef and Morning Star, were officially conglomerated into one megaresort with an excellent location on a bluff overlooking both the harbor and the Caribbean. This is a full-service, American-style resort; it's not suited to those seeking a cozy island ambience (go to Hotel 1829 or Hotel Mafolie for that). Facilities devoted to the good life are everywhere: To reach the private beach, for example, you take a glass-enclosed elevator. The accommodations have all you'll need for comfort, and the bathrooms, with combo tub/shower, are generally spacious. The bedrooms at Frenchman's Reef are traditionally furnished and comfortable, while those at the Morning Star are more luxurious. All have private balconies with sea views. There is enough variety in dining to keep you on the premises, and the cuisine has become better and better. In general, we prefer the seafood to the frozen meat imported from the U.S. mainland.

No. 5 Estate Bakkeroe, Flamboyant Point (P.O. Box 7100), St. Thomas, U.S.V.I. 00801. ℂ 800/524-2000 or 340/776-8500. Fax 340/716-6191. www.marriott.com. 504 units. Winter $239–$369 double; off season $229–$309 double. AE, DC, DISC, MC, V. **Amenities:** 5 restaurants; 5 bars; 2 outdoor pools; 2 tennis courts; health club; spa; sauna; watersports equipment/rentals; business center; 24-hr. room service; babysitting; laundry service; dry cleaning; nonsmoking rooms; rooms for those w/ limited mobility. *In room:* A/C, TV, dataport, fridge, beverage maker, hair dryer, iron.

The Ritz-Carlton, St. Thomas ★

This hotel's architecture evokes a *palazzo* in Venice. Fronted by white-sand beaches, it stands on 30 acres of an oceanfront estate at the island's southeastern tip, 4 miles from Charlotte Amalie. The Ritz is set amid landscaped gardens, with fountains and hidden courtyards evoking the feel of a sprawling villa. Guests register in a palace-like reception area. Most of the accommodations are in several three-story villas designed with Italian Renaissance motifs and the pastels of the Mediterranean. Added to this roster are 48 new guest rooms and suites. The finest are a series of club-level units. The least desirable are those on the ground floor, with only partial views. Each room features a private balcony and quality linens. All this would be great if room maintenance and service were better. The St. Thomas Ritz-Carlton is not run on as high a standard as many other Ritz-Carlton hotels—hence, its demotion from three Frommer's stars to one.

The elegant dining room, **The Great Bay Grill,** captures the best scenic views of Great Bay and St. John and serves refined cuisine that's complimented by a first-rate wine list.

6900 Great Bay, St. Thomas, U.S.V.I. 00802. (℃) **800/241-3333** or 340/775-3333. Fax 340/775-4444. www.ritzcarlton.com. 200 units. Winter $489–$995 double, $1,500 suite; off season $535–$665 double, $565 suite. AE, DC, DISC, MC, V. **Amenities:** 5 restaurants; 3 bars; 2 outdoor pools; 2 tennis courts; health club; spa; Jacuzzi; watersports equipment rental; children's programs; 24-hr. room service; massage; babysitting; laundry service; dry cleaning. *In room:* A/C, TV, minibar, beverage maker, safe.

EXPENSIVE

Bolongo Bay Beach Club ⭐ *Kids*   This is an unpretentious, barefeet-welcome kind of place. You'll find a half-moon-shaped white-sand beach, and a cluster of pink two- and three-story buildings, plus some motel-like units closer to the sands. There's also a social center consisting of a smallish pool and a beachfront bar, replete with palm fronds. It's a relatively small property, but it offers all the facilities of a big resort. Many guests check in on the continental plan, which includes breakfast; others opt for all-inclusive plans that include all meals, drinks, a sailboat excursion to St. John, and use of scuba equipment. Rooms are simple, summery, and filled with unremarkable but comfortable furniture. Each unit has its own balcony or patio, a refrigerator, and one king-size or two double beds. Some of the units on the beach come with kitchenettes, and apartment-style condos, in a three-story building, have full kitchens.

7150 Bolongo, St. Thomas, U.S.V.I. 00802. (℃) **800/524-4746** or 340/775-1800. Fax 340/775-3208. www.bolongobay.com. 65 units. Winter $245 double (room only), $470 double (all inclusive); off season $175–$195 double (room only), $400 double (all inclusive). Ask about packages and various meal plans. AE, MC, V. **Amenities:** 2 restaurants; 2 bars; 3 outdoor pools; 2 tennis courts; fitness center; sauna; children's programs (ages 4–12); babysitting; basketball courts; boating; deep-sea fishing; dive shop; scuba diving; snorkeling; windsurfing. *In room:* A/C, TV, kitchen or kitchenette (in some), fridge, beverage maker, hair dryer, iron, safe.

THE EAST END
VERY EXPENSIVE

Wyndham Sugar Bay Beach Resort & Spa ⭐⭐   At the east end of the island, a 5-minute ride from Red Hook, this all-inclusive hotel is much improved but still lags behind the Marriott. It has panoramic views, although its secluded beach is really too small for a resort of this size. After a $5-million renovation, guest rooms have modern carpeting, furnishings, electronics, wall treatments, and plumbing. Many of the attractive rooms are decorated with rattan pieces and pastels, and all boast roomy marble bathrooms with shower stalls. The hotel's spa, Journeys, is the largest full-service spa in the U.S. Virgins, and the first to offer hydrotherapy treatments. The spa is also open to non-visitors who call for an appointment.

6500 Estate Smith Bay, St. Thomas, U.S.V.I. 00802. © **800/WYNDHAM** in the U.S., or 340/777-7100. Fax 340/777-7200. www.wyndham.com. 297 units. Winter $688–$744 double (all-inclusive), $365–$432 double (room only), from $900 suite (all-inclusive), from $542 suite (room only); off season $524–$660 double (all-inclusive), $185–$326 (room only), from $700 suite (all-inclusive), from $355 suite (room only). AE, DC, DISC, MC, V. **Amenities:** 3 restaurants; 2 bars; 3 outdoor pools; 4 lit tennis courts; fitness center; spa; sauna; children's club; secretarial services; babysitting; laundry service; dry cleaning; nonsmoking rooms; rooms for those w/limited mobility; dive shop; kayaks; sailing; snorkeling; windsurfing. *In room:* A/C, TV, dataport, fridge, beverage maker, hair dryer, iron, safe.

EXPENSIVE

Elysian Beach Resort ✿   This time-share resort on Cowpet Bay, a 30-minute drive from Charlotte Amalie, is imbued with a certain European resort chic. If you seek tranquillity and seclusion without all the razzle-dazzle of other East End competitors, stay here. The beautiful white-sand beach is another compelling reason to choose this place. The resort offers an open-air shuttle to town.

The thoughtfully planned bedrooms have balconies, and 14 offer sleeping lofts reached by a spiral staircase. The decor is tropical, with rattan and bamboo furnishings, ceiling fans, and natural-wood ceilings. The rooms are in a bevy of four-story buildings connected to landscaped gardens. Of the various units, 43 can be converted into one-bedroom suites, 43 into two-bedroom suites, and 11 into three-bedroom suites. Designer fabrics and white ceramic-tile floors make the tropical living quite luxurious. Try to avoid rooms in buildings V, W, X, Y, and Z, as they are some distance from the beach.

6800 Estate Nazareth, Cowpet Bay, St. Thomas, U.S.V.I. 00802. © **800/438-6499** or 340/775-1000. Fax 340/776-0910. www.equivest.com. 182 units. Winter $195–$239 double, $399 suite; off season $149–$199 double, $319 suite. AE, DC, DISC, MC, V. **Amenities:** 2 restaurants; 2 bars; outdoor pool; tennis court; fitness center; sauna; massage; laundry service; dry cleaning; nonsmoking rooms; rooms for those w/limited mobility; open-air shuttle to town; snorkeling gear; Sunfish sailboats; volleyball. *In room:* A/C, TV, kitchenette, beverage maker, hair dryer, iron, safe.

Pavilions and Pools ✿   Ideal for a honeymoon, this resort lets you have your own villa, with floor-to-ceiling glass doors opening onto your own private swimming pool. It's ideal for those who want to run around nude as Adam and Eve, Eve and Eve, or Adam and Adam. The resort, 7 miles east of Charlotte Amalie, is a string of condominium units, tastefully rebuilt and furnished. After checking in and following a wooden pathway to your attached villa, you don't have to see another soul until you leave if you so wish—the fence and gate around your space are that high. Your swimming pool is encircled by a deck and plenty of tropical greenery. Inside, a room divider screens a well-equipped kitchen. The place is not posh, and an average good motel in the States will have better-quality furniture. The bathroom has an outdoor garden shower where you can rinse off after a swim or trip to the beach. The resort adjoins Sapphire Bay, which boasts one of the island's best beaches and many watersports concessions. Honeymooning couples should inquire about packages.

6400 Estate Smith Bay, St. Thomas, U.S.V.I. 00802. ℂ **800/524-2001** or 340/775-6110. Fax 340/775-6110. www.pavilionsandpools.com. 25 units. Winter $250–$275 double; off season $180–$195. Rates include continental breakfast. AE, MC, V. **Amenities:** Restaurant; 25 outdoor pools; laundry service; nonsmoking rooms; rooms for those w/limited mobility; day sails; snorkeling gear. *In room:* A/C, TV, dataport, kitchen, fridge, beverage maker, hair dryer, iron, safe.

4 Where to Dine

The dining scene in St. Thomas is among the best in the West Indies, but it has its drawbacks: Fine dining (and even not-so-fine dining) tends to be expensive, and the best spots (with a few exceptions) are not right in Charlotte Amalie and can only be reached by taxi or car.

You'll find an eclectic mix of cuisines on St. Thomas, including American, Italian, Mexican, Asian, and other options. We recommend digging into some of the local Caribbean dishes at least once or twice, especially the seafood specialties like "ole wife" and yellowtail, which are usually prepared with a spicy Creole mixture of peppers, onions, and tomatoes. The winner among native side dishes is *fungi* (pronounced *foon*-gee), made with okra and cornmeal. Most local restaurants serve johnnycake, a popular fried, unleavened bread.

IN CHARLOTTE AMALIE
EXPENSIVE

Banana Tree Grill INTERNATIONAL   This place offers candlelit dinners, sweeping views over the harbor, and a decor that includes banana plants scattered through the two dining rooms. The cuisine is creative, the patrons often hip and laid-back. Start off with

Where to Dine in St. Thomas

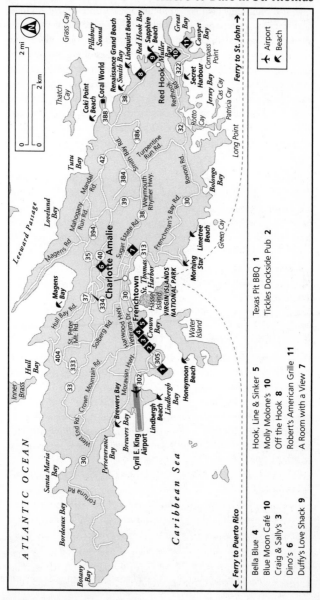

Bella Blue **4**
Blue Moon Café **10**
Craig & Sally's **3**
Dino's **6**
Duffy's Love Shack **9**

Hook, Line & Sinker **5**
Molly Molone's **10**
Off the Hook **8**
Robert's American Grille **11**
A Room with a View **7**

Texas Pit BBQ **1**
Tickles Dockside Pub **2**

← Ferry to Puerto Rico

Ferry to St. John →

✈ Airport
⚓ Beach

one of the accurately named "fabulous firsts," such as tuna wontons with a zippy orange-pepper sauce, or bacon-wrapped horseradish shrimp grilled and dancing over a mango glaze. Main dishes are filled with flavor, especially the house specialties of sugar-cane-and-cocoa-lacquered tuna, lobster tail tempura with an orange-pepper sauce, and the divine mango-and-mustard-glazed salmon. Try the aioli shank, a house specialty, if it's offered: A shank of lamb is slowly braised in Chianti and served with an aioli sauce over white beans and garlic mashed potatoes. The desserts are truly decadent.

In Bluebeard's Castle, Bluebeard's Hill. ✆ **340/776-4050.** Reservations recommended. Main courses $17–$39. AE, MC, V. Tues–Sun 6–9:30pm.

Beni Iguana's Sushi Bar ✿ JAPANESE   It's the only sushi restaurant on St. Thomas, a change of pace from the Caribbean, steak, and seafood nearby. Along with a handful of shops, it occupies the courtyard and an old cistern across from Emancipation Square Park. You can eat outside, or pass through Danish colonial doors into a red-and-black-lacquered interior devoted to a sushi bar and a handful of simple tables. A perennial favorite is the "13" roll, stuffed with spicy crabmeat, salmon, lettuce, cucumbers, and scallions.

In the Grand Hotel Court, Veteran's Dr. ✆ **340/777-8744.** Reservations recommended. Sushi $4–$18 per portion (2 pieces); main courses $8–$17; combo plates for 4 to 5 diners $26–$36 each. AE, DC, MC, V. Mon–Sat 11:30am–3pm and 5–9pm.

Hervé Restaurant & Wine Bar ✿✿ AMERICAN/ CARIBBEAN/CONTINENTAL   This is the hottest restaurant on St. Thomas. A panoramic view of Charlotte Amalie and a historic setting are minor benefits—it's the cuisine that matters here. Hervé P. Chassin, whose expertise has touched such stellar properties as the Hotel du Cap d'Antibes, is a restaurateur with a vast classical background. Here, in his own unpretentious setting, he offers high-quality food at reasonable prices.

There are two dining areas: a large open-air terrace, and a more intimate wine room. Contemporary American and classic French dishes are served, many with Caribbean touches. Start with the pistachio-encrusted Brie, shrimp in a stuffed crab shell, or conch fritters with mango chutney. From here, you can let your taste buds indulge in such treats as the house special bouillabaisse, or a delectable black sesame–crusted tuna with ginger-raspberry sauce. Well-prepared specials of game, fish, and pasta are also featured. Desserts here are equally divine—you'll rarely taste a creamier crème caramel or a lighter, fluffier mango or raspberry cheesecake.

Next to Hotel 1829, Government Hill. ℂ **340/777-9703.** Reservations requested. Main courses $5.50–$17 lunch, $19–$28 dinner. AE, MC, V. Daily 11am–3pm and 6–10pm.

Tavern on the Waterfront ℝ *Finds* CARIBBEAN/FRENCH Yes, that was Walter Cronkite you saw dining at the next table. And was that Michael Jordan at the far end of the room? This is often the place of choice for celebrities visiting the island. The cuisine is Caribbean style with a French flair, and the chefs are inventive but cook with a solid technique, and attractive presentation. All the dishes have a distinctive flavor, beginning with such appetizers as conch fritters or coconut shrimp with mango chutney. Main dishes include the award-winning barbecue pork ribs that take 120 hours—from the marinade to the cooking—to prepare. We've also enjoyed their exotic pork platter, with espresso and cinnamon–encrusted pork medallions covered with a passion fruit demi-glaze. The blackened seafood linguini, another winner, comes with mahimahi, jumbo sea scallops, New Zealand mussels, and shrimp, bathed in a Cajun cream sauce.

Live entertainment is often featured, which you can enjoy while taking in harbor views. The setting is relatively simple but still elegant, with tables resting under African mahogany vaulted ceilings. Original artwork hangs on the white walls.

Waterfront at Royal Dane Mall. ℂ **340/776-4328.** Reservations required. Main courses $19–$42. AE, DISC, MC, V. Mon–Sat 11am–3pm and 5:30–10pm.

Virgilio's ℝ NORTHERN ITALIAN This is the best northern Italian restaurant in the Virgin Islands. Virgilio's neo-baroque interior is sheltered under heavy ceiling beams and brick vaulting. Owner Virgilio del Mare serves meals against a backdrop of stained-glass windows, crystal chandeliers, and soft Italian music. A well-trained staff attends to the tables. The *cinco peche* (clams, mussels, scallops, oysters, and crayfish simmered in a saffron broth) is a house special, and the lobster ravioli is the best there is. Classic dishes are cooked with flair—the rack of lamb shank, for example, is filled with a porcini mushroom stuffing and glazed with a roasted garlic aioli. The marinated grilled duck is served chilled.

18 Dronningens Gade (entrance on a narrow alley running between Main and Back sts.). ℂ **340/776-4920.** Reservations recommended. Main courses $11–$26 lunch, $20–$40 dinner. AE, MC, V. Mon–Sat 11:30am–10:30pm.

MODERATE

Cuzzin's Caribbean Restaurant & Bar 🎯 *Finds* CARIBBEAN
For some real, old-fashioned Virgin Islands cooking, head to this offbeat place in an 18th-century stable on Back Street. The dining room is comfortable, with stone and brick walls. The restaurant boasts island dishes, with a focus on seafood, especially conch, lobster, and freshly caught fish. Native dishes include stews and curries, such as island-style mutton, curried chicken, and conch stewed in onion butter sauce. The signature dish is Cuzzin' Nemo, a mélange of lobster, conch, scallops, and shrimp served over pasta. Fried green bananas or fried plantains accompany most dishes, and desserts are rich and luscious. The drinks of choice include local beverages such as ginger beer, mauby, and sea moss.

7 Wimmelskafts Gade (Back St.). ✆ 340/777-4711. Reservations recommended. Main courses $14–$28. AE, DISC, MC, V. Tues–Sat 11am–5pm and 6–9pm.

The Green House AMERICAN/CARIBBEAN   Fronted by big windows, this waterfront restaurant attracts cruise-ship passengers who have shopped and need a place to drop. The food here is not the island's best, but it's satisfying if you're not too demanding. The house specializes in chicken, often with exotic fruit flavors, such as mango banana chicken or coconut chicken. The excellent appetizers range from conch fritters to stuffed jalapeño peppers. A kettle of soup is always on the stove, and you can make a meal of the freshly made salads. The most popular item on the menu is the big, juicy burger, the island's finest, made with certified Angus beef. There's a wide selection of seafood, like the baked stuffed swordfish with garlic cream sauce, plus chef's specialties such as baby back ribs.

Every day, happy hour from 4:30 to 7pm seduces party animals with 2-for-1 drinks. On Tuesday nights after 9:30pm, the Green House turns into a hip nightclub attracting a 21-and-over crowd. These "Two-for-Tuesdays" are the biggest events on Tuesday night in St. Thomas, when, again, you can get two drinks for the price of one. On Friday nights you can hear live reggae music here; on other nights the sounds are selected by a DJ.

Veterans Dr. ✆ 340/774-7998. Main courses $10–$30. AE, DISC, MC, V. Daily 11:30am–10pm; bar daily 11:30–2am.

INEXPENSIVE

Diamond Barrel AMERICAN/CARIBBEAN   This popular local eatery and hangout is active throughout the day. The decor (what there is of it) is nautical. Breakfast is fairly standard fare, but at lunch you can sample some good regional dishes, including the catch of the day and various chicken dishes. You might begin with whatever was thrown in the kettle that day. If you want to go really local, opt for the stewed mutton or the pickled pigs' feet, although you might settle for the salmon patties. On-site is a bakery providing fresh pastries and other baked goods. Expect cafeteria-style service.

18 Norre Gade. © **340/774-5071.** Breakfast $4–$10; lunch main courses $6–$12. No credit cards. Mon–Sat 6:30am–6pm.

Gladys's Café ☺ *Finds* CARIBBEAN/AMERICAN Antigua-born owner Gladys Isles is a warm, gracious woman who makes a visit here all the more special. Her Café is in a 1700 pump house with a stonework courtyard that has a well (one of only three on the island) in the middle. Breakfast here is the best value in town. The lunch offerings feature various sandwiches, salads, and fresh seafood, including an excellent swordfish and dumplings. The house specialty is the hot chicken salad, made with pieces of sautéed breast with red-wine vinegar, pine nuts, and dill, all nestled on a bed of lettuce. Or try a local lobster, shrimp, fresh pasta, fresh fish, or steak.

Royal Dane Mall. © **340/774-6604.** Reservations required for groups of 6 or more. Breakfast $5.50–$11; lunch main courses $11–$16. AE, MC, V. Mon–Sat 7am–5pm; Sun 8am–2pm.

Hard Rock Cafe AMERICAN Go here if you must. Occupying the second floor of a pink-sided mall whose windows overlook the ships in the harbor, this restaurant is a member of the chain that defines itself as the Smithsonian of rock 'n' roll. Walls are devoted to memorabilia of John Lennon, Eric Clapton, Bob Marley, and others. Throughout most of the day this place functions as a restaurant, serving salads, sandwiches, burgers (including a well-flavored veggie burger), fish, steaks, barbecued meats, and the best fajitas in the Virgin Islands. The hamburgers are good; as for the other stuff, you've had better. But the food is incidental to the good times. On Friday and Saturday, a live band performs, at which time a small dance floor gets busy, and the bar trade picks up considerably.

In International Plaza, Waterfront Hwy. © **340/777-5555.** Main courses $9–$20. AE, DC, DISC, MC, V. Daily 10:30am–11pm.

EAST OF CHARLOTTE AMALIE
EXPENSIVE

A Room with a View ☺ INTERNATIONAL The finest restaurant in Bluebeard's Castle Hotel attracts diners who come for the succulent food and a wide-angle hillside view that some patrons, especially after a few drinks, have described as mystical. The intimate (40 seats) restaurant is outfitted in tones of burgundy and green, with floor-to-ceiling windows that sweep westward over the sunset, the harbor front of Charlotte Amalie, and as far away as the airport. There's a small bar on the premises (the kind of five-stool bar that's appropriate for an aperitif, but not as an all-night hangout).

Your meal might begin with such choices as steamed littleneck clams in either a white wine or red wine–based Provençal sauce, spinach pie *(spanikopita)* as you might remember it tasting in Greece, grilled portobello mushrooms with goat cheese, and *dolmades* (stuffed vine leaves) with dill and sun-dried tomatoes. Main courses feature fresh fish, including an excellent yellowfin tuna, with teriyaki and ginger sauce; and locally caught lobster prepared Thermidor style (removed from its shell, simmered with butter, cream, sherry, and Romano cheese). Carnivores will enjoy the tender, succulent filet steak with peppercorn sauce. The chef is especially proud of the pork Marsala, simmered in butter with mushrooms, Marsala wine, and cream. Attentive service adds to the evening's charms.

In Bluebeard's Castle Hotel (p. 45), Bluebeard's Hill. ℭ **340/774-2377.** Reservations recommended. Main courses $22–$32. AE, MC, V. Mon–Sat 5pm–midnight.

MODERATE

Dino's MEDITERRANEAN/PIZZA   This restaurant doesn't necessarily have the best food on St. Thomas, but it's got the best view. Built in the 1950s on some of the island's highest terrain, it stands in an isolated spot with panoramic views over Magens Bay. Over the years, various chefs and owners have experimented with different cuisines; the present occupants decided to go trendy with Mediterranean. Many guests prefer to arrive when the bar opens at 5pm, to enjoy the greatest place in St. Thomas for sunset cocktails. By the time dinner is served, it's "Who cares?" Others come for the cuisine, which is more familiar than imaginative but quite satisfying. The appetizer of crab cakes with an endive salad is delicious, and portobello mushrooms with fresh mozzarella please the palate. For a main course, most of the ingredients are imported but taste just fine in such dishes as grilled yellowfin tuna with ginger, soy sauce, and wasabi. Many patrons come here just for the New York–style pizzas.

Rte. 33, Crown Mountain Rd. ℭ **340/774-6800.** Reservations recommended. Pizza $11–$16; main courses $11–$25. MC, V. Mon–Sat 5–10pm.

WEST OF CHARLOTTE AMALIE
MODERATE

Bella Blue ℛ MEDITERRANEAN/SEAFOOD   West of Charlotte Amalie, this restaurant's 12 tables overlook the harbor. For years this restaurant enjoyed fame throughout the Caribbean when it was called Alexander's and served a heavy (for the Tropics) Austrian cuisine. Under its new owners, the fare is lighter and focuses on the sunny flavors of the Mediterranean. To begin with, you might try the tuna tartare or a Moroccan dish. The cooks are excellent at concocting superb creations from lamb, veal, and seafood. The menu is seasonal and features what's good and fresh at the marketplace.

French Town Mall. ℂ **340/774-4349.** Reservations recommended. Main courses $8–$20 lunch, $16–$25 dinner. AE, MC, V. Mon–Sat 11:30am–5pm and 5:30–10pm.

Craig & Sally's ℛ INTERNATIONAL

This Caribbean cafe is set in an airy, open-sided pavilion in Frenchtown. Its eclectic cuisine is, according to the owner, "not for the faint of heart, but for the adventurous soul." Views of the sky and sea are complemented by a cuisine that ranges from pasta to seafood, with influences from Europe and Asia. Roast pork with clams, filet mignon with macadamia-nut sauce, and grilled swordfish with a sauce of fresh herbs and tomatoes are examples from a menu that changes every day. The lobster-stuffed, twice-baked potatoes are inspired. The wine list is the most extensive and sophisticated on St. Thomas.

3525 Honduras, Frenchtown. ℂ **340/777-9949.** Reservations recommended. Main courses $16–$43. MC, V. Wed–Fri 11:30am–3pm; Wed–Sun 5:30–10pm.

Hook, Line & Sinker AMERICAN/SEAFOOD

Locals and visitors flock to this rendezvous, where they get friendly service, good food at reasonable prices, and a panoramic view of the harbor. The setting evokes a New England seaport village; the building has a pitched roof and skylights, along with wraparound French doors and windows. A *Cheers*-like crowd frequents the bar. Breakfast, except for Sunday brunch, is standard. Lunch choices range from a Caesar salad to grilled chicken dishes. The dinner menu is usually a delight, featuring delicious dishes such as mango-rum tuna, jerk swordfish, and yellowtail stuffed with mushrooms and red peppers and covered in a garlic sauce. Locals call the hearty soups "outrageous."

62 Honduras, Frenchtown. ℂ **340/776-9708.** Main courses $7–$11 lunch, $13–$22 dinner; Sun brunch $7–$13. AE, MC, V. Mon–Sat 11am–4pm and 6–10pm; Sun 10am–2:30pm.

INEXPENSIVE

Tickles Dockside Pub AMERICAN   This joint is dedicated to the concept of fun, comfort, and reasonably-priced food in a friendly atmosphere. Diners at this open-air restaurant can sit back and relax while watching the sailboats and cruise ships on the water.

The menu features a simple American fare of burgers (not as good as Hard Rock's), including a vegetarian burger, and other sandwiches. The renowned Reuben is made with your choice of ham, turkey, or corned beef, grilled with Tickles's own Russian dressing, Swiss cheese, and sauerkraut. Start off with a plate of "gator eggs" (lightly breaded jalapeño peppers stuffed with cheese) or "sweet lips" (strips of sweet, fried chicken with a honey-mustard sauce), or a local version of conch chowder. If you're in the mood for seafood, try the beer-battered whitefish, which is fried and served with Swiss-fried potatoes. The cooks also turn out an array of dishes found in different places throughout America: chicken Alfredo, prime rib, baby back ribs, fried catfish, and a fisherman's platter served over pasta.

Crown Bay Marina. ✆ **340/776-1595.** Main courses $8–$15 lunch, $10–$28 dinner. AE, MC, V. Daily 7am–10:30pm (Bar until midnight).

THE EAST END
EXPENSIVE

Blue Moon Café ✦ CREATIVE AMERICAN   This open-air restaurant is truly an idyllic dining spot. The beachfront restaurant claims, with some degree of accuracy, one of the most memorable settings for panoramic sunset views. *The Wine Spectator* honored the restaurant twice for having the most romantic setting in St. Thomas. In winter, there is piano music on Wednesday nights, and a steel drum band on Fridays. The menu, based on market-fresh ingredients, is changed twice seasonally. The list of dishes is geared to appeal to a wide range of palates. Begin with such tropical starters as coconut-honey shrimp with a guava dipping sauce or a portobello mushroom-and-goat cheese tart with field onions. Tip-top foodstuffs are handled with imagination and used in zestful combinations such as mahimahi with pecans, bananas, and a coconut-rum sauce, and grilled scallops with a tomato-basil risotto with fresh asparagus. For lunch, you may want to confine yourself to burgers, wraps, salads, and sandwiches.

In the Secret Harbour Beach Resort, 6280 Estate Nazareth Bay. ✆ **340/779-2262.** Reservations required. Main courses $14–$35. AE, DC, DISC, MC, V. Daily 8–10am, 11am–3pm, and 6–10pm.

Robert's American Grille ✦ *Finds* AMERICAN   When the shopping bazaars and the glut of cruise-ship passengers flooding Charlotte Amalie have got you down, head to this retreat. Robert's offers cuisine, decor, and service that have a subtle flair. The restaurant opens onto the beach at Cowpet Bay. In an open-air setting, you can enjoy chef/owner Kevin Kuepper's cuisine. He takes regional American dishes and applies his own creative, imaginative interpretations. You might start with his Elysian salad (mesclun greens with roasted walnuts, Bermuda onions, chopped tomatoes, and a house-made dried-cranberry-poppyseed dressing, garnished with shredded Gruyère). His "cherry chicken" is a delight: a boneless breast of chicken sautéed with Michigan dried cherries and tarragon, simmered in a cream sauce, and served with buttermilk mashed potatoes. His pan-fried pork loin medallions are also excellent; the boneless center cut is sautéed and then deglazed with a honey-lime wasabi. Another treat is pan-seared tandoori-marinated filet of mahimahi with Thai purple sticky rice and a West Indian curry sauce.

In Elysian Beach Resort (p. 49), 6800 Estate Nazareth, Cowpet Bay. ⓒ **340/775-1000**. Reservations recommended. Main courses $14–$29. AE, MC, V. Tues–Sat 5:30–10:30pm; Sun 11:30am–2:30pm and 5:30–9pm.

MODERATE

Molly Malone's IRISH/CARIBBEAN   At the Red Hook American Yacht Harbor, you can join the good ol' boys and dig into some of the best baby back ribs on the island. If you're nostalgic for the Emerald Isle, go for the shepherd's pie. The conch fritters are the best in the East End, and you can launch yourself with a bowl of savory conch chowder. In one of the wildest culinary offerings we've seen lately, an "Irish/Caribbean stew" is a nightly feature. If the catch that day netted a big wahoo, those game fish steaks will be on the menu. No one can drink more brew than the boisterous crowd that assembles here every night to let the good times roll. You can dine outdoors under a canopy, right on the dock at the eastern end of Red Hook, where the ferry from St. John pulls in.

6100 Red Hook Quarters. ⓒ **340/775-1270**. Main courses $15–$25. AE, MC, V. Daily 7am–1am.

Off the Hook ⓖ ASIAN/CARIBBEAN   Diners here enjoy an eclectic medley of specialties inspired by Asia, which the chefs concoct using some of the freshest and finest ingredients in the West Indies. In an open-air dining room near the American Yacht Harbor, close to the departure point for the ferry to St. John, the fresh catch of the day—hauled off the little fishing boats that pull in—is delivered to the kitchen, where it's grilled to perfection. The yellowfin tuna keeps us coming back. The chef is adept at preparing a tuna and salmon sushi platter, and the Black Angus steak is always a pure delight. The decor is rustic, with outdoor dining and wooden tables.

6300 Estate Smith Bay. ⓒ **340/775-6350**. Reservations required. Main courses $18–$26. AE, MC, V. Daily 6–10pm. Closed Sept 15–Oct 15.

INEXPENSIVE

Duffy's Love Shack ★ *Finds* AMERICAN/CARIBBEAN   This is a fun and happening place where you can mingle with the locals. As the evening wears on, the customers become the entertainment, often dancing on tables or forming conga lines. Yes, Duffy's also serves food, a standard American cuisine spiced up with Caribbean flair and flavor. The restaurant is open-air, with lots of bamboo and a thatched roof over the bar. Even the menu appears on a bamboo stick, like an old-fashioned fan. Start with the honey-barbequed ribs, then move on to cowboy steak or junkanoo chicken (in a coconut-and-pineapple sauce). After 10pm, a late-night menu appears, mostly featuring sandwiches. The bar business is huge, and the bartender is known for his lethal rum drinks.

650 Red Hook Plaza, Rte. 38. (C) **340/779-2080.** Main courses $8–$16. No credit cards. Daily 11:30am–2am.

5 Beaches

Chances are that your hotel will be on the beach, or very close to one. All the beaches in the Virgin Islands are public, and most St. Thomas beaches lie anywhere from 2 to 5 miles from Charlotte Amalie.

THE NORTH COAST

The gorgeous white sands of **Magens Bay** ★★—the family favorite of St. Thomas—lie between two mountains 3 miles north of the capital. The turquoise waters are calm and ideal for swimming, though the snorkeling isn't as good. The beach is no secret, and it's usually overcrowded, though it gets better in the mid-afternoon. Changing facilities, snorkeling gear, lounge chairs, paddleboats, and kayaks are available. There is no public transportation to get here (though some hotels provide shuttle buses); from Charlotte Amalie, take Route 35 north all the way. The gates to the beach are open daily from 6am to 6pm. After 4pm, you'll need insect repellent. Admission is $1 per person and $1 per car. Don't bring valuables, and certainly don't leave anything of value in your parked car. Break-ins of cars and a few muggings are reported monthly.

A marked trail leads to **Little Magens Bay,** a separate, clothing-optional beach that's especially popular with gay and lesbian visitors. This is former president Clinton's preferred beach on St. Thomas (no, he doesn't go nude).

Coki Point Beach, in the northeast near Coral World, is good but often very crowded with both singles and families. It's noted for its warm, crystal-clear water, ideal for swimming and snorkeling; you'll see thousands of rainbow-hued fish swimming among the corals. Locals sell small bags of fish food, so you can feed the sea creatures while you're snorkeling. From the beach, there's a view of offshore Thatch Cay. Concessions can arrange everything from waterskiing to parasailing. A Vitrans East End bus runs to Smith Bay and lets you off at the gate to Coral World and Coki. Watch out for pickpockets.

Also on the north side of the island is luscious **Grand Beach,** one of St. Thomas's most beautiful, attracting mainly families and couples. It opens onto Smith Bay and is near Coral World. Many watersports are available here. The beach is right off Route 38.

THE EAST END

Small and special, **Secret Harbour** is near a collection of condos and has long been favored by singles of either sex and by those of all sexual persuasions. With its white sand and coconut palms, it's the epitome of Caribbean charm. The snorkeling near the rocks is some of the best on the island. No public transportation stops here, but it's an easy taxi ride east of Charlotte Amalie heading toward Red Hook.

Sapphire Beach 𝕣 is set against the backdrop of the Sapphire Beach Resort & Marina, where you can have lunch or order drinks. Like Magens Beach, this good, wide, safe beach is one of the most frequented by families. There are good views of offshore cays and St. John, and a reef is close to the shore. Windsurfers like this beach a lot. Snorkeling gear and lounge chairs can be rented. Take the Vitrans East End bus from Charlotte Amalie, via Red Hook. Ask to be let off at the entrance to Sapphire Bay; it's not too far a walk from here to the water.

White-sand **Lindquist Beach** isn't a long strip, but it's one of the island's prettiest beaches. It's between Wyndham Sugar Bay Resort & Spa and the Sapphire Beach Resort. Many films and TV commercials have used this photogenic beach as a backdrop. It's not likely to be crowded, as it's not very well known. Couples in the know retreat here for sun and romance.

THE SOUTH COAST

Morning Star 𝕣—also known as Frenchman's Bay Beach—is near the Frenchman's Reef & Marriott Morning Star Beach Resort, about 2 miles east of Charlotte Amalie. Here, among the hip, savvy, often young crowds (many of whom are gay singles and couples), you can don your skimpiest bikini. Sailboats, snorkeling equipment, and lounge chairs are available for rent. The beach is easily reached by a

Taking to the Seas

On St. Thomas, most of the boat business centers around the Red Hook and Yacht Haven marinas.

The 50-foot *Yacht Nightwind,* Sapphire Marina (© 340/775-4110), offers full-day sails, from 9am to 4pm, to St. John and the outer islands. The $120 price for adults ($85 for kids 12 and under) includes continental breakfast, a champagne buffet lunch, and an open bar aboard. You're also given free snorkeling equipment and instruction.

New Horizons, 6501 Red Hook Plaza, Suite 16, Red Hook (© 340/775-1171), offers wind-borne excursions amid the cays and reefs. The two-masted, 65-foot sloop has circumnavigated the globe, and has been used as a design prototype for other boats. Owned and operated by Canadian Tim Krygsveld, it contains a hot-water shower, serves a specialty drink called a "New Horizons Nooner" (with a melon-liqueur base), and carries a complete line of snorkeling equipment for adults and children. A full-day excursion, from 9:15am to 4pm, with a continental breakfast, Italian buffet lunch and an open bar, costs $110 per person ($55 for children ages 2–12). Excursions depart daily, weather permitting, from the Sapphire Beach Resort & Marina (© 800/524-2090 or 340-775-6100; www.sapphire beachresort.com). Call ahead for reservations and information.

New Horizons also offer *New Horizons II,* a 44-foot custom-made speedboat that takes you on a full-day trip, from 7:30am to 4:30pm, to some of the most scenic highlights of the British Virgin Islands. Trips cost $125 for adults or $95 for children ages 2 to 12.

You can avoid the crowds by sailing aboard the *Fantasy,* 6100 Leeward Way, no. 28 (© 340/775-5652; fax 340/775-6256), which departs daily from the American Yacht Harbor

cliff-front elevator at Frenchman's Reef. **Limetree Beach,** set against a backdrop of seagrape trees and shady palms, also lures hip folks. On this spread of sand, you can bask in the sun and even feed hibiscus blossoms to the iguanas. Snorkeling gear, lounge and beach chairs, towels, and drinks are available. There's no public transport, but the beach can easily be reached by taxi from Charlotte Amalie.

at Red Hook at 9:30am and returns at 3pm. The boat takes a maximum of six passengers to St. John and nearby islands for swimming, snorkeling, and beachcombing. Snorkel gear and expert instruction is provided, as is a champagne lunch; an underwater camera is available. The full-day trip costs $125 per person for adults and children. A half-day sail, usually only offered during the low season, departs in the morning or afternoon, lasts 3 hours, and costs $80 for adults and children.

American Yacht Harbor, Red Hook (© **340/775-6454**), offers both bareboat and fully crewed charters. Boats leave from a colorful yacht-filled harbor set against the backdrop of Heritage Gade, a reproduction of a Caribbean village. The harbor is home to numerous boat companies, including day-trippers, fishing boats, and sailing charters like **Nauti Nymph Powerboat Rentals** (© **800/734-7345**). There are also four restaurants on the property, serving everything from Continental to Caribbean cuisine. Another reliable charter boat outfitter is **Charteryacht League,** at Flagship (© **800/524-2061** or **340/774-3944**).

Sailors may want to check out the *Yachtsman's Guide to the Virgin Islands,* available at major marine outlets, at bookstores, through catalog merchandisers, or direct from **Tropic Isle Publishers,** P.O. Box 610938, North Miami, FL 33261-0938 (© **877/923-9653**; www.yachtsmansguide.com). This annual guide, which costs $11, is supplemented by photographs; landfall sketches and charts showing harbors and harbor entrances, anchorages, channels, and landmarks; and information on preparations necessary for cruising the islands.

WEST OF CHARLOTTE AMALIE

Near the University of the Virgin Islands, in the southwest, **Brewers Bay** is one of the island's most popular beaches for families. The strip of white coral sand is almost as long as the beach at Magens Bay. Unfortunately, this isn't a good place for snorkeling. Vendors sell light meals and drinks. From Charlotte Amalie, take the Fortuna bus heading west; get off at the edge of Brewers Bay, across from the Reichhold Center.

Lindbergh Beach, with a lifeguard, restrooms, and a bathhouse, is at the Island Beachcomber Hotel (p. 44) and is used extensively by locals, who stage events from political rallies to Carnival parties here. Beach-loving couples are also attracted to this beach. It's not good for snorkeling. Drinks are served on the beach. Take the Fortuna bus route west from Charlotte Amalie.

6 Fun in the Surf & Sun

WATERSPORTS

DEEP-SEA FISHING   The U.S. Virgins have excellent deep-sea fishing—some 19 world records (8 for blue marlin) have been set in these waters. Outfitters abound at the major marinas like Red Hook. We recommend angling off the *Fish Hawk* (© 340/775-9058), which Captain Al Petrosky sails out of Fish Hawk Marina Lagoon on the east end. His 48-foot diesel-powered craft is fully equipped with rods and reels. For the trip, all equipment, and drinks (but not meals) you'll pay $550 per half-day for up to six passengers. Full-day excursions start at $1,100.

KAYAK TOURS   Virgin Island Ecotours/Mangrove Adventures (© 340/779-2155) offers half-day kayak trips through a mangrove lagoon on the southern coastline. The cost is $60 per person. The tour is led by professional naturalists who allow for 30 to 45 minutes of snorkeling.

SCUBA DIVING & SNORKELING   The best scuba diving site off St. Thomas, especially for novices, is **Cow and Calf Rocks,** off the southeast end (45 min. from Charlotte Amalie by boat); here, you'll discover a network of coral tunnels filled with caves, reefs, and ancient boulders encrusted with coral. The *Cartanser Sr.,* a sunken World War II cargo ship that lies in about 35 feet of water, is beautifully encrusted with coral and is home to myriad colorful resident fish. Another popular wreck dive is the *Maj. General Rogers,* the stripped-down hull of a former Coast Guard cutter.

Experienced divers may want to dive at exposed sheer rock pinnacles like **Sail Rock** and **French Cap Pinnacle,** which are encrusted with hard and soft corals, and are frequented by lobsters and green and hawksbill turtles. Both spots are to open-ocean currents, making these very challenging dives.

St. Thomas Diving Club, 7147 Bolongo Bay (© 877/538-8734 in the U.S., or 340/776-2381), is a full-service, PADI five-star IDC

Finds **A Thrilling Dive for Non-Divers**

Virgin Islands Snuba Excursions (© 340/693-8063; www.vi snuba.com) are ideal for beginning swimmers. These excursions are offered both at Coral World on St. Thomas, and at Trunk Bay, on St. John. With Snuba's equipment—an air line that attaches to an air tank floating on the surface—even novices can breathe easily underwater without the use of restrictive dive gear. The Snuba operations begin in waist-deep water and make a gradual descent to a depth of 20 feet. It's fun for the entire family, from ages 8 and up, and no snorkeling or scuba experience is needed. Most orientation and guided underwater tours take 1½ hours, costing $57 per person on St. John. On St. Thomas, a pass to Coral World is included, and the rate is $59 for adults and $57 for children 8 to 12.

center, the best on the island. An open-water certification course, including four dives, costs $385. An advanced open-water certification course, including five dives that can be accomplished in 2 days, goes for $275. On request, divers are taken on an excursion that includes a two-tank dive to the wreck of the **HMS *Rhone*** in the British Virgin Islands; the trip costs $130, and the company must have a minimum of 6 divers to arrange the trip. A scuba tour of the 350-foot wreck of the *Witshoal* is offered for experienced divers; the cost is $88. You can also enjoy local snorkeling for $40.

DIVE IN!, in the Sapphire Beach Resort & Marina, Smith Bay Road, Route 36 (© 866/434-8346, ext. 2144, in the U.S., or 340/777-5255), is a well-recommended diving center that offers some of the finest services in the U.S. Virgin Islands, including professional instruction (beginner to advanced), beach and boat dives, custom packages, snorkeling trips, and a full-service PADI dive center. An introductory course is $75, with a one-tank dive for $65 and two-tank dives costing $85. A six-dive pass costs $230.

MORE OUTDOOR ADVENTURE

GOLF   Mahogany Run, on the north shore at Mahogany Run Road (© 800/253-7103), is an 18-hole, par-70 course. It rises and drops like a roller coaster on its journey to the sea; cliffs and crashing waves are the ultimate hazards at the 13th and 14th holes. Former President Clinton pronounced this course very challenging. Greens fees are $140 to $160 for 18 holes, reduced to $100 to $125 in the late afternoon. Carts are included. Club rental costs $40.

Moments **Under the Sea (Without Getting Wet)**

The air-conditioned *Atlantis* submarine will take you on a 1-hour voyage (the whole experience is really 2 hr., when you include transportation to and from the sub) to depths of 90 feet, where an amazing world of marine life unfolds. You'll have close-up views of coral reefs and sponge gardens through the sub's 2-foot windows. On some voyages, *Atlantis* divers swim with the fish and bring them close to the windows for photos.

Passengers take a surface boat from the West Indies Dock, right outside Charlotte Amalie, to the submarine, which is near Buck Island (the St. Thomas version, not the more famous Buck Island near St. Croix). The fare is $84 for adults, $42 for children ages 4 to 17; children 3 and under are not allowed. The *Atlantis* operates daily. Reservations are a must (the sub carries only 48 passengers). For tickets, go to the Havensight shopping mall, building 6, or call © **340/776-5650.**

TENNIS   The best tennis on the island is at the **Wyndham Sugar Bay Beach Club** *★★*, 6500 Estate Smith Bay (© **340/777-7100**), which has four Laykold courts lit at night, and a pro shops. Nonguests pay $8 per hour.

Another good resort for tennis is the **Bolongo Bay Beach Resort,** Bolongo Bay (© **340/775-1800**), which has two courts that are lit until 6pm. They're free to members and hotel guests, but cost $10 per hour for nonguests.

Marriott Frenchman's Reef Tennis Courts, Flamboyant Point (© **340/776-8500**), has two courts. Again, nonguests are charged $10 per hour per court. Lights stay on until 10pm.

7 Seeing the Sights

ATTRACTIONS IN CHARLOTTE AMALIE

The color and charm of the Caribbean come to life in the waterfront town of **Charlotte Amalie,** capital of St. Thomas, where most visitors begin their visit to the island. Seafarers from all over used to flock to this old-world Danish town, as did pirates and sailors of the Confederacy, who used the port during the American Civil War. At one time, St. Thomas was the biggest slave market in the world.

What to See in Charlotte Amalie

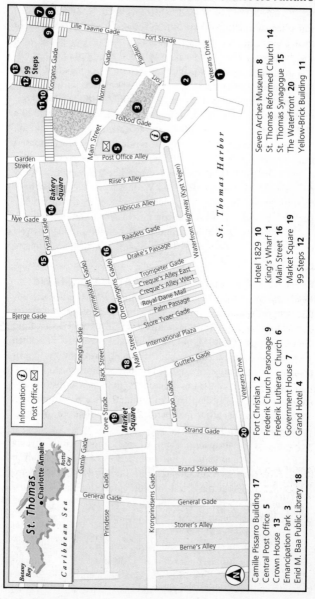

Camille Pissarro Building **17**
Central Post Office **5**
Crown House **13**
Emancipation Park **3**
Enid M. Baa Public Library **18**

Fort Christian **2**
Frederik Church Parsonage **9**
Frederik Lutheran Church **6**
Government House **7**
Grand Hotel **4**

Hotel 1829 **10**
King's Wharf **1**
Main Street **16**
Market Square **19**
99 Steps **12**

Seven Arches Museum **8**
St. Thomas Reformed Church **14**
St. Thomas Synagogue **15**
The Waterfront **20**
Yellow-Brick Building **11**

Old warehouses, once used for storing pirate goods, have been converted to shops. The main streets, called "Gade" (a reflection of their Danish heritage), now coalesce into a virtual shopping mall, and are often packed. Sandwiched among these shops are a few historic buildings, most of which can be seen on foot in about 2 hours. Try the walking tour below to visit the city's attractions.

The **Paradise Point Tramway** (© **340/774-9809**) affords visitors a dramatic view of Charlotte Amalie's harbor with a ride to a 697-foot peak. The tramway operates six cars, each with a 8-person capacity, for the 15-minute round-trip ride. It transports customers from the Havensight area to Paradise Point, where you can visit shops and the popular restaurant and bar. The tramway runs Friday to Tuesday from 9am to 5pm, and Wednesday and Thursday from 9am to 10pm. You'll pay dearly for the experience: the cost is $16 per adult round-trip, $8 round-trip for children under 12.

Charlotte Amalie is also worth exploring on foot, though we recommend that you do it early (before 10am) to avoid the throng of cruise-ship passengers.

PLACES OF INTEREST IN CHARLOTTE AMALIE

Places you might want to visit include **King's Wharf**, site of the Virgin Islands Legislature, which is housed in an apple-green military barracks dating from 1874, which is just down Fort Pladsen from **Fort Christian** (© **340/776-4566**) which dates from 1672. Named after Danish king Christian V, this structure was a governor's residence, police station, court, and jail until it became a historic landmark in 1977. A museum illuminates the island's history and culture. Cultural workshops and an exhibit of Victorian furnishings are just some of the attractions here. A museum shop features local crafts, maps, and prints.

Nearby is Emancipation Park, where a proclamation freeing African slaves and indentured European servants was read on July 3, 1848. Near the park is the Grand Hotel, built in 1837, where a visitor center dispenses travel information about the island. Around the corner, and up Post Office Alley, is the Central Post Office. On display here are murals by Stephen Dohanos, who became famous as a *Saturday Evening Post* cover artist.

Other buildings of interest you might wish to visit include **Frederik Lutheran Church,** built between 1780 and 1793, a Georgian-style building, financed by a free black parishioner, Jean Reeneaus.

If you head down Norre Gade and make a left at Lille Taavne Gade, just after you cross Kongens Gade, you'll see **Government**

House. This is the administrative headquarters for the U.S. Virgin Islands. It's been the center of political life in the islands since it was built around the time of the American Civil War. Visitors are allowed on the first two floors Monday through Saturday from 8am to noon and from 1 to 5pm.

Also on Government Hill, right next to Government House, you can visit the **Seven Arches Museum** (© **340/774-9295**). Browsers and gapers love checking out this museum, which is the private home of longtime residents Philibert Fluck and Barbara Demaras. This 2-century-old Danish house has been restored and furnished with antiques. Walk through the yellow ballast arches into the Great Room, which has a wonderful view of the Caribbean's busiest harbor. The $5 admission fee includes a cold tropical drink served in a beautiful, walled flower garden. It's open daily from 10am to 4pm, or by appointment.

Directly across from the Seven Arches Museum and Government House is the **Frederik Church Parsonage.** This building dates from 1725. It's one of the oldest houses on the island, and the only structure in the Government Hill district to retain its simple 18th-century lines.

Heading back down Kongens Gade, at the foot of the 99 Steps, you'll see **Hotel 1829.** Formerly known as the Lavalette House, this place was designed in 1829 by one of the leading merchants of Charlotte Amalie. This is a landmark building and a charming hotel that has attracted many of the island's most famous visitors over the years. (**Hotel 1829** provides the perfect veranda, with a spectacular view, for a midday drink or a sundowner.)

After your break, before you climb the 99 Steps, you may wish to stop in next door at the **Yellow-Brick Building.** This structure was built in 1854 in what local architects called "the style of Copenhagen." You can go inside and browse the many shops within.

Then, if you're up for it, you can climb the **99 Steps** (actually 103), which were erected in the early 1700s, and take you to the summit of Government Hill, from where you'll see the 18th-century **Crown House.** This stately private house was the home of von Scholten, the Danish ruler who issued the famous proclamation of emancipation in 1848.

Walk back down the steps and continue west along Kongens Gade, then down a pair of old brick steps until you reach Garden Street. Go right (north) on Garden Street and take a left onto Crystal Gade. There are two houses of worship you might want to see: **St. Thomas Reformed Church,** which dates from 1844. Much of its original structure, which was designed like a Greek temple, has been preserved intact, nearby is **St. Thomas Synagogue,** the oldest synagogue in continuous use under the American flag, and the second oldest in the Western Hemisphere. It was erected in 1833 by Sephardic Jews, and it still maintains the tradition of having sand on the floor, commemorating the exodus from Egypt. The structure was built of local stone, ballast brick from Denmark, and mortar made of molasses and sand. It's open to visitors Monday to Friday 9am to 4pm. Next door, the **Weibel Museum** showcases 300 years of Jewish history. It keeps the same hours.

On Main Street, you can also visit the Camille Pissarro Building at the Amsterdam Sauer Jewelry Store. Pissarro, a Spanish Jew who was one of the founders of French Impressionism, was born here as Jacob Pizarro in 1830. Before moving to Paris, he worked for his father in a store on Main Street.

Further down Main Street, you'll see Market Square. This was the center of a slave-trading market before the 1848 emancipation. Today it's an open-air fruit and vegetable market, selling, among other items, *genips* (grape-type fruit; to eat one, break open the skin and suck the pulp off the pit). The wrought-iron roof covered a railway station at the turn of the 20th century. The market is open Monday to Saturday, its busiest day; hours vary, but it's busiest from 9am to 3pm.

ATTRACTIONS IN THE WEST

Route 30 (Veterans Dr.) will take you west of Charlotte Amalie to **Frenchtown** (turn left at the sign to the Admiral's Inn). Early French-speaking settlers arrived on St. Thomas from St. Bart's. Many of today's residents are the direct descendants of those immigrants, who were known for speaking a distinctive French patois. This colorful village contains a bevy of restaurants and taverns. Because Charlotte Amalie has become somewhat dangerous at night, Frenchtown has picked up its after-dark business and is the best spot for dancing, drinking, and other local entertainment.

Further west, Harwood Highway (Rte. 308) will lead you to **Crown Mountain Road,** a scenic drive opening onto the best views of the hills, beaches, and crystal-clear waters around St. Thomas. Eventually, you'll arrive at **Mountain Top,** Crown Mountain (© **340/774-2400**). This building has a hot dog cart and a bar, plus eight shops. Most people come to enjoy the view and sip the banana daiquiris—the bar here supposedly invented them in 1949! This is perhaps the most scenic perch in St. Thomas, featuring a view of Sir Francis Drake Channel, which separates the U.S. Virgin Islands from the British Virgin Islands. It's open daily from 9am to 5pm.

ATTRACTIONS AROUND THE ISLAND

Coral World Marine Park & Undersea Observatory ⚡ (Kids

This marine complex, which is St. Thomas's number-one tourist attraction, features a three-story underwater observation tower 100 feet offshore. Inside, you'll see sponges, fish, coral, and other aquatic creatures in their natural state. An 80,000-gallon reef tank features exotic marine life of the Caribbean; another tank is devoted to sea predators, with circling sharks and giant moray eels. Activities include daily fish and shark feedings. The latest addition to the park is a semi-submarine that lets you enjoy the panoramic view and the "down under" feeling of a submarine without truly submerging.

Nondivers can get some of the thrill long known to scuba afi-cionados by participating in **Sea Trek.** For $68, you can get a full immersion undersea with no experience necessary. Participants are given a helmet and a tube to breathe through. The tube is attached to an air source at the observatory tower. You then enjoy a 20-minute stroll in water that's 18 feet deep, observing rain-bow-hued tropical fish and the coral reefs as you move along the sea floor. It's a marvelous way to experience the world through the eyes of a fish.

Coral World's guests can take advantage of **Coki Beach** for snorkel rentals, scuba lessons, or swimming and relaxing. Lockers and showers are available. Also included in the marine park are the Tropical Terrace Restaurant, duty-free shops, and a nature trail.

6450 Estates Smith Bay, a 20-min. drive from Charlotte Amalie off Rte. 38. ℂ **340/775-1555.** www.coralworldvi.com. Admission $18 adults, $9 children ages 3–12. Daily 9am–5pm.

Estate St. Peter Greathouse Botanical Gardens

This estate consists of 11 acres set at the foot of volcanic peaks on the northern rim of the island. The grounds are laced with self-guided nature walks that will acquaint you with some 200 varieties of plants and trees, including an umbrella plant from Madagascar. From a deck in the gardens, you can see some 20 of the Virgin Islands, including Hans Lollick, an uninhabited island between Thatched Cay and Madahl Point. The house itself, filled with local art, is worth a visit.

EXCURSIONS FROM ST. THOMAS

Water Island, ¾ mile off the coast from the harbor at Charlotte Amalie, is the fourth-largest island in the U.S. Virgins, with 500 acres of land. At palm-shaded **Honeymoon Beach,** you can swim, snorkel, sail, water-ski, or sunbathe, then order lunch or a drink from the beach bar (on Sat–Sun only). A ferry runs between Crown Bay Marina and Water Island several times a day, $4.50 one-way, $9 round-trip. (Crown Bay Marina, © 340/774-2255, is part of the St. Thomas submarine base.)

In the same bay is **Hassel Island.** This island is almost completely deserted, and is protected as part of a U.S. National Park. There are no hotels or services of any kind, and swimming is limited to narrow, rocky beaches. Even so, many visitors hire a boat to drop them off for an hour or two. A hike along part of the shoreline is a relief from the cruise-ship congestion of Charlotte Amalie. Bring water and food if you plan to spend more than 3 hours here.

An even better option is a **day trip to St. John,** home of world-famous Trunk Bay Beach. To get there, you can take one of many ferry services. Boats depart from Charlotte Amalie or, more frequently, from Red Hook, and arrive in St. John's Cruz Bay. The one-way fare is $3 for adults, $1 for children under age 11. Near the access ramp of the pier in Cruz Bay, you'll find rows of taxis that will take you on a tour of the island. A 4-hour guided tour costs about $60, a full day (7 hr.) is $75 ($65 for children 12 and under). If you want to skip the tour of St. John and head right to the beach at Trunk Bay for the day, simply negotiate a fare with one of the taxi drivers at the pier. Be sure to arrange a time to be picked up at the end of the day, too. The cost of a one-way trip is usually around $5 to $10 per person. See chapter 3 for more on St. John.

8 Shopping

The discounted, duty-free shopping in the Virgin Islands makes St. Thomas a shopping mecca. It's possible to find well-known brand names here at savings of up to 60% off mainland prices. But be warned—savings are not always good, so make sure you know the price of the item back home to determine if you are getting a good deal. Having sounded that warning, we'll mention some St. Thomas shops where we have found really good buys.

Most shops, some of which occupy former pirate warehouses, are open Monday to Saturday 9am to 5pm. Some stores are open Sunday and holidays if a cruise ship is in port.

SHOPPING DISTRICTS

Nearly all the major shopping in St. Thomas is along the harbor of Charlotte Amalie. Cruise-ship passengers shop at the **Havensight Mall,** where they disembark. The principal shopping street is **Main Street** or Dronningens Gade (its old Danish name). To the north is another merchandise-loaded street called **Back Street** or Vimmelskaft. Many shops are also spread along the **Waterfront Highway** (also called Kyst Vejen). Between these major streets is a series of side streets, walkways, and alleys—all filled with shops. Other shopping streets are Tolbod Gade, Raadets Gade, Royal Dane Mall, Palm Passage, Storetvaer Gade, and Strand Gade.

THE BEST BUYS & WHERE TO FIND THEM

The best buys include china, crystal, perfumes, jewelry (especially emeralds), Haitian art, fashion, watches, and items made of wood. Cameras and electronic items, based on our experience, are not the good buys they're reputed to be. St. Thomas is also the best place in the Caribbean for discounts in porcelain, but remember that U.S. brands may often be purchased for 25% off the retail price on the mainland. Look for imported patterns for the biggest savings.

It is illegal for most street vendors (food vendors are about the only exception) to ply their trades outside of the designated area called **Vendors Plaza,** at the corner of Veterans Drive and Tolbod Gade. Hundreds of vendors converge here Monday through Saturday at 7:30am; they usually pack up around 5:30pm. (Very few hawk their wares on Sun, unless a cruise ship is scheduled to arrive.)

When you tire of French perfumes and Swiss watches, head for **Market Square,** as it's called locally, or more formally, Rothschild Francis Square. Here, under a Victorian tin roof, locals with machetes slice open fresh coconuts so you can drink the milk, and women wearing bandannas sell akee, cassava, and breadfruit.

Other noteworthy shopping districts include **Tillett Gardens,** a virtual oasis of arts and crafts—pottery, silk-screened fabrics, candles, watercolors, jewelry, and more—located on the highway across from Four Winds Shopping Center. The Jim Tillett Gallery here is a major island attraction in itself (see listing below).

At **Mountain Top,** near the center of the island, there's a modern shopping mall—a bit too tourist-tacky for us—that contains about eight shops; the views are much better than the merchandise.

All the major stores in St. Thomas are located by number on an excellent map in the center of the publication *St. Thomas This Week,* distributed to all arriving plane and boat passengers, and available at the visitor center. A lot of the stores on the island don't have street numbers or don't display them, so look for their signs instead.

SHOPPING A TO Z
ART

Bernard K. Passman 𝕬𝕬   Bernard K. Passman is the world's leading sculptor of black coral art and jewelry. He's famous for his *Can Can Girl* and his four statues of Charlie Chaplin. On Grand Cayman, he learned to fashion exquisite treasures from black coral found 200 feet under the sea. After being polished and embellished with gold and diamonds, some of Passman's work has been treasured by royalty. There are simpler and more affordable pieces for sale as well. 38A Main St. ℭ 340/777-4580.

Gallery Camille Pissarro   This art gallery, accessible by stairs, is in the house where Pissarro, a paragon of Impressionism, was born in 1830. In three high-ceilinged and airy rooms, you can see Pissarro paintings relating to the islands. Many prints by local artists are available, and the gallery also sells original batiks, alive with vibrant colors. Caribbean Cultural Centre, 14 Main St. ℭ 340/774-4621.

Gallery St. Thomas 𝕬   This is a showcase for the works of Virgin Islands painters, notably Lucinda Schutt, who is best known for her Caribbean land- and seascapes. At this gallery, to the west of Hotel 1829, Schutt not only sells artwork beginning at $18, but also teaches watercolor painting to students. First building on Garden St., Government Hill. ℭ 340/774-9440. www.gallerystthomas.com.

Jim Tillett Art Gallery & Silk Screen Print Studio 𝕬𝕬   Since 1959, Tillett Gardens, once an old Danish farm, has been the island's arts-and-crafts center. This tropical compound is a series of buildings housing studios, galleries, and an outdoor garden restaurant and bar. Prints in the galleries start as low as $10. The best work of local artists is displayed here—originals in oils, watercolors, and acrylics. The Tillett prints on fine canvas are all one-of-a-kind. The famous Tillett maps on fine canvas are priced from $40. Tillett Gardens, 4126 Anna's Retreat, Tutu. ℭ 340/775-1929. Take Rte. 38 east from Charlotte Amalie.

Mango Tango Art Gallery   This is one of the largest art galleries in St. Thomas, connected with several internationally recognized artists. Original artwork begins at $300; prints and posters are cheaper. Represented are artists who spend at least part of their year in the Virgin Islands, many of them sailing during breaks from their studio time. Examples include Don Dahlke, Max Johnson, Anne

Miller, David Millard, Dana Wylder, and Shari Erickson. Al Cohen's Plaza, Raphune Hill, Rte. 38. ✆ **340/777-3060.**

Native Arts & Crafts Cooperative ✪   This is the largest arts and crafts emporium in the U.S. Virgin Islands, combining the output of 90 different artisans into one sprawling shop. Contained within the former headquarters of the U.S. District Court, a 19th-century brick building adjacent to Charlotte Amalie's tourist information office, it specializes in items small enough to be packed into a suitcase or trunk. Examples include spice racks, paper towel racks, lamps crafted from conch shells, salad utensils and bowls, crocheted goods, and straw goods. Tarbor Gade 1. ✆ **340/777-1153.**

BOOKS
Dockside Bookshop   If you need a beach read, head for this well-stocked store near the cruise-ship dock. It has the best selection of books on island lore, as well as a variety of general reading selections. Havensight Mall. ✆ **340/774-4937.**

BRIC-A-BRAC
Carson Company Antiques   This shop's small spaces are loaded with merchandise, tasteless and otherwise, from everywhere. Its clutter and eclectic nature just might be part of the attraction. Bakelite jewelry is cheap and cheerful, and African artifacts are often interesting. Royal Dane Mall, off Main St. ✆ **340/774-6175.**

CAMERAS & ELECTRONICS
Boolchand's   This is the place to go when you're in the market for a camera. Famous throughout the Caribbean, this is the major retailer of not only cameras, but also electronics and digital products throughout the West Indies. Now into its 8th decade, it sells all the big names, from Kodak to Leica, and from Nikon to Fuji. In the electronics division are the latest in DVDs, minidiscs, and other items. There is also a jewelry department and a wide selection of watches. 31 Main St. ✆ **340/776-0794.**

Royal Caribbean ✪ *Value*   This is the largest camera and electronics store in the Caribbean. It carries Nikon, Minolta, Pentax, Canon, and Panasonic products. It's a good source for watches, too, featuring such brands as Seiko, Movado, Corum, Fendi, and Zodiac. There's also a collection of Philippe Charriol watches, jewelry, and leather bags, and a selection of Mikimoto pearls, 14- and 18-karat jewelry, and Lladró figurines. Another branch is at Havensight Mall (✆ **340/776-8890**). 33 and 35 Main St. ✆ **340/776-4110.**

CHOCOLATES

Caribbean Chocolate   A collection of fresh chocolates, many of which are made fresh daily, await your taste buds at this store. The claim here is that the outlet sells "anything under the sun with chocolate." What a delight to tuck into some of their homemade fudge. Trompeter Gade. ℂ **340/774-6675.**

CLOTHING

Local Color   Located at the waterfront, this retail outlet has a wide selection of affordable clothing for men, women, and children, as well as island furnishings and accessories such as handbags, hats, and jewelry. Royal Dane Mall at the waterfront. ℂ **340/774-2280.**

Tommy Hilfiger Boutique   The world now knows this merchandise, of course, but prices here might be cheaper than Stateside. There is a selection of sportswear for men and women, footwear, jeans, children's clothing, furnishings, and fragrances. Waterfront Hwy. at Trompeter Gade 30 ℂ **340/777-1189.**

CRYSTAL & CHINA

The Crystal Shoppe ⭐ *Finds*   This family-run store offers a dazzling array of crystal from around the world. All the big names in glass—Wedgwood, Hümmel, Royal Copenhagen, Swarovski, and Rosenthal—are here, along with some particularly good pieces from the Swedish firm of Kosta Boda. The porcelain Lladró figurines from Spain are also a fast-moving item. 14 Main St. ℂ **340/777-9835.**

The English Shop   The Queen of England buys some of the brand name products carried here, including Royal Doulton, Wedgwood, and Spode. You can make your selection from the extensive catalogs, and the merchandise will be shipped to you from the factory. The products aren't just from England, but from around the world, including Japan. This outlet carries perhaps the largest selection of dinnerware in the Caribbean, and is one of the best importers of the biggest trade names in crystal, china, and figurines. Havensight Mall (Rte. 30). ℂ **340/776-1555.**

Scandinavia Center   This family owned and operated shop specializes in some of the most famous products of Scandinavia, including glassware, silver, and crystal. You'll recognize such names as Bing & Grøndahl, Georg Jensen, Kosta Boda, Orrefors, and Royal Copenhagen. The jewelry department is especially enticing, with its 14-karat and 18-karat designs in white and yellow gold. Havensight Mall, Building III. ℂ **800/524-2063** or 340/776-5030.

EYEWEAR

Davante On the waterfront near the cruise-ship docks, this retail outlet offers a large collection of sunglasses and prescription eyewear from more than 70 designers. High-fashion superstars on display include products of Dolce & Gabanna, Christian Roth, and Versace. Riise Mall. ✆ **340/714-1220.**

Fashion Eyewear On the waterfront, this outlet displays all the big names in eyewear, and even sells prescription sunglasses that can be readied here in only 30 minutes. Make a selection from 20 top designers. International Plaza. ✆ **340/776-9005.**

FABRICS

Fabric in Motion Fabric in Motion searches the globe for fabrics, and delights shoppers with its selection of silklike cottons from the fabled Liberty's of London, the best of linens from Italy, and flamboyant batiks from Indonesia. Many tempting items are for sale, including leather handbags from Colombia, and fun bags for the beach. Storetvaer Gade. ✆ **340/774-2006.**

FRAGRANCES

Tropicana Perfume Shoppe 👉 *Value* This outlet is billed as the largest perfumery in the world. It offers all the famous names in perfumes, skin care, and cosmetics, including Lancôme. Men will find Europe's best colognes and aftershave lotions here. A very friendly and attentive staff will enhance your shopping experience. 2 Main St. ✆ **800/233-7948** or 340/774-0010.

GIFTS & LIQUORS

A.H. Riise Gift & Liquor Stores This is St. Thomas's oldest outlet for luxury items, such as jewelry, crystal, china, and perfumes. It also offers the widest sampling of liquors on the island. Everything is displayed in a 19th-century Danish warehouse that extends from Main Street to the waterfront. The store boasts a collection of fine jewelry and watches from Europe's leading names, as well as a wide selection of Greek gold, platinum, and jewelry. Imported cigars are stored in a walk-in humidor. There's also a vast selection of fragrances for men and women, along with the world's best-known names in cosmetics and treatment products. Waterford, Lalique, Baccarat, and Rosenthal, among others, are featured in the china and crystal department. Specialty shops in the complex sell Caribbean gifts, books, clothing, food, art prints, note cards, and designer sunglasses. Delivery to cruise ships and the airport is free. 37 Main St. at A. H. Riise Gift & Liquor Mall (perfume and liquor branch stores at the Havensight Mall). ✆ **800/524-2037** or 304/776-2303.

Al Cohen's Discount Liquors One of St. Thomas's most famous outlets occupies a warehouse at Havensight, across from the West Indian Company docks, where cruise-ship passengers disembark. Inside is a huge storehouse of liquor and wine. After an expansion and remodeling, there are more brands and items on sale than ever before. You can also purchase fragrances, T-shirts, and souvenirs. Long Bay Rd. ℂ 340/774-3690.

Caribbean Marketplace The best selection of Caribbean spices are found here, including Sunny Caribbee products, a vast array of condiments (ranging from spicy peppercorns to nutmeg mustard), and botanical products. Do not expect very attentive service. Havensight Mall (Building III). ℂ 340/776-5400.

Down Island Traders ✦ (Finds The aroma of spices will lead you to this market, which has Charlotte Amalie's most attractive array of spices, teas, seasoning, candies, jellies, jams, and condiments, most of which are packaged from Caribbean products. The owner also carries a line of local cookbooks, as well as silk-screened T-shirts and bags, Haitian metal sculptures, jewelry, Caribbean folk art, and gifts. Veterans Dr. ℂ 340/776-4641.

JEWELRY

Artistic Jewelers This outlet is a leading merchant of jewelry and gems. 32 Main St. ℂ 800/653-3113.

Azura Jewels Replacing the Colombian Emeralds shop is another fine jewelry store carrying just about the same products, including emeralds, sapphires, tanzanite, and fine watches. Havensight Mall. ℂ 340/774-2442.

Cardow Jewelers Often called the Tiffany's of the Caribbean, Cardow Jewelers boasts the largest selection of fine jewelry in the world. This fabulous shop, displaying more than 20,000 rings, offers savings because of its worldwide direct buying, large turnover, and duty-free prices. Unusual and traditional designs are offered in diamonds, emeralds, rubies, sapphires, and Brazilian stones, as well as pearls. The Treasure Cove has cases of gold jewelry priced under $300. 39 Main St. ℂ 340/776-1140.

Dynasty Jewelers A 20-year survivor of the jewelry trade, this shop offers diamond, tanzanite, ruby, emerald, sapphire, and blue diamond jewelry in one half, and liquor in the other. There's no better combination if you're in a luxurious mood. There are three other branch locations at the **Havensight Mall** (ℂ 800/225-7052). 1 Main St. ℂ 340/774-2222.

H. Stern Jewelers   This international jeweler is one of the most respected in the world, with some 175 outlets. It's Cardow's leading competitor (see above). Besides this branch, there are two more on Main Street. Stern gives worldwide guaranteed service, including a 1-year exchange privilege. Havensight Mall. (© **800/524-2024** or 340/776-1223.

Pierre's ⭐   Connoisseurs of colored gemstones consider this store one of the most impressive repositories of collector's items in the Caribbean. In its inventory are glittering and mystical-looking gemstones you might never have heard of before. Look for alexandrites (garnets in three shades of green); spinels (pink and red); sphenes, yellow-green sparklers from Madagascar (as reflective as high-quality diamonds); and tsavorites, a green stone from Tanzania. 24 Palm Passage. (© **800/300-0634** or 340/776-5130.

LINENS
Mr. Tablecloth   This shop constantly receives new shipments of top-quality linens from China, including Hong Kong. It has the best selection of tablecloths and accessories, plus doilies, in Charlotte Amalie. Also check out the display of placemats, aprons, and runners. 6 Main St. (© **340/774-4343**.

MUSIC
Modern Music   This store features nearly every genre of music, from rock to jazz to classical, and especially Caribbean. You'll find new releases from Caribbean stars such as Jamaica's Byron Lee and the Virgin Islands' The Violators, as well as U.S. artists. There's one other branch at the Nisky Center (© **340/777-7878**). Across from Havensight Mall and cruise-ship docks. (© **340/774-3100**.

9 St. Thomas After Dark

St. Thomas has more nightlife than any other island in the U.S. or British Virgin Islands, but it's not as extensive as you might think. Many Charlotte Amalie streets are dangerous after dark, so visitors have stopped visiting the area for nightlife, with the exception of a few places, such as the Green House. Much of the action has shifted to **Frenchtown** ⭐⭐, which has some great restaurants and bars. However, just as in Charlotte Amalie, some of these hot spots are along dark, badly lit roads. The primary problem is mugging. Some of the criminal activity appears drug-related. Sexual assault is known to occur, but happens rather infrequently.

The big hotels, such as Frenchman's Reef & Marriott Morning Star Beach Resort and Bluebeard's, have the most lively after-dark scenes. After a day of sightseeing and shopping in the hot West Indies sun, sometimes your best bet is just to stay at your hotel in the evening, perhaps listening to a local fungi band playing traditional music on homemade instruments.

THE PERFORMING ARTS

Pistarckle Theater   On the grounds of Jim Tillett Art Gallery & Silk Screen Print Studio (p. 74), this professional theater presents four plays as part of its season. Occupying a vacant print shop, the 100-seat theater is air-conditioned. A drama camp for children is run during the summer. Tillet Gardens, 4126 Anna's Retreat, Tutu. ℂ 340/775-7877. www.pistarckletheater.vi. Tickets $18–$20.

Reichhold Center for the Arts ℞   The premier performing arts venue in the Caribbean is west of Charlotte Amalie. Call the theater or check with the tourist office to see what's on. The lobby displays a free exhibit of paintings and sculptures by Caribbean artists. A Japanese-inspired amphitheater, permeated by the scent of gardenias, is set into a natural valley, with seating for 1,196. Several different music, dance, and drama companies perform here. Performances usually begin at 8pm. University of the Virgin Islands, 2 John Brewers Bay. ℂ 340/693-1559. Tickets $7.50–$60.

BARS & CLUBS

The Bar at Paradise Point   Any savvy insider will tell you to head here to watch the sunset. It's 740 feet above sea level, across from the cruise-ship dock, and provides excellent photo ops and panoramic sunset views. Cruise-ship passengers, usually a middle-aged crowd, flock to this bar. A tram takes you up the hill. Get the bartender to serve you a "Bushwacker" (his specialty). You can also order inexpensive food here during the day, such as pizza, hot dogs, and hamburgers, beginning at $4. There's fine dining on Thursdays through Sundays, with main courses ranging from a doable $15 to $21. Happy hour, with discounted drinks, is on Wednesdays. Open Monday and Tuesday from 9am to 7pm, Wednesday through Sunday from 9am to 9pm. Paradise Point. ℂ 340/777-4540. No cover.

Cabana Bar   There's piano-bar entertainment nightly at this scenic spot overlooking the yacht harbor. It's a popular gathering spot for both residents and visitors, who are mainly in their 30s and 40s. You can dance from 8pm to midnight on Thursday and from 8pm to 1am on Saturday. Entertainment varies from month to month, but many nights are devoted to jazz. Open daily from 5pm to midnight. Bluebeard's Hill. ℂ 340/774-1600. No cover.

Epernay This stylish watering hole, with an ocean view, adds a touch of Europe to the neighborhood. You can order glasses of at least six champagnes, and vintage wines come by the glass. Appetizers include sushi and caviar. You can also order main courses, plus desserts such as chocolate-dipped strawberries. A mature, sophisticated crowd gathers here. Open Monday to Wednesday 11:30am to 11pm, Thursday to Saturday 11:30am to midnight. Rue de St. Barthélemy, Frenchtown. ℂ 340/774-5348. Fri–Sat cover $5.

The Greenhouse On the waterfront, this bar and restaurant is one of the few night spots we recommend in the heart of Charlotte Amalie. You can park nearby and walk to the entrance. Each night, a different type of entertainment is featured, ranging from reggae to disco. Open Sunday through Thursday 10:30am to 10pm, Friday and Saturday 11am to 1am. Veterans Dr. ℂ 340/774-7998. No cover.

Happy Buzzard Attracting a wide range of ages, this bar (formerly known as Fat Tuesday) is along the waterfront in the center of Charlotte Amalie. The bartenders offer a variety of beer, highballs, and shooters, including the "Head Butt," which contains Jagermeister, Bailey's, and amaretto. Special events are often presented, with live music on Tuesday nights. Open daily from 10am to 8pm, later on Friday and Saturday. 26A Royal Dane Mall. ℂ 340/777-8676.

Hull Bay Hideaway A longtime favorite, this retreat has a laid-back, casual atmosphere, attracting, in the words of a bartender, "people from all walks of life, from boaters to condo renters." Many locals and regulars like to spend Sunday afternoons here, when there's often live music. It's a cheap place to eat—hot dogs and hamburgers are served until 4:30pm. After 5:30pm, you can order affordable main courses in the restaurant, including the catch of the day and the chef's pork stew. There's also some gambling machines and a volleyball court. Bar open daily 9am to 10pm; restaurant open daily 5:30 to 9:30pm. 10 Hull Bay. ℂ 340/777-1898.

Iggie's Bolongo This place functions during the day as an informal, open-air restaurant serving hamburgers, sandwiches, and salads. After dark, it presents karaoke and occasional live entertainment. It attracts the broadest spectrum of age groups and professions in Charlotte Amalie. Call to find out what's happening. Bolongo Bay Beach Club, 7150 Bolongo. ℂ 340/779-1800.

Latitude 18 This is the hot spot of the east coast, where the ferry boats depart for St. John. The restaurant/bar, featuring a ceiling adorned with boat sails, offers live entertainment, especially on

Tuesday and Saturday nights. The bar is open daily from 3 to 11pm; the restaurant is open Sunday and Monday 5 to 9pm and Tuesday to Saturday 6 to 10pm. Red Hook Marina. ℂ 340/779-2495.

The Sugar Mill ℛ   This is the largest and newest entertainment complex on the island, with three separate venues. The courtyard sports bar offers a variety of games. The more elegant wine and champagne bar is where guests can relax to the sounds of jazz and blues. In a restored 18th-century sugar mill, the bar features more than 100 different types of wines and champagnes. There's also a dance club, featuring a sunken dance floor combined with a state-of-the-art lighting and sound system. Open Thursday to Sunday, with no set closing time—go after 10pm. 193 Contant. ℂ 340/776-3004. Fri–Sat cover $15–$20.

Turtle Rock Bar   This popular bar offers live music and karaoke to a young crowd. There's space to dance, but most patrons just sway and listen. The steel-drum bands that play from 2pm to closing on Sundays are excellent. Burgers, salads, steaks, and grilled fish are available at the Iguana Grill, a few steps away. In the Iguana Grill at the Wyndham Sugar Bay Resort & Spa, 6500 Estate Smith Bay (a few minutes' drive west of Red Hook). ℂ 340/777-7100. No cover.

Walter's Livingroom ℛ   This intimate, dimly lit, two-level bar attracts locals, often gay men, in season, drawing more off-island visitors in winter. It's in a clapboard town house built around 1935. The music here ranges from the 1970s to current top hits. 3 Trompeter Gade. ℂ 340/774-5025. Sun–Thurs cover $1, Fri–Sat cover $3.

3

St. John

East of St. Thomas, across a glistening turquoise channel known as Pillsbury Sound, lies St. John, the smallest and least densely populated of the three main U.S. Virgin Islands.

St. John is a wonder of unspoiled beauty. Along its rocky coastline are crescent-shaped bays and white-sand beaches, and the interior is no less impressive. The variety of wildlife is the envy of naturalists around the world. And there are miles of hiking trails, leading past the ruins of 18th-century Danish plantations to panoramic views. You can even find mysteriously geometric petroglyphs of unknown age and origin incised into boulders and cliffs.

Today, St. John (unlike the other U.S. islands) remains pristine, its preservation enforced by the National Park Service. Thanks to the efforts of Laurance Rockefeller, who purchased many acres and donated them to the United States, the island's shoreline waters, as well as more than half of its surface area, make up the Virgin Islands National Park. The hundreds of coral gardens that surround St. John are rigorously protected—any attempt to damage or remove coral is punishable with large and strictly enforced fines.

Despite the unspoiled beauty, the island manages to provide visitors with modern amenities and travel services, including a sampling of restaurants, car-rental kiosks, yacht-supply facilities, hotels, and campgrounds. Cinnamon Bay, founded by the National Park Service in 1964, is the most famous campsite in the Caribbean. In addition, the roads are well maintained; there's even a small commercial center, Cruz Bay, on the western tip. Don't come here for nightlife: St. John is sleepy, and that's why people love it.

One of the most exciting ways to see St. John is by four-wheel-drive vehicle, which you can rent in town (in winter it's best to reserve in advance). The steep roadside panoramas are richly tinted with tones of forest green and turquoise and liberally accented with flashes of silver and gold from the strong Caribbean sun.

St. John is the friendliest of the U.S. Virgin Islands, although it is only a short ferry ride from more commercialized St. Thomas. There isn't even an airport, and life is more laid-back than in the other U.S. Virgins. People have time to talk and perhaps provide you with directions. Whereas you'll never meet the managers of most East End properties on St. Thomas, you may end up sitting up, drinking, and talking with a St. John innkeeper until late into the night. If you come for a visit same time next year, you might even be welcomed as one of the family; you'll certainly be considered a "regular."

1 Orientation

ARRIVING

The easiest way to get to St. John is by **ferry** (© 340/776-6282), which leaves from the Red Hook pier on St. Thomas's eastern tip; the trip takes about 20 minutes each way. Beginning at 6:30am, boats depart more or less every hour. The last ferry back to Red Hook departs from St. John's Cruz Bay at 11pm. The service is frequent and efficient enough that even cruise-ship passengers temporarily anchored in Charlotte Amalie can visit St. John for a quick tour. The one-way fare is $3 for adults, $1 for children 12 and under. Schedules change without notice, so call in advance.

To reach the ferry, take the **Vitran** bus from a point near Market Square (in Charlotte Amalie) to Red Hook. The cost is $1 per person each way. In addition, privately owned taxis will negotiate a price to carry you from virtually anywhere to the docks at Red Hook.

If you've just landed on St. Thomas and want to go to the ferry dock, your best bet is to take a cab from the airport (Vitran buses run from Charlotte Amalie but don't serve the airport area). After disembarking from the ferry on St. John, you'll have to get another cab to your hotel. Depending on the traffic, the cab ride on St. Thomas could take 30 to 45 minutes, at a fare between $20 and $22.

It's also possible to board a **boat** for St. John at the Charlotte Amalie waterfront for a cost of $7 each way. The ride takes 45 minutes. The boats depart from Charlotte Amalie at 9am and continue at intervals of between 1 and 2 hours, until around 5:30pm. (The last boat to leave St. John's Cruz Bay for Charlotte Amalie departs at 3:45pm.) Call © 340/776-6282 for more information.

VISITOR INFORMATION

The **tourist office** (© 340/776-6450) is near the Battery, a 1735 fort that's a short walk from the St. Thomas ferry dock. It's open Monday to Friday from 8am to 1pm and 2 to 5pm. A **National Park visitor center** (© 340/776-6201) is found at Cruz Bay, offering two

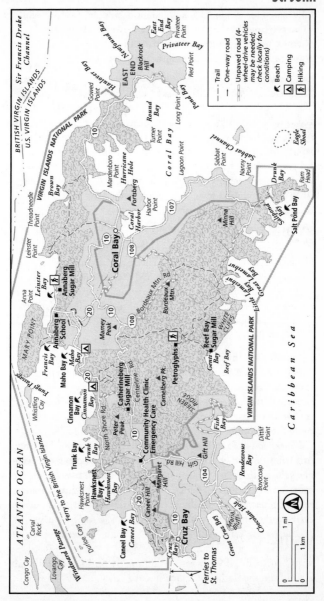

St. John

Legend:
- - - - Trail
One-way road
Unpaved road (4-wheel-drive vehicles may be needed; check locally for conditions)
🏖 Beach
△ Camping
🧍 Hiking

ATLANTIC OCEAN

Caribbean Sea

VIRGIN ISLANDS NATIONAL PARK

BRITISH VIRGIN ISLANDS
U.S. VIRGIN ISLANDS

Sir Francis Drake Channel

Hurricane Hole

Coral Bay

Cruz Bay

Ferries to St. Thomas

Ferry to the British Virgin Islands

0 1 mi
0 1 km

floors of information and wall-mounted wildlife displays, plus a video presentation about the culture of the Virgin Islands.

You can pick up a map of the island from the tourist office and also a copy of *St. John This Week,* which is distributed free.

2 Getting Around

The 20-minute ferry ride from St. Thomas will take you to **Cruz Bay,** the capital of St. John, which seems a century removed from the life you left behind. Cruz Bay is so small that its streets have no names, but it does have the **Mongoose Junction** shopping center (worth a visit), a scattering of restaurants, and a park. Cruise ships are nonexistent here, so you won't find hordes of milling shoppers. After a stroll around town, seek out the natural attractions of the island.

BY BUS & TAXI

The most popular way to get around is by the **Vitran** service, the same company that runs the buses on St. Thomas. Buses run between Cruz Bay and Coral Bay, for $1 for adults and 75¢ for children.

An open-air **surrey-style taxi** is more fun, however. Typical fares are $4 to Trunk Bay, $4.50 to Cinnamon Bay, or $5 to Maho Bay. Between midnight and 6am, fares are increased by 50%. Call (C) **340/ 693-7530** for more information.

BY CAR OR JEEP

The island's undeveloped roads offer some of the best views anywhere. Because of this, many people opt to rent a vehicle (sometimes with four-wheel-drive) to tour the island. Most visitors need a car for only a day or two. *Remember:* Drive on the left and follow posted speed limits, which are generally very low.

Unless you need to carry luggage, which should be locked away in a trunk, you might consider one of the sturdy, open-sided, jeep-like vehicles that offer the best view of the surroundings and are the most fun way to tour St. John. Note that most of these vehicles have manual transmission, which can be especially tricky in a car built to drive on the left side of the road. They cost $76 to $84 a day.

The largest car-rental agency on St. John is **Hertz** ((C) **800/ 654-3131** in the U.S., or 340/693-7580 or 340/776-6171; www.hertz.com). If you want a local firm, try **St. John Car Rental,** across from the Catholic Church in Cruz Bay ((C) **340/776-6103**).

FAST FACTS: St. John

American Express You'll have to visit St. Thomas for service. The representative is **Caribbean Travel Agency/Tropic Tours,** 9716 Estate Thomas, Havensight (✆ **340/774-1855**).

Banks **First Bank Virgin Islands** is at 90C Cruz Bay (✆ **340/776-6881**).

Business Hours Stores are generally open Monday to Friday 9am to 5pm, Saturday 9am to 1pm.

Cameras & Film To purchase film or have it developed, go to **Sparky's,** Cruz Bay Park (✆ **340/776-6284**).

Currency Exchange Go to the branch of **First Bank Virgin Islands** in Cruz Bay (✆ **340/776-6881**).

Dentists The **Virgin Islands Dental Association** (✆ **340/775-9110**) is a member of the American Dental Association and is also linked with various specialists. Call for information or an appointment.

Doctors Call ✆ **911** for an emergency. Otherwise, go to **St. John Myrah Keating Smith Community Health Center,** 3B Sussanaberg (✆ **340/693-8900**).

Drugstores Go to **St. John Drugcenter,** Boulon Shopping Center, Cruz Bay (✆ **340/776-6353**). The staff here not only fills prescriptions but also sells film, cameras, magazines, and books. Hours are Monday through Saturday from 9am to 6pm. The pharmacy is open Monday through Saturday from 10am to 5pm.

Emergencies For the police, an ambulance, or in case of fire, call ✆ **911**.

Internet Access Go to **Connections,** Parcel Street, Suite 6D (✆ **340/776-6922**). This computer lounge doesn't serve drinks, but you can bring your own as long as you don't spill it; expect to pay $5 for 30 minutes. You can also use the computers at the **Elaine Ione Sprauve Public Library,** Enighted Street (✆ **340/776-6359**), for a charge of $2 for 30 minutes.

Laundry Try **Santo's Laundromat,** 1321 Cruz Bay Valley (✆ **340/693-7733**); and **Super Clean,** Enighted Street (✆ **340/693-7333**).

Maps See "Orientation," above.

Newspapers & Magazines Copies of U.S. newspapers, such as the *New York Times* and the *Miami Herald* arrive daily and are for sale at **Mongoose Junction, Caneel Bay,** and the **Westin Resort St. John.** The latest copies of *Time* and *Newsweek* are also for sale. *What to Do: St. Thomas/St. John,* the official guidebook of the St. Thomas and St. John Hotel Association, is available at the tourist office (see "Orientation," above) and at various hotels.

Post Office The **Cruz Bay Post Office** is at Cruz Bay (℅ **340/ 779-4227**).

Safety There is some crime, but it's relatively minor compared to St. Thomas. Most crime against tourists consists of muggings or petty theft, but rarely violent attacks. Precautions, of course, are always advised. You are most likely to be the victim of a crime if you leave valuables unguarded on Trunk Bay, as hundreds of people seem to do every year.

Taxes The only local tax is an 8% surcharge added to all hotel rates.

Telephone & Fax All island phone numbers have seven digits. It is not necessary to use the 340 area code when dialing within St. John.

3 Where to Stay

The number of accommodations on St. John is limited, and that's how most die-hard fans like it. There are four basic choices here: luxury resorts, condominiums and villas, guesthouses, and campgrounds. Prices are often slashed in summer by 30% to 60%.

Chances are your location will be determined by your choice of resort. However, if you're dependent on public transportation and want to make one or two trips to St. Thomas by ferry, Cruz Bay is the most convenient place to stay. It also offers easy access to shopping, bars, and restaurants if you want to walk.

LUXURY RESORTS

Caneel Bay 𝒜𝒜𝒜 Conceived by megamillionaire Laurance S. Rockefeller in 1956, this is the Caribbean's first ecoresort. Though it's long been one of the premier resorts of the Caribbean, Caneel Bay is definitely not one of the most luxurious. A devoted fan once told us, "It's like living at summer camp." That means no phones or TVs in the rooms. Nevertheless, the movers and shakers of the

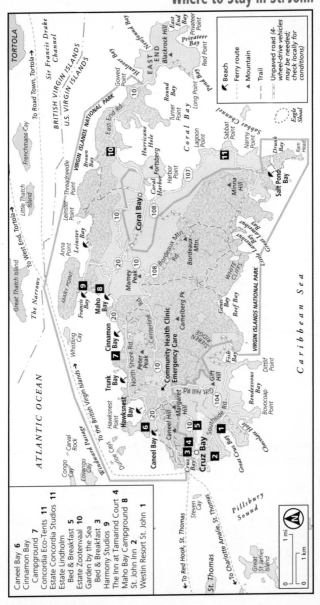

Caneel Bay **6**
Cinnamon Bay
Campground **7**
Concordia Eco-Tents **11**
Estate Concordia Studios **11**
Estate Lindholm
Bed & Breakfast **5**
Estate Zootenvaal **10**
Garden by the Sea
Bed & Breakfast **3**
Harmony Studios **9**
The Inn at Tamarind Court **4**
Maho Bay Campground **8**
St. John Inn **2**
Westin Resort St. John **1**

world continue to descend on this place, though younger people tend to head elsewhere. To attract more families, young children are now allowed here. Go to Westin Resort St. John (see below) for glitz and glitter; head here for a touch of class.

The resort lies on a 170-acre portion of the national park, offering a choice of seven beaches. Surrounded by lush greenery, the main buildings are strung along the bays, with a Caribbean lounge and dining room at the core. Other buildings housing guest rooms stand along the beaches. Try to get one of the six rooms in cottage no. 7, overlooking two of the most idyllic beaches, Scott and Paradise. Most rooms, however, are set back on low cliffs or headlands. The decor within is understated, with Indonesian wicker furniture, hand-woven fabrics, sisal mats, and plantation fans.

The resort has consistently maintained a high level of cuisine, often quite formal for the laid-back Caribbean. In recent years the food has been considerably improved and modernized, with more variety and more healthy choices on the menu.

Virgin Islands National Park, St. John, U.S.V.I. 00831. ☎ **340/776-6111.** Fax 340/693-8280. www.caneelbay.com. 166 units. Winter $450–$1,150 double; off season $325–$895 double. MAP (breakfast and dinner) $80 per person, per day extra. 1 child under 16 can stay free in parent's room. AE, DC, MC, V. **Amenities:** 3 restaurants; 2 bars; outdoor pool; 11 tennis courts; fitness center; spa; children's center; business center; limited room service; babysitting; laundry service; dry cleaning; nonsmoking rooms; rooms for those w/limited mobility; afternoon tea; boating; deep-sea fishing; dive shop; kayaks; snorkeling; Sunfish sailboats; windsurfing. *In room:* A/C, minibar, beverage maker, hair dryer, iron/ironing board, safe, ceiling fan, no phone.

Westin Resort St. John 🐾🐾🐾 (Kids)

Come here if you like megaresort flash and glitter as opposed to the "old school ties" of Caneel Bay. (Madonna would check in here; Walter Cronkite would prefer Caneel Bay.) This is the most architecturally dramatic and visually appealing hotel on St. John. The complex is set on 34 gently sloping, intricately landscaped acres on the southwest side of the island. It consists of 13 cedar-roofed postmodern buildings, each with ziggurat-shaped angles, soaring ceilings, and large windows. Herringbone-patterned brick walkways connect the gardens (with 400 palms imported from Puerto Rico) with the 1,200-foot white-sand beach and the largest pool in the Virgin Islands. Some of the accommodations contain fan-shaped windows and curved ceilings. Most units open onto private balconies, and some have their own whirlpools. All bedrooms come with full state-of-the-art bathrooms.

Cuisine options here are more varied than those at Caneel, featuring nouvelle cuisine, buffets, and even New York deli sandwiches.

Great Cruz Bay, St. John, U.S.V.I. 00831. ☎ **800/808-5020** in the U.S., or 340/693-8000. Fax 340/779-4500. www.westinresortstjohn.com. 349 units. Winter $406–$679 double, $939–$1,589 suite; off season $299–$500 double, $739–$1,189 suite. AE, DC, DISC, MC, V. Round-trip shuttle and private ferryboat transfers from St. Thomas airport $70 per adult, $50 per child. **Amenities:** 3 restaurants; 2 bars; outdoor pool; nearby golf; 6 lit tennis courts; fitness center; sauna; business center; children's programs, 24-hr. room service; babysitting; laundry service; nonsmoking rooms; rooms for those w/limited mobility; dive shop; fishing; sailboats; hiking; snorkeling; windsurfing. *In room:* A/C, TV, dataport, minibar, kitchenette (in some), beverage maker, hair dryer, iron/ironing board, safe.

EXPENSIVE

Estate Zootenvaal ⚲   This property is located on 30 acres within the boundaries of the national park at the edge of a horseshoe-shaped bay. It's a good choice for escapees from urban areas who want privacy. The accommodations have been renovated, now sporting designer fabrics in muted tones. Each has its own color scheme and comes with a fully equipped kitchen and a shower-only bathroom. Rooms have ceiling fans, but no telephones or televisions. Maid service can be arranged at an extra cost. Guests can use the private beach that's known for its great snorkeling.

Hurricane Hole, St. John, U.S.V.I. 00830. ☎ **340/776-6321** or 216/861-5337. www.usviguide.com/zootenvaal. 4 units. Year-round $290 1-bedroom for 2; $350 2-bedroom for 2. Extra person $75–$90. No credit cards. *In room:* Kitchen, coffeemaker, fridge, no phone.

MODERATE

Estate Concordia Studios   This environmentally sensitive 51-acre development is praised for its integration with the local ecosystem. Its elevated structures were designed to coexist with the stunning southern edge of St. John. The secluded property is on a low cliff above a salt pond, surrounded by hundreds of acres of pristine national park. It's best for those with a rental vehicle. Each building was designed to protect mature trees, and is connected to its neighbors with boardwalks. The nine studios are in six postmodern cottages. Each unit comes with a kitchen, shower-only bathroom, balcony, and ceiling fan; some have an extra bedroom. On-site management assists with activity suggestions. For information on the on-site **Eco-Tents,** refer to "Campgrounds," below.

20–27 Estate Concordia, Coral Bay, St. John, U.S.V.I. 00830. ☎ **800/392-9004** in the U.S. and Canada, 212/472-9453 in New York City, or 340/776-6226. Fax 340/776-6504. www.maho.org. 9 units. Winter $135–$210 studio for 2; off season $95–$150 studio for 2. Extra person $25 winter, $15 off season. MC, V. **Amenities:** Outdoor pool; coin-operated laundry. *In room:* Kitchen, ceiling fan, no phone.

Garden by the Sea Bed & Breakfast ⚡ *Finds*   Overlooking the ocean, this B&B is a 10-minute walk south from the little port of Cruz Bay. It has easy access to the north shore beaches and lies between Frank and Turner bays. From the gardens of the house, a 1-minute path along Audubon Pond leads to Frank Bay Beach. Be sure to reserve as it offers only three bedrooms. Each bedroom features elephant bamboo canopy beds, Japanese fountains, ceiling fans, and hardwood floors. Artifacts from around the world furnish the units. Don't expect phones or TVs, as this is a getaway, not a communications center. The 1970s house is designed in a Caribbean gingerbread style with cathedral beamed ceilings. Breakfast is served on the veranda (try their homemade muffins and quiche).

P.O. Box 37, Cruz Bay, St. John, U.S.V.I. 00830. ⓒ 340/779-4731. www.garden bythesea.com. 3 units. Winter $200–$215 double; off season $125–$150 double. No credit cards. **Amenities:** Nonsmoking rooms. *In room:* Ceiling fan, no phone.

Harmony Studios ⚡   On a hillside above the Maho Bay Campground, this is a small-scale cluster of 12 luxury studios in six two-story houses with views down to the sea. The complex is designed to combine both ecological technology and comfort; it's one of the few resorts in the Caribbean to operate exclusively on sun and wind power. Most of the building materials are made from recycled materials, including plastic and glass containers, newsprint, old tires, and scrap lumber. The managers and staff are committed to offering educational experiences, as well as the services of a small-scale resort. The studios contain ceiling fans, tiled shower-only bathrooms, kitchenettes, dining areas, and outdoor terraces. Guests can walk a short distance downhill to use the restaurant, grocery store, and watersports facilities at the Maho Bay campground.

P.O. Box 310, Cruz Bay, St. John, U.S.V.I. 00831. ⓒ 800/392-9004 in the U.S. and Canada, 212/472-9453 in New York City, or 340/776-6226. Fax 340/776-6504. www.maho.org. 12 units. Winter $195–$220 studio for 2; off season $120–$145 studio for 2. Extra person $25. MC, V. **Amenities:** Sailing; snorkeling; windsurfing. *In room:* Kitchenette, ceiling fan, no phone.

INEXPENSIVE

Estate Lindholm Bed & Breakfast ⚡ *Finds*   The island's best B&B grew out of an estate originally settled by Dutch planters in the 1720s. Set amongst the Danish ruins, Estate Lindholm is a charming guesthouse on a hill overlooking Cruz Bay, each of its bedrooms opening onto a view. The spacious bedrooms (all non-smoking) are attractively and comfortably furnished, many resting under ceiling beams. Guests can enjoy private balconies as well. On the property is the **Asolare** restaurant, one of the island's best (see below). The staff is helpful in hooking you up with any number of outdoor activities, including everything from sea kayaking to windsurfing.

Cruz Bay, St. John, U.S.V.I. 00831. © **800/322-6335** or 340/776-6121. www. estatelindholm.com. 10 units. Winter $290-$340 double; off season $140-$240 double. Rates include continental breakfast. AE, DISC, MC, V. **Amenities:** Restaurant; freshwater outdoor pool; fitness room; all nonsmoking rooms. *In room:* A/C, TV, beverage maker, fridge, microwave.

GUESTHOUSES

The following places offer just the basics, but they're fine if you're not too finicky.

The Inn at Tamarind Court   Right outside Cruz Bay but still within walking distance of the ferryboat dock, this modest place consists of a small hotel and an even simpler West Indian inn. Bedrooms are small, evoking those in a little country motel; most have twin beds. Shower-only bathrooms in the inn are shared; units in the hotel have small private bathrooms. The social life here revolves around its courtyard bar and restaurant, **Pa Pa Bulls**. From the hotel, you can walk to shuttles that take you to the beaches.

South Shore Rd. (P.O. Box 350), Cruz Bay, St. John, U.S.V.I. 00831. © **800/221-1637** or 340/776-6378. Fax 340/776-6722. www.tamarindcourt.com. 20 units, 14 with bathroom. Winter $148 double with bathroom, $240 apt, $240 suite; off season $110-$120 double with bathroom, $170-$190 apt, $190 suite. Rates include continental breakfast. AE, DISC, MC, V. **Amenities:** Restaurant; bar. *In room:* A/C, TV, fridge, ceiling fan, no phone.

St. John Inn *(Value)*   The old Cruz Inn, once the budget staple of the island, enjoys a new lease on life. Although its rates have gone up, it has also been much improved. The inn overlooks Enighed Pond, only a few blocks from the Cruz Bay Dock area. Accommodations have a light, airy, California feel. The small- to medium-size bedrooms have wrought-iron beds, handcrafted pine armoires, and a touch of Ralph Lauren flair to make for an inviting nest. The junior suites contain full sofa beds, kitchenettes, and sitting areas. The shower-only bathrooms are small. The inn offers a 43-foot motor yacht, *Hollywood Waltz,* for daily excursions to private snorkeling spots and private beaches on uninhabited islands.

P.O. Box 37, Cruz Bay, St. John, U.S.V.I. 00831. © **800/666-7688** in the U.S., or 340/693-8688. Fax 340/693-9900. www.stjohninn.com. 11 units. Winter $140–$225 double; off season $80–$150 double. Extra person $15. Rates include continental breakfast. AE, MC, V. **Amenities:** Bar; outdoor pool; babysitting; nonsmoking rooms; grill. *In room:* A/C, TV, dataport, kitchenette, fridge, beverage maker, hair dryer, iron, microwave.

CAMPGROUNDS

Cinnamon Bay Campground ⏣ *Kids*   This National Park Service campground is the most complete in the Caribbean. The site is directly on the beach, surrounded by thousands of acres of tropical vegetation. Life is simple here: You have a choice of a tent, a cottage, or a bare site. At the bare campsites, nothing is provided except general facilities. The canvas tents are 10×14 feet with a floor, and come with a number of extras, including all cooking equipment; even your linen is changed weekly. The cottages are 15×15 feet, consisting of a room with two concrete walls and two screen walls. They contain cooking facilities and four twin beds with thin mattresses; one cot can be added. Lavatories and cool-water showers are in separate buildings nearby. Camping is limited to a 2-week period in winter in any given year, 3 weeks the remainder of the year. Near the road is the office, with a grocery and a cafeteria.

P.O. Box 720, Cruz Bay, St. John, U.S.V.I. 00831. © **340/776-6330.** Fax 340/776-6458. www.cinnamonbay.com. 126 units, none with bathroom. Winter $110–$140 cottage for 2, $80 tent site, $27 bare site; off season $70–$90 cottage for 2, $58 tent site, $27 bare site. Extra person $7–$17. AE, MC, V. **Amenities:** Restaurant; message center; grocery store; grill; kayaks; lockers; safe deposit boxes; sailing; snorkeling; windsurfing. *In room:* No phone.

Concordia Eco-Tents   This is the most recent addition to Stanley Selengut's Concordia development project on the southern tip of St. John, overlooking Salt Pond Bay and Ram Head Point. These solar- and wind-powered tent-cottages combine sustainable technology with some of the most spectacular views on the island. The light framing, fabric walls, and screened-in windows lend a treehouse atmosphere to the experience. Set on the windward side of the island, the tent-cottages enjoy natural ventilation from the cooling trade winds. Inside, each has two twin beds with rather thin mattresses in each bedroom, one or two twin mattresses on a loft platform, and a queen-size futon in the living-room area (each unit can sleep up to six people). Each kitchen comes equipped with a running-water sink, propane stove, and cooler. In addition, each Eco-Tent has a small private shower, rather meager towels, and a composting toilet.

The secluded hillside location, surrounded by hundreds of acres of pristine park land, requires guests to arrange for a rental vehicle. Beaches, hikes, and the shops and restaurants of Coral Bay are only a 10-minute drive from the property. For a recommendation of regular on-site studios, see the Estate Concordia Studios review on p. 91.

20–27 Estate Concordia, Coral Bay, St. John, U.S.V.I. 00830. © **800/392-9004,** or 212/472-9453 for reservations. Fax 212/861-6210. www.maho.org. 18 tent-cottages (4 are wheelchair accessible). Winter $125–$135 tent for 2; off season $95 tent for 2. Extra person $25 winter, $15 off season. MC, V. **Amenities:** Outdoor pool. *In room:* No phone.

Maho Bay Campground *◈* *Kids* An 8-mile drive northeast of Maho Bay, this is an interesting concept in ecology vacationing, where you camp close to nature but with considerable comfort. It's set on a hillside above the beach surrounded by the Virgin Islands National Park. To preserve the existing ground cover, all 114 tent-cottages are on platforms above a thickly wooded slope. Utility lines and pipes are hidden under wooden boardwalks and stairs. Each tent-cottage, covered with canvas and screens, has two twin beds with thin mattresses, a couch, electric lamps and outlets, a dining table, chairs, a propane stove, an ice chest (cooler), linen, thin towels, and cooking and eating utensils. Guests share communal bathhouses. Maho is more intimate and slightly more luxurious than its nearest competitor, Cinnamon Bay (see above).

P.O. Box 310, Cruz Bay, St. John, U.S.V.I. 00830. © **800/392-9004,** 212/472-9453 in New York City, or 340/715-0501. Fax 340/776-6504, or 212/861-6210 in New York City. www.maho.org. 114 tent-cottages, none with bathroom. Winter $115–$120 tent-cottage for 2 (minimum stay of 7 nights); off season $75 tent-cottage for 2. Extra person $15 in winter, $12 off season. AE, MC, V. **Amenities:** Restaurant; sailing; snorkeling; windsurfing. *In room:* No phone.

4 Where to Dine

St. John has some posh dining, particularly at the luxury resorts like Caneel Bay, but it also has West Indian restaurants with plenty of local color and flavor. Many of the restaurants command high prices, but you can lunch reasonably almost anywhere. Dinner is often quite an event, since it's about the only form of nightlife the island has.

EXPENSIVE

Asolare *◈* FRENCH/ASIAN This is the most beautiful and elegant restaurant on St. John, with the hippest and best-looking staff. Asolare sits on top of a hill overlooking Cruz Bay and some of the British Virgin Islands. *Asolare* translates as "the leisurely passing of time without purpose," and that's what many diners prefer to do here. The chef roams the world for inspiration and cooks with flavor and flair, using some of the best and freshest ingredients available on island. To begin, try the grilled Asian barbecued shrimp or the squid and shrimp medley. For a main course, you might be tempted by the ginger lamb or the peppercorn dusted filet of beef. Two truly excellent dishes are the chicken Kiev and the sashimi tuna on a sizzling plate with a plum–passion fruit sake vinaigrette. For dessert, try the fresh berry dishes or the chocolate pyramid cake.

Cruz Bay. ℂ 340/779-4747. Reservations required. Main courses $30–$50. AE, MC, V. Daily 5:30–9pm.

Chloe & Bernard's ⭑⭑ INTERNATIONAL   At the Westin Resort, this luxurious restaurant features one of the island's best dining experiences. Lying on the upper level of the open-air lobby, the restaurant offers intimate, relaxed dining. Chloe and Bernard are named after two fictional characters who spend their time traveling the world in search of delectable recipes to add to their mouth-watering menu. The talented chefs turn out savory dishes redolent of Caribbean sunshine and full of flavor. This is best evoked by such dishes as steamed Chilean sea bass in tomato sauce with caramelized onions in white-wine shallots; oven-roasted beef tenderloin with green, white, and red-peppercorn sauce; and oven-roasted duck breast topped with Roquefort cheese and crushed walnuts.

In the Westin Resort St. John (p. 90), Great Cruz Bay. ℂ 340/693-8000. Reservations recommended. Main courses $34–$42; fixed-price 3-course dinner $65-$95. AE, MC, V. Daily 6–9:30pm.

Equator ⭑ CARIBBEAN   This restaurant lies behind the tower of an 18th-century sugar mill, where ponds with waterlilies fill former crystallization pits for hot molasses. A flight of stairs leads to a monumental circular dining room, with a wraparound veranda and sweeping views of a park. In the center rises the stone column that horses and mules once circled to crush sugar-cane stalks. In its center, the restaurant grows a giant poinciana-like Asian tree of the *Albizia lebbeck* species. Islanders call it "woman's tongue tree."

The cuisine is the most daring on the island, and for the most part, the chefs pull off their transcultural dishes. A spicy and tantalizing opener is lemon grass–and-ginger-cured salmon salad. A classic Caribbean callaloo soup is offered, and the salads use fresh ingredients such as Roma tomatoes and endive. Daily Caribbean selections are offered, or you can opt for such fine dishes as seared Caribbean tuna, or penne pasta with shiitake mushrooms and roasted tomatoes in an herb-garlic-cream sauce. There's always a dry, aged Angus steak or a grilled veal chop for the more traditional palate.

In the Caneel Bay hotel, Caneel Bay. ℂ 340/776-6111. Reservations required. Main courses $22–$42. Year-round Tues–Sun 6:30–9pm.

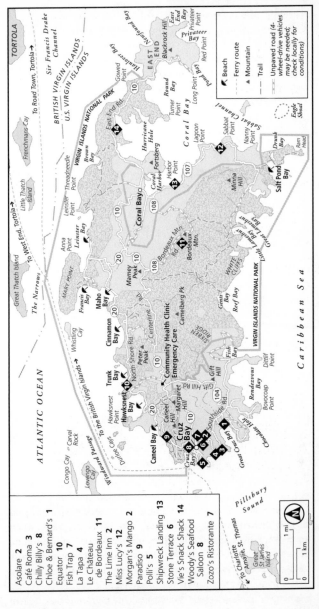

Asolare **2**
Café Roma **3**
Chilly Billy's **8**
Chloe & Bernard's **1**
Equator **10**
Fish Trap **7**
La Tapa **4**
Le Château
de Bordeaux **11**
The Lime Inn **2**
Miss Lucy's **12**
Morgan's Mango **2**
Paradiso **9**
Polli's **5**
Shipwreck Landing **13**
Stone Terrace **6**
Vie's Snack Shack **14**
Woody's Seafood
Saloon **8**
Zozo's Ristorante **7**

Le Château de Bordeaux ✸ CONTINENTAL/CARIBBEAN
This restaurant is 5 miles east of Cruz Bay, near the geographical center of the island and close to one of its highest points. It's known for having some of the best views on St. John. A lunch grill on the patio serves burgers and drinks Monday through Saturday. In the evening, amid a Victorian decor with lace tablecloths, you can begin with a house-smoked chicken spring roll or a velvety carrot soup. After that, move on to one of the saffron-flavored pastas or a savory West Indian seafood chowder, the island's best. Smoked salmon and filet mignon are a bow to the international crowd, although the wild-game specials are more unusual. The well-flavored Dijon mustard and pecan-crusted roast rack of lamb with a shallot port reduction is also a good choice. For dessert, there's a changing array of cheesecakes, among other options. The specialty drink is a passion-fruit daiquiri.

Junction 10, Bordeaux Mountain. ✆ **340/776-6611.** Reservations recommended. Main courses $28–$34. AE, MC, V. Daily 6–9pm.

Paradiso ✸✸ CONTEMPORARY AMERICAN   This is the most talked-about restaurant on St. John, other than Asolare (see above), and one of the few that's air-conditioned. The interior has lots of brass, glowing hardwoods, and nautical antiques, not to mention the most beautiful bar on the island, crafted from mahogany, purpleheart, and angelique. Try such appetizers as grilled chicken spring rolls with roasted sweet peppers. Roasted garlic Caesar salad with sun-dried tomatoes and Parmesan grissini is a new twist on this classic dish. But the main dishes truly shine, especially a pan-seared local yellowfin tuna with baby arugula, fennel, pear, and radicchio, and a grilled Kansas City sirloin marinated in garlic and fresh herbs. Another enticing choice is oven-roasted free-range chicken breast with roasted potatoes, carrots, and butternut squash.

Mongoose Junction. ✆ **340/693-8899.** Reservations recommended. Main courses $28–$38. AE, MC, V. Daily 6–9:30pm. Bar daily 5–10:30pm.

Stone Terrace ✸ ECLECTIC   On the waterfront at Cruz Bay this charmer overlooks the sea where the ferries from St. Thomas dock. Named for the native stone-built structure it occupies, it serves some of the freshest and best dishes on island. For inspiration, the chef roams the world. As the pelicans dive in the bay, you can peruse Chef Aaron Willis's eclectic menu. Dinner seating is on a covered archway with a terrace. The lively repertoire of dishes is crafted with a generous, personal touch. We especially like the appetizer of crab cakes with lime aioli over jicama and mango slaw, and have equal affection for goat cheese-filled pumpkin crepe, and exotic greens in a light Parmesan dressing. Soups and salads play a large role on the menu, the shrimp bisque with a sherry crème fraîche worthy of a recipe in *Gourmet*. On our most recent rounds, the chef heightened our enjoyment with such main courses as grilled breast of duck confit and molasses-rubbed pork tenderloin.

Our party was also captivated by the macadamia-and-tamarind-encrusted pork tenderloin with plantain mashed potatoes and chipotle-braised fennel. But what really won our hearts was the arrival of a Dijon and dried Vidalia onion–encrusted rack of lamb with Gorgonzola sauce, carrot gnocchi, and wilted greens.

Cruz Bay. © **340/693-9370.** Reservations recommended. Main courses $25–$36. MC, V. Tues–Sun seatings at 6 and 8pm.

Zozo's Ristorante ℝ ITALIAN   An in-the-know crowd of locals and visitors flocks to this delightful Italian restaurant with an open-air terrace. If you don't want to hear street noise, head inside this cool enclave. First-rate ingredients, style, and flavorful dishes make for a winning combination. Our party recently ordered an array of appetizers, sampling an eggplant tower (layers of eggplant, Fontina, and mozzarella topped with marinara), black mussels in white wine, garlic, and plum tomatoes, and lump crab cakes with a roasted pepper aioli. The pastas are the island's best, especially the lobster ravioli with wild mushrooms and toasted pine nuts. Tuck into such fish dishes as a grilled sea bass with an eggplant tapenade in a roasted garlic shrimp sauce. The veal shank *(osso buco)* is simmered in red wine, tomato, and veal stock and is a tasty main course.

Gallows Point. © **340/693-9200.** Reservations recommended. Main courses $27–$36. AE, MC, V. Daily 5:30–9pm.

MODERATE

Café Roma *Kids* ITALIAN   This restaurant in the center of Cruz Bay is not a place for great finesse in the kitchen, but it's a longtime favorite and has pleased a lot of diners such as families who just want a casual meal. To enter, you have to climb a flight of stairs. You might arrive early and have a strawberry colada, then enjoy a standard pasta, veal, seafood, or chicken dish. There are usually 30 to 40 vegetarian items on the menu. The owner claims, with justification, that his pizzas are the best on the island; try the white pizza. Italian wines are sold by the glass or bottle, and you can end the evening with an espresso.

Cruz Bay. © **340/776-6524.** Main courses $11–$25. MC, V. Daily 5–10pm.

Fish Trap ⦿ SEAFOOD   This aptly named place serves St. John's best seafood. It's a casual, laid-back atmosphere with tables placed on a covered patio open to the trade winds, an easy walk up from the ferry dock. Chef Aaron Willis is the island's favorite, bringing his New York culinary training with him but showing a total familiarity with West Indian seasonings and flavors. Nobody on St. John does conch fritters better than this skilled cook, and he's been praised by such national magazines as *Vogue* and *Gourmet.* Depending on the catch of the day, six fresh fish specials are featured nightly, most likely wahoo, shark, mahimahi, or snapper. The grilled tuna, for example, comes in a wasabi sauce and the swordfish is made more appetizing by the use of lemon grass. An array of steaks, tasty pastas, chicken cutlets, and burgers are always served.

Cruz Bay, next to Our Lady of Mount Carmel Church. ⓒ **340/693-9994.** Reservations required only for groups of 6 or more. Main courses $10–$42. MC, V. Tues–Sun 4:30–9:30pm.

La Tapa INTERNATIONAL   This is one of our favorite restaurants in Cruz Bay, where you can sample the tapas, Spanish-inspired bite-size morsels of fish, meat, or marinated vegetables, accompanied by pitchers of sangria. There's a tiny bar with no more than five stools, a two-tiered dining room, and lots of original paintings (the establishment doubles as an art gallery for local artists). Menu items are thoughtful and well conceived, and include fast-seared tuna with a Basque-inspired relish of onions, peppers, garlic, and herbs; filet *poivre,* a steak soaked with rum and served with a cracked-pepper sauce and mashed potatoes. Live jazz is offered on Mondays, and on Wednesdays, merengue and salsa music is played.

Centerline Rd. (across from Scotia Bank), Cruz Bay. ⓒ **340/693-7755.** Reservations recommended. Main courses $19–$32. AE, MC, V. Daily 5:30–10pm.

The Lime Inn SEAFOOD   This open-air restaurant is in the Lemon Tree Mall in the heart of Cruz Bay. It's known for its fresh grilled Caribbean-style lobster. Other grilled seafood choices range from shrimp to the fresh catch of the day. The seared whole snapper, when served, is a delight. If you're not in the mood for seafood, try one of the daily chicken and pasta specials or one of the grilled steaks. There's also a grilled filet mignon stuffed with crabmeat. A beautifully prepared chicken Wellington is one of the chef's specialties. The most popular night is Wednesday when the Lime Inn offers an all-you-can-eat, peel-and-eat shrimp feast for $19.

In the Lemon Tree Mall, Konges Gade, Cruz Bay. ☎ **340/776-6425.** Reservations recommended. Main courses $7–$13 lunch, $16–$25 dinner. AE, MC, V. Mon–Fri 11:30am–3pm and 5:30–10pm; Sat 5:30–10pm. Closed 3 weeks in Sept.

Miss Lucy's 🜲 *(Kids)* CARIBBEAN   For the broadest array of island cookery, nobody does it better than Miss Lucy. Her food is made the way it used to be in the Caribbean long before anyone heard of high-rise resorts. Her paella is the most scrumptious on the island, a kettle brimming with hot Italian sausage, deep-fried chicken, shrimp, and mussels over saffron rice. Traditional conch fritters appear with a picante sauce, and you can gobble them down with Miss Lucy's callaloo soup. She has a magic touch with this soup. Her fish is pulled from Caribbean waters, and does she ever know how to cook it! When a fisherman catches a wahoo, he is often likely to bring it here for Miss Lucy to cook. Main dishes come with *fungi,* a corn-meal-and-okra side dish. At one of her "full moon parties," she'll cook a roast suckling pig. Before becoming the island's most famous woman chef, Miss Lucy was a big hit with tourists as St. John's first female taxi driver. For dessert, try her banana pancakes.

Salt Pond Rd., near Estate Concordia, Coral Bay. ☎ **340/693-5244.** Reservations recommended. Main courses $16–$24. AE, MC, V. Tues–Sat 11am–3pm and 6–9pm; Sun 10am–2pm.

Morgan's Mango CARIBBEAN   The chefs here roam the Caribbean for tantalizing flavors, which they adapt for their ever-changing menu. The restaurant is easy to spot, with its big canopy, the only protection from the elements. The bar wraps around the main dining room and offers some 30 frozen drinks. Thursday is Margarita Night, when soft music plays. Some think the kitchen tries to do too much, but it does produce some zesty fare—everything from Anegada lobster cakes to a spicy Jamaican pickapepper steak. Try flying fish served as an appetizer, followed by Haitian voodoo snapper pressed in Cajun spices, then grilled and served with fresh fruit salsa. Equally delectable is mahimahi in a Cruzan rum and mango sauce. The knockout dessert is the mango-banana pie.

Cruz Bay (across from the National Park dock). ☎ **340/693-8141.** Reservations recommended. Main courses $10–$25. AE, MC, V. Daily 5–10pm.

Shipwreck Landing SEAFOOD/CONTINENTAL   Eight miles east of Cruz Bay on the road to Salt Pond Beach, Shipwreck Landing offers palms and tropical plants on a veranda overlooking the sea. The intimate bar specializes in tropical frozen drinks. Lunch isn't ignored, and there's a lot more than sandwiches, salads, and burgers—try pan-seared blackened snapper in Cajun spices, or conch fritters, or different vegetarian dishes to get you going. The chef shines brighter at night, though, offering a pasta of the day along with such specialties as a tantalizing Caribbean blackened shrimp. A lot of the fare is routine, but the grilled mahimahi in lime butter is worth the trip. Entertainment, including jazz and rock, is featured Wednesday night, with no cover.

34 Freeman's Ground, Rte. 107, Coral Bay. ⓒ 340/693-5640. Reservations requested. Main courses $6–$25; lunch from $6–$12. AE, DISC, MC, V. Daily 11am–10pm. Bar until 11pm.

INEXPENSIVE

Chilly Billy's INTERNATIONAL   Islanders view this eatery as their favorite place for a filling breakfast and a savory lunch. We prefer its breakfasts, especially the "monkey bread toast," which wins new converts every week. The chefs sauté raisin and apple bread that has first been soaked in an egg batter and Bailey's Irish Cream. Of course, you can have the usual assortment of flavored pancakes (often berry) and omelets. But you may prefer something more exotic, like a Mexican-styled burrito with jalapeño jack cheese. Freshly made salads, some of the best on the island, are served at lunch, or else you can order an assortment of sandwiches, including one made of mahimahi, another a St. John Reuben with the works, including turkey and that jalapeno jack cheese again.

Lumberyard Shopping Center, Boulon Center Rd. ⓒ 340/693-8708. Reservations not required. Breakfast $4.50–$11; lunch $7–$12; salads $6.50–$11. MC, V.

Polli's _Kids_ TEX-MEX   This likable restaurant is across from the ferry dock in Cruz Bay, with an air-conditioned indoor dining area, as well as an open-air dining area with panoramic views. Its roster of frozen margaritas (try the golden margarita) is tailor-made as a preface to a savory Tex-Mex meal. Menu items include fajitas (made with your choice of beef, chicken, seafood, or tofu), burritos supreme, seafood enchilada platters, quesadillas, and some of the best-price barbecue on the island. Children's plates, including tacos and cheese quesadillas or enchiladas, are also dished up, along with some juicy, smoked ribs with a fiery Texas barbecue sauce.

Cruz Bay (in a lumberyard across from the ferry dock). ⓒ 340/775-4550. Main courses $10–$20. AE, DC, MC, V. Mon–Sat 11am–9:30pm.

Vie's Snack Shack _Finds_ CARIBBEAN   Vie's looks like little more than a plywood-sided hut, but its charming and gregarious owner is known as one of the best local chefs on St. John. Her garlic chicken is famous. She also serves conch fritters, johnnycakes, island-style beans and rice with meat sauce, and coconut and pineapple tarts. Don't leave without a glass of homemade limeade. The place is open most days, but as Vie says, "Some days, we might not be here at all"—so you'd better call before you head out.

East End Rd., Rte. 10 (13 miles east of Cruz Bay). ✆ 340/693-5033. Main courses $5–$6. AE. Tues–Sat 10am–5pm (but call first!).

Woody's Seafood Saloon SEAFOOD/AMERICAN   This local dive and hangout at Cruz Bay is more famous for its beers on tap than its cuisine. A mix of local fishermen, taxi drivers, tour guides, island drifters, and an occasional husband and wife show up here to sample the spicy conch fritters. Shrimp appears in various styles, and you can usually order fresh fish and other dishes, including burgers, blackened shark, drunken shellfish, and mussels and clams steamed in beer. There's reggae on Wednesday, and, as a patron said, "a little bit of everything and anything" on Saturday night.

Cruz Bay (50 yards from the ferry dock). ✆ 340/779-4625. Reservations not accepted. Main courses $8–12 lunch, $9–$16 dinner. AE, DC, DISC, MC, V. Sun–Thurs 11:50am–1am; Fri–Sun 11:50am–2am.

5 Beaches

The best beach, hands down, is **Trunk Bay** ⨀⨀⨀, the biggest attraction on St. John. To miss its picture-perfect shoreline of white sand would be like touring Paris and skipping the Eiffel Tower. One of the loveliest beaches in the Caribbean, it offers ideal conditions for diving, snorkeling, swimming, and sailing. The only drawback is the crowds (watch for pickpockets). Beginning snorkelers are attracted to the underwater trail near the shore (see "Fun in the Surf & Sun," below); you can rent snorkeling gear here. Lifeguards are on duty. Admission is $4 per person for those over age 16. If you're coming from St. Thomas, both taxis and safari buses to Trunk Bay meet the ferry from Red Hook when it docks at Cruz Bay.

Caneel Bay, the stamping ground of the rich and famous, has seven beaches on its 170 acres, and all are open to the public. **Caneel Bay Beach** is easy to reach from the main entrance of the Caneel Bay resort. A staff member at the gatehouse will provide directions. **Hawksnest Beach** is one of the most beautiful beaches near the Caneel Bay properties. It's not wide, but it's choice. Since it's near Cruz Bay, where the ferry docks, it is the most crowded, especially when cruise-ship passengers come over from St. Thomas. Safari buses and taxis from Cruz Bay will take you along Northshore Road.

The campgrounds of **Cinnamon Bay** have their own beach, where forest rangers sometimes have to remind visitors to put their swim trunks back on. This is our particular favorite, a beautiful strip of white sand with hiking trails, windsurfing, ruins, and wild donkeys (don't feed or pet them!). Changing rooms and showers are available, and you can rent watersports equipment. Snorkeling is popular; you'll often see big schools of purple triggerfish. This beach is best in the morning and at midday, as afternoons are likely to be windy. A marked **nature trail,** with signs identifying the flora, loops through a tropical forest on even turf before leading up to Centerline Road.

Maho Bay Beach is immediately to the east of Cinnamon Bay, and it also borders campgrounds. As you lie on the sand, you can see a whole hillside of pitched tents. This is also a popular beach.

Francis Bay Beach and **Watermelon Cay Beach** are just a few more of the beaches you'll encounter traveling eastward along St. John's curving coastline. The beach at **Leinster Bay** is another haven for those seeking a private sunny retreat. You can swim in the bay's shallow water or snorkel over the spectacular and colorful coral reef, perhaps in the company of an occasional turtle or stingray.

The remote **Salt Pond Bay** is known to locals but often missed by visitors. It's on the beautiful coast in the southeast, adjacent to **Coral Bay.** The bay is tranquil, but the beach is somewhat rocky. It's a short walk down the hill from a parking lot. (*Beware:* A few cars have recently been broken into.) The snorkeling is good, and the bay has some fascinating tidal pools. The Ram Head Trail begins here and, winding for a mile, leads to a belvedere overlooking the bay. Facilities are meager but include an outhouse and a few picnic tables.

If you want to escape the crowds, head for **Lameshur Bay Beach,** along the rugged south coast, west of Salt Pond Bay and accessible only via a bumpy dirt road. The sands are beautiful and the snorkeling is excellent. You can also take a 5-minute stroll down the road past the beach to explore the nearby ruins of an old plantation estate that was destroyed in a slave revolt.

Does St. John have a nude beach? Not officially, but lovely **Solomon Bay Beach** is a contender, although park rangers of late have sometimes asked people to put their swimwear back on. Leave Cruz Bay on Route 20 and turn left at the park service sign, about ¼ mile past the visitor center. Park at the end of a cul-de-sac, then walk along the trail for about 15 minutes. Go early, and you'll practically have the beach to yourself. As mentioned earlier, people sometimes shed their swimwear at **Cinnamon Bay** (p. 104). Again, rangers frequently ask beachgoers to put their bathing suits back on.

6 Fun in the Surf & Sun

St. John offers some of the best snorkeling, scuba diving, swimming, fishing, hiking, sailing, and underwater photography in the Caribbean. The island is known for Virgin Islands National Park, as well as for its coral-sand beaches, winding mountain roads, hidden coves, and trails that lead past old, bush-covered sugar-cane plantations. Just don't visit St. John expecting to play golf.

WATERSPORTS

The most complete line of watersports equipment available, including rentals for windsurfing, snorkeling, kayaking, and sailing, is offered at the **Cinnamon Bay Watersports Center,** on Cinnamon Bay Beach (② **340/776-6330**). One- and two-person sit-on-top kayaks rent for $15 to $20 per hour. You can also sail away in a 14-foot or 16-foot Hobie monohull **sailboat,** for $55 to $70 per hour.

BOAT EXCURSIONS   You can take half- and full-day boat trips, including a full-day excursion to the Baths at Virgin Gorda, for $95 (plus a $25 customs fee for B.V.I). A snorkel excursion on St. John costs $100 to $110 per person (plus $20 Customs fee). Call **Vacation Vistas and Motor Yachts** (② **340/776-6462**) for details. **Cruz Bay Watersports** (② **340/776-6234**) offers trips to the British Virgin Islands (bring your passport) for $90, including food and beverages.

FISHING   Outfitters located on St. Thomas offer sport-fishing trips here—they'll come over and pick you up. Call the **Charter Boat Center** (② **340/775-7990**) at Red Hook. Count on spending from $450 to $650 per party for a half-day of fishing.

SCUBA DIVING & SNORKELING   **Cruz Bay Watersports,** P.O. Box 252, Cruz Bay, St. John (② **340/776-6234**), is a PADI and NAUI five-star diving center. Certifications can be arranged through a dive master, for $350. Beginner scuba lessons start at $100. Two-tank reef dives with all dive gear cost $85, and wreck dives, night dives, and dive packages are available. In addition, snorkel tours are offered daily for $65.

Divers can ask about scuba packages at **Low Key Watersports,** Wharfside Village (② **800/835-7718** in the U.S., or 340/693-8999). All wreck dives offered are two-tank/two-location dives and cost $83. One-tank dives cost $58 per person, with night dives going for $70.

Moments **A Water Wonderland**

At Trunk Bay, divers and snorkelers can follow the **National Park Underwater Trail** (© **340/776-6201**), which stretches for 650 feet and helps you identify what you see—everything from false coral to colonial anemones. You'll pass lavender sea fans and schools of silversides. Rangers are on hand to provide information. There is a **$4** admission fee to access the beach.

Snorkel tours are available at $40 per person. The center rents watersports gear, including masks, fins, snorkels, and dive skins, and arranges day sailing trips, kayaking tours, and deep-sea fishing.

The best place for snorkeling is **Trunk Bay** (see "Beaches," above). Snorkeling gear can be rented from the Cinnamon Bay Watersports Center (see above) for $5, plus a $25 deposit. Two of the best **snorkeling spots** around St. John are **Leinster Bay** 🐟🐟 and **Haulover Bay** 🐟🐟. Usually uncrowded Leinster Bay offers some of the best snorkeling in the U.S. Virgins. The water is calm, clear, and filled with brilliantly hued tropical fish. Haulover Bay is a favorite among locals. It's often deserted, and the waters are often clearer than in other spots around St. John. The ledges, walls, and nooks here are set very close together, making the bay a lot of fun for anyone with a little bit of experience.

SEA KAYAKING   Arawak Expeditions, based in Cruz Bay (© **800/238-8687** in the U.S., or 340/693-8312), provides kayaking gear, healthful meals, and experienced guides for full- and half-day outings. Trips cost $75 and $40, respectively. Multiday excursions with camping are also available; call their toll-free number if you'd like to arrange an entire vacation with them. These trips range in price from $995 to $1,295.

WINDSURFING   The windsurfing at Cinnamon Bay is some of the best anywhere, for either the beginner or the expert. The **Cinnamon Bay Watersports Center** (see above) rents high-quality equipment for all levels, even for kids. Boards cost $30 an hour; a 2-hour introductory lesson costs $80.

MORE OUTDOOR ADVENTURE

St. John has the most rewarding hiking in the Virgin Islands. The terrain ranges from arid and dry (in the east) to moist and semi-tropical (in the northwest). The island boasts more than 800 species of plants, 160 species of birds, and more than 20 trails maintained in fine form by the island's crew of park rangers. Much of the land on the island is designated as **Virgin Islands National Park.** Visitors must stop by the **Cruz Bay Visitor Center,** where you can pick up the park brochure, which includes a map of the park, and the *Virgin Islands National Park News,* which has the latest information on park activities. It's important to carry a lot of water and wear sunscreen and insect repellent when you hike.

St. John is laced with a wide choice of clearly marked walking paths. At least 20 of these originate from Northshore Road (Rte. 20) or from the island's main east-west artery, Centerline Road (Rte. 10). Each is marked at its starting point with a preplanned itinerary; the walks can last anywhere from 10 minutes to 2 hours. Maps are available from the national park headquarters at Cruz Bay.

One of our favorite hikes, the **Annaberg Historic Trail** (identified by the U.S. National Park Service as trail no. 10), requires only about a half-mile stroll. It departs from a clearly marked point along the island's north coast, near the junction of routes 10 and 20. This self-guided tour passes the partially restored ruins of a manor house built during the 1700s. Signs along the way give historical and botanical data. Visiting the ruins is free. If you want to prolong your hiking experience, take the **Leinster Bay Trail** (trail no. 11), which begins near the point where trail no. 10 ends. It leads past mangrove swamps and coral inlets rich with plant and marine life; markers identify some of the plants and animals.

Near the beach at **Cinnamon Bay,** there's a marked nature trail, with signs identifying the flora. It's a relatively flat walk through a tropical forest, eventually leading straight up to Centerline Road.

The **National Park Service** (© 340/776-6201) provides a number of ranger-led activities. One of the most popular is the guided 2.5-mile **Reef Bay Hike.** Included is a stop at the only known petroglyphs on the island and a tour of the sugar-mill ruins. A park ranger discusses the area's natural and cultural history along the way. The hike starts at 9:30am on Monday, Tuesday, Thursday, and Friday and costs $20 per person. Reservations are required and can be made by phone (at least 2–3 weeks in advance).

Another series of hikes traversing the more arid eastern section of St. John originates at clearly marked points along the island's **southeastern tip,** off Route 107. Many of the trails wind through the grounds of 18th-century plantations, past ruined schoolhouses, rum distilleries, molasses factories, and great houses, many of which are covered with lush, encroaching vines and trees.

7 Exploring St. John

The best way to see St. John quickly, especially if you're on a cruise-ship layover, is to take a 2-hour **taxi tour.** The cost is $45 for one or two passengers, or $16 per person for three or more. Almost any taxi at Cruz Bay will take you on these tours, or you can call the **St. John Taxi Association** (© 340/693-7530).

Many visitors spend time at **Cruz Bay,** where the ferry docks. This village has bars, restaurants, boutiques, and pastel-painted houses. It's a bit sleepy, but relaxing after the pace of St. Thomas.

Most cruise-ship passengers dart through Cruz Bay and head for the island's biggest attraction, **Virgin Islands National Park** 🍁🍁 (© 340/776-6201). The park totals 12,624 acres including submerged lands and water adjacent to St. John, and has more than 20 miles of hiking trails to explore. See "More Outdoor Adventure," above, for information on trails and organized park activities.

Other major sights on the island include **Trunk Bay** (see "Beaches," earlier in this chapter), one of the world's most beautiful beaches, and **Fort Berg** (also called Fortsberg), at Coral Bay, which served as the base for the soldiers who brutally crushed the 1733 slave revolt. Finally, try to make time for the **Annaberg Ruins** on Leinster Bay Road, where the Danes maintained a thriving plantation and sugar mill after 1718. It's located off Northshore Road, east of Trunk Bay. Admission is free. On certain days of the week (dates vary), guided walks of the area are given by park rangers. For information on the **Annaberg Historic Trail,** see p. 107.

8 Shopping

Compared to St. Thomas, St. John's shopping isn't much, but what's here is interesting. The boutiques and shops of Cruz Bay are individualized and quite special. Most of the shops are clustered at Mongoose Junction, in a woodsy area beside the roadway, about a 5-minute walk from the ferry dock. See "Where to Dine," earlier in this chapter, for our restaurant recommendations in this complex.

Before you leave the island, you'll want to visit the recently expanded **Wharfside Village,** just a few steps from the ferry-departure point. Here in this complex of courtyards, alleys, and shady patios is a mishmash of all sorts of boutiques, along with some restaurants, fast-food joints, and bars.

Bajo El Sol, Mongoose Junction, North Shore Road, Cruz Bay (© 340/693-7070), is a cooperative and award-winning gallery displaying the work of many island artists. For sale are paintings,

Tips **The Best Shopping Day**

The most fun shopping on the island takes place on **St. John Saturday** ⍟, a colorful, drum-beating, spice-filled feast for the senses, held on the last Saturday of every month. This daylong event begins in the morning in the center of town and spills across the park. Vendors hawk handmade items, ranging from jewelry to handicrafts and clothing, and food made from local ingredients. One vendor concocts soothing salves from recipes passed on by her ancestors; another designs and makes porcelain earrings; another flavors chicken and burgers with her own secret hickory barbecue sauce; yet another hollows out and carves gourds from local calabash trees.

---

sculpture, ceramics, and jewelry. Aimee Trayser with her paintings and collages and Les Anderson produce exceptional work.

Bamboula, Mongoose Junction (② **340/693-8699**), has an exotic and very appealing collection of gifts from St. John, the Caribbean, India, Indonesia, and Central Africa. The store also has clothing for both men and women under its own label—hand-batiked soft cottons and rayons made for comfort in a hot climate.

Here's your chance to pick up a unique item. A total of 100 artists, artisans, and designers have their work showcased here at **Best of Both Worlds,** at Mongoose Junction. The shop is one of the best places for gifts and art, including metal sculptures. Many award-winning designers display their unique art and pieces of jewelry here, along with art glass, lamps, dishware, and clocks. There are especially good buys in artistic glasswork.

If you're planning to hike the trails of lush St. John, and you've arrived unprepared, **Big Planet Adventure Outfitters,** Mongoose Junction, North Shore Road, Cruz Bay (② **340/776-6638**) is the best place to go stock up on outdoor clothing. Reef footware and Naot sandals are sold, along with a selection of other durable items, including backpacks, luggage, sunglasses, and the like.

The Canvas Factory, Mongoose Junction (② **340/776-6196**), produces its own handmade, rugged, colorful canvas bags, as well as sailing hats, soft-sided luggage, and cotton hats.

Clothing Studio, Mongoose Junction (② **340/776-6585**), is the Caribbean's oldest hand-painted-clothing studio. Here you can watch talented artists create original designs on fine tropical clothing, including swimwear and daytime and evening clothing, mainly for women and babies, with a few items for men.

Donald Schnell Studio ⊛, Mongoose Junction (© 340/776-6420), is a working studio and gallery where Mr. Schnell and his assistants have created one of the finest collections of handmade pottery, sculpture, and blown glass in the Caribbean. They're known for their rough-textured coral work. Water fountains are a specialty item, as are house signs and coral-pottery dinnerware. The studio will ship its work all over the world. Go in and discuss any particular design you may have in mind.

Every Ting, Bay St., Cruz Bay (© 340/693-5820), is the best of all-purpose stores, and it's also a gathering point for locals and visitors alike. It's like a nerve center where you can drop in for a "cuppa" or to use the Internet. You can find reading material here for the beach along with music CDs, cotton resort wear, and even campy picture frames decorated with pinkish shells gathered on the beach.

Fabric Mill, Mongoose Junction (© 340/776-6194), features silk-screened and batik fabrics from around the world. Vibrant rugs and bed, bathroom, and table linens can add a Caribbean flair to your home. Whimsical soft sculpture, sarongs, scarves, and handbags are also made here.

The Marketplace, Cruz Bay (© 340/776-6455), with its dramatic architecture and native stone, is a cool place to shop on a hot day and enjoy its verandas and courtyards. It's ideal if you're renting a condo on St. John, as many visitors do, as the market here includes everything from a hardware shop to a video store, plus health care needs and a lot more.

R and I Patton Goldsmithing, Mongoose Junction (© 340/776-6548), is one of the oldest businesses on the island. Three-quarters of the merchandise here is made on St. John. There's a large selection of island-designed jewelry in sterling silver, gold, and precious stones. Also featured are the works of goldsmiths from outstanding American studios, as well as Spanish coins.

The location of the **Shop at Caneel Bay,** in the Caneel Bay resort (© 340/776-6111), guarantees both an upscale clientele and an upscale assortment of merchandise. Scattered over two simple, elegant floors are drugstore items, books, sundries, and handicrafts, as well as some unusual artwork and pieces of expensive jewelry. There are also racks of resort wear and sportswear for men and women. The shop carries handbags and watches by top designers.

9 St. John After Dark

Bring a good book. When it comes to nightlife, St. John is no St. Thomas, and everybody here seems to want to keep it that way. Most people are content to have a leisurely dinner and then head for bed.

The **Caneel Bay Bar,** at the Caneel Bay resort (© 340/ 776-6111), has live music Thursday to Saturday 8 to 10:30pm. The most popular drinks are the Cool Caneel (local rum with sugar, lime, and anisette) and the trademark Plantation Punch (lime and orange juice with three different kinds of rum, bitters, and nutmeg).

The two places above are very touristy. If you'd like to drink and gossip with the locals, try **JJ's Texas Coast Café,** Cruz Bay (© 340/ 776-6908), a real dive, across the park from the ferry dock. The margaritas here are lethal. Also at Cruz Bay, check out the action at **Fred's** (© 340/776-6363), across from the Lime Inn. Fred's brings in bands and has dancing on Wednesday and Friday nights. It's just a little hole-in-the-wall and can get crowded fast.

The best sports bar is **Skinny Legs,** Emmaus, Coral Bay, beyond the fire station (© 340/779-4982). This shack made of tin and wood has the best burgers in St. John. (The chili dogs aren't bad, either.) The yachting crowd hangs out here, though you wouldn't know it at first glance—it often seems that the richer they are, the poorer they dress. The bar has a satellite dish, dartboard, and horseshoe pits. There's live music on Thursday, Friday, and Saturday nights during high season and on Saturday night year-round.

Morgan's Mango (© 340/693-8141), a restaurant, is also one of the hottest watering holes on the island. It's in Cruz Bay, across from the National Park dock. Count yourself lucky if you get in on a crowded night in winter. The place became famous locally when it turned away Harrison Ford, who was vacationing at Caneel Bay. Thursday is Margarita Night, and Tuesday night is Lobster Night.

Woody's Seafood Saloon *₢*, Cruz Bay (© 340/779-4625), is the previously recommended local dive and hangout at Cruz Bay, 50 yards from the ferry dock (p. 103). It draws both visitors and a cross-section of island life from expats to villa owners. Michigan-born Woody Mann, the bartender, is often compared to the character of the same name on the sitcom *Cheers.* You can come here to eat or drink. The place is particularly popular during happy hour from 3 to 6pm. It's about the only place on island you can order food at 10pm. The joint jumps Sunday to Thursday 11:50am to 1am, Friday and Saturday 11:50am to 2am.

4

St. Croix

At 84 square miles, St. Croix is the largest of the U.S. Virgin Islands. At the east end—the easternmost point of the United States—the terrain is rocky and arid. The west end is more lush and even includes a small "rain forest" of mango, mahogany, tree ferns, and dangling lianas. Between the two extremes are beautiful beaches, rolling hills, pastures, and, increasingly, miles of condos.

Christopher Columbus named the island *Santa Cruz* (Holy Cross) when he landed on November 14, 1493. He anchored his ship off the north shore but was quickly driven away by the spears, arrows, and axes of the Carib Indians. The French laid claim to the island in 1650; the Danes purchased it from them in 1773. Under their rule, the slave trade and sugar cane fields flourished until the latter half of the 19th century. Danish influence still permeates the island today.

St. Croix is more relaxed with friendlier people than St. Thomas. It is nowhere near as inviting or welcoming as St. John, and St. Croix doesn't approach the graciousness of the British Virgin Islands. Additionally, the introduction of gambling has brought a more jaded type of tourist to the island. Even with gambling, St. Croix has a long way to go to reach the experience of mass tourism of St. Thomas.

1 Orientation

ARRIVING
BY PLANE

All flights to St. Croix land at the **Henry E. Rohlsen Airport,** Estate Mannings Bay (© **340/778-1012**), on the southern coast of the island. There are no ATMs at the airport, but the major car-rental firms maintain kiosks here. Do reserve a car before you arrive.

American Airlines (© **800/433-7300;** www.aa.com) currently offers the most frequent and reliable service to St. Croix. Passengers connect through San Juan from either New York City's JFK airport or from Newark, New Jersey. From San Juan, **American Eagle**

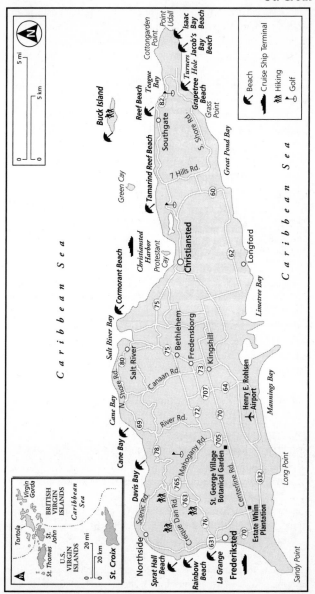

N

5 mi

5 km

Beach
Cruise Ship Terminal
Hiking
Golf

Point Udall
Cottongarden Point
Isaac
Turners Hole Jacob's Bay Beach
Teague Bay
Reef Beach
82
Grapetree Beach
Grass Point
Southgate
Tamarind Reef Beach
S. Shore Rd.
Great Pond Bay

Buck Island

7 Hills Rd.
60

Green Cay

Christiansted

Caribbean Sea

Christiansted Harbor
Protestant Cay
62
Longford

Cormorant Beach

Salt River Bay
75
Limetree Bay

80
Salt River
Bethlehem
75
Fredensborg
Kingshill
73
Manning Bay
Cane Bay
69
Canaan Rd.
707
64
N. Shore Rd.
72
70
River Rd.
Henry E. Rohlsen Airport
78
70

Caribbean Sea

Davis Bay
765
Mahogany Rd.
705
St. George Village Botanical Garden
632
Long Point
Northside
Scenic Rd.
Cinque Dan Rd.
763
Centerline Rd.
76
Estate Whim Plantation
Sprat Hall Beach
631
70
Rainbow Beach
La Grange
Frederiksted
Sandy Point

Caribbean Sea

N

Virgin Gorda
Tortola
BRITISH VIRGIN ISLANDS
Caribbean Sea
St. Thomas St. John
U.S. VIRGIN ISLANDS
St. Croix
20 mi
20 km

offers several daily nonstop flights. There's also one flight daily from Miami, with one stop (but no change of plane) in St. Thomas. The flight originates in Dallas–Fort Worth, American's biggest hub.

Travel time to St. Croix from New York is 4 hours, from Chicago 5½ hours, from Miami 3½ hours, and from Puerto Rico 20 minutes. There are no direct flights to St. Croix from Canada or the United Kingdom; connections are made via Miami.

There are also easy air links between St. Thomas and St. Croix. **American Eagle** (© **800/433-7300;** www.aa.com) has three daily flights; in addition, **Seaborne Airlines** (© **888/359-8687** or 340/773-6442; www.seaborneairlines.com) offers 17 flights daily. Flight time is only 25 minutes.

BY BOAT

Virgin Islands Fast Ferry (© **877/733-9425;** www.virginislands fastferry.com) operates a high-speed catamaran service linking Charlotte Amalie in St. Thomas with Christiansted on St. Croix in 75 minutes. The service operates from mid-December to May 2. Schedules are subject to change and dependent on the weather, so check before you make plans to go this way. Most departures are from St. Croix at 7am or from St. Thomas at 9am. Fares are $38 one-way, $64 round-trip; children under 2 ride free.

Departures on St. Croix are from the Gallows Bay Terminal and on St. Thomas from Blyden Terminal along Veterans Avenue. Since only cruise ships with fewer than 200 passengers land directly at the port at Christiansted, most vessels arrive at Frederiksted, where the Abrahson Pier has room for two megaships to arrive at the same time. Most visitors spend little time in Frederiksted, heading instead to Christiansted some 17 miles to the northeast.

VISITOR INFORMATION

VISITOR INFORMATION   You can begin your explorations at the **visitor bureau,** 53A Company St., in Christiansted (© **340/ 773-0495**), a yellow building across from the open-air market. It's open Monday to Friday 8am to 5pm. The U.S. Virgin Islands Division of Tourism has an office at the Customs House Building, Strand Street (© **340/772-0357**) in Frederiksted.

Tourist offices provide free maps to the island. *St. Croix This Week,* distributed free to cruise-ship and air passengers, has detailed maps of Christiansted, Frederiksted, and the entire island, pinpointing individual attractions, hotels, shops, and restaurants. If you plan to do extensive touring of the island, purchase *The Official Road Map of the U.S. Virgin Islands,* available at island bookstores.

ISLAND LAYOUT

St. Croix has two sizable towns: Christiansted on the north central shore and Frederiksted in the southwest. The Henry E. Rohlsen Airport is on the south coast, directly west of the Hess Oil Refinery, the major industry on the island. No roads circle St. Croix's coast.

To continue east from Christiansted, take Route 82 (also called the East End Rd.). Route 75 will take you west from Christiansted through the central heartland, then south to the Hess Oil Refinery. Melvin H. Evans Highway, Route 66, runs along the southern part of the island. You can connect with this route in Christiansted and head west all the way to Frederiksted.

CHRISTIANSTED

This town's historic district is in the center bordering Veterans Drive, which runs along the waterfront. The district is split by Kronprindsens Gade (Rte. 308 or Main St.), which is connected to Veterans Drive by a number of shop-filled little streets, including Gutters Gade, Trompeter Gade, and Raadets Gade. The visitor information center is located at 53A Company St.. The center of Christiansted can get very congested, and driving around is difficult because of the one-way streets. It's usually more practical to park your car and cover the relatively small district on foot. You will find open-air parking on both sides of Fort Christiansvaern.

THE NORTH SHORE

This coastal strip that stretches from Cottongarden Point, the eastern tip of the island, all the way west past Christiansted and up and around Salt River Bay, comes to an end as it reaches the settlement of Northside in the far west. It is the most touristy region of St. Croix, site of the best beaches, the most hotels, and the finest resorts and shopping. It is also the takeoff point (at Christiansted Harbor) for excursions to Buck Island, St. Croix's most popular attraction. Many visitors confine their stay in St. Croix entirely to the north coast. The northern coastline is not only long but also diverse, going from a lush rainforest that envelops most of the northwest to the eastern sector, which is dry with palm-lined beaches.

THE EAST END

The East End begins east of Christiansted, the capital, taking in Tamarind Reef Beach and Reef Beach before it reaches Teague Bay, coming to an end at Cottongarden Point, the far eastern tip of St. Croix. This section is linked by Route 82 (also called East End Rd.). The Buccaneer, the island's major resort, is here, along with such other resorts as Tamarind Reef Hotel. The area is far less congested than the section immediately to the west of Christiansted, and many visitors prefer the relative isolation and tranquillity of the East End. This section of St. Croix is relatively dry, the landscape a bit arid, but its compensating factor is a number of palm-lined beaches. The best place for a beach picnic is Cramer's Park at the far eastern tip, a U.S.V.I. territorial beach popular with the islanders themselves.

FREDERIKSTED

It's hard to get lost in tiny Frederiksted. Most visitors head for the central historic district, where the Frederiksted Pier juts out into the sea. The two major streets, both of which run parallel to the water, are Strand Street and King Street. See the "St. Croix" map on p. 113 to help get your bearings.

2 Getting Around

If you plan to do some serious sightseeing, you'll need to rent a car, as getting around by public transportation is a slow, uneven process. There is bus service, but you might end up stranded somewhere and unable to reach your destination without a taxi.

BY TAXI

At Henry E. Rohlsen Airport, official taxi rates are posted. From the airport, expect to pay about $14 to $26 to Christiansted and about $12 to $24 to Frederiksted. Cabs are unmetered, so agree on the rate before you get in. The **St. Croix Taxicab Association** (© 340/778-1088) offers door-to-door service.

BY BUS

Air-conditioned **buses** run between Christiansted and Frederiksted about every 45 minutes daily between 5:30am and 9pm. They start at Tide Village, to the east of Christiansted, and go along Route 75 to the Golden Rock Shopping Center. They transfer along Route 70, with stopovers at the Sunny Isle Shopping Center, La Reine Shopping Center, St. George Village Botanical Garden, and Whim Plantation Museum, before reaching Frederiksted. The fare is $1, or 55¢ for seniors. For more information, call © 340/778-0898.

BY CAR

Remember to *drive on the left.* In most rural areas, the speed limit is 35 mph; certain parts of the major artery, Route 66, are 55 mph. In towns and urban areas, the speed limit is 20 mph. Keep in mind that if you're going into the "bush country," you'll find the roads very difficult. Sometimes the government smoothes the roads out before the rainy season begins (often in Oct or Nov), but they still deteriorate rapidly.

St. Croix offers moderately priced car rentals, even on cars with automatic transmissions and air-conditioning. However, because of the island's higher-than-normal accident rate (which is partly the result of visitors who forget to drive on the left-hand side of the road), insurance costs are higher than elsewhere. **Avis** (© **800/ 331-1212** or 340/778-9355; www.avis.com), **Budget** (© **800/ 472-3325** or 340/778-9636; www.budgetrentacar.com), and **Hertz** (© **800/654-3131** or 340/778-9744; www.hertz.com) all have desks at the airport; look for their kiosks near the baggage-claim areas. Collision-damage insurance costs $14 per day, depending on the company and size of car, and we feel that it's a wise investment. Some credit card companies grant you collision-damage protection if you pay for the rental with their card. Verify coverage before you go.

FAST FACTS: St. Croix

American Express The American Express travel representative is **Southerland,** Queens Cross Street, Carvelle Arcade Building (© **800/260-2603** or 340/773-9500).

Banks Several major banks are represented in St. Croix. Chase Manhattan Bank is at 1101 King St. in Christiansted (© **340/ 773-1200**). Most are open Monday through Thursday from 9am to 3pm and Friday from 9am to 4pm. Virgin Islands Community Bank has a branch at 12 King's St. (© **340/773-0440**) in Christiansted and another branch on Strand Street in Frederiksted.

Bookstores Head to the **Bookie,** 3 Strand St. (© **340/773-2592**), in Christiansted. The shop is open Monday to Friday from 8am to 5pm.

Business Hours Typical business hours are Monday to Friday 9am to 5pm, Saturday 9am to 1pm.

Cameras & Film There is no specific outlet devoted to cameras and film. The best stock, however, is found at **Kmart** at the Sunny Isles Shopping Center, Space 1 (© **340/719-9190**).

Dentists Call the **Sunny Isle Medical Center,** Sunny Isle (© **340/778-6356**) for an appointment.

Doctors For a referral, call **Sunny Isle Medical Center** (✆ **340/778-0069**).

Drugstores Try the **Golden Rock Pharmacy,** Golden Rock Shopping Center (✆ **340/773-7666**), open Monday to Saturday 8am to 7pm, and Sunday 8am to 3pm. There's also **People's Drugstore,** Sunny Isle Shopping Center (✆ **340/778-5537**), open Monday to Saturday 8am to 9pm, and Sunday 9am to 9pm.

Emergencies To reach the police, fire department, or an ambulance, call ✆ **911.**

Hospitals The main facility is **Governor Juan F. Luis Hospital & Medical Center,** 4007 Estate Diamond Ruby (✆ **340/778-6311**).

Internet Access Go to **Strand Street Station,** 1002 Strand St., Christiansted (✆ **340/719-6245**), which charges $5 for 30 minutes. You can also go to **A Better Copy,** 52 Company St., Christiansted (✆ **340/692-5303**), which also charges $5 for every half-hour.

Laundry Try **Tropical Cleaners & Launderers,** 16–17 King Cross St. (✆ **340/773-3635**), in Christiansted. Hours are Monday to Saturday 7:30am to 6pm.

Newspapers & Magazines Newspapers such as the *Miami Herald* are flown into St. Croix daily. St. Croix has its own newspaper, *St. Croix Avis. Time* and *Newsweek* are widely sold as well. Your best source of local information is *St. Croix This Week,* distributed free by the tourist offices.

Police The police headquarters is on Market Street in Christiansted. In case of emergency, dial ✆ **911;** for non-emergency assistance, call ✆ **340/778-2211.**

Post Office The post office is on Company Street (✆ **340/773-3586**), in Christiansted. The hours of operation are Monday to Friday 7:30am to 4:30pm and Saturday 7:30am to noon.

Restrooms There are few public restrooms, except at the major beaches and airport. In Christiansted, the National Park Service maintains some restrooms within the public park beside Fort Christiansvaern.

Safety St. Croix is safer than St. Thomas. Although there have been random acts of violence against tourists, even murder, most crime on the island is petty theft, usually of possessions left unguarded at the beach while vacationers go into the water for a swim, or muggings (rarely violent) of visitors wandering the dark streets and back alleys of Frederiksted and

Christiansted at night. Exercise caution at night by sticking to the heart of Christiansted and not wandering around in Frederiksted. Avoid night strolls along beaches. Night driving in remote parts of the island can also be risky; you might be car-jacked and robbed at knifepoint.

Taxes The only local tax is an 8% surcharge added to all hotel rates.

Taxis For an airport taxi, call ✆ **340/778-1088;** in Christiansted call ✆ **340/773-5020.**

Telephone & Fax You can dial direct to St. Croix from the mainland by using the 340 area code. Omit the 340 for local calls. A local call at a phone booth costs 25¢. The bigger hotels will send telexes and faxes, or you can go to the post office (see above).

3 Where to Stay

St. Croix's deluxe resorts are along the North Shore, its charming old waterfront inns mostly in Christiansted. You may also stay at a former plantation or in a condo complex, which offers privacy and the chance to save money by preparing your own meals. The choice is yours: a location in Christiansted or Frederiksted close to shops and nightlife, but away from the beach; or an isolated resort where, chances are, your accommodations will be either on the beach or a short walk away from it. From such resorts, you'll have to drive into one of the towns for a shopping binge or for restaurants and clubs.

In general, rates are steep, but in summer, hotels slash prices by about 25% to 50%. All rooms are subject to an 8% hotel room tax, which is not included in the rates given below.

Note: If you need a hair dryer, you should pack your own. Apparently, a lot of visitors have packed up hotel hair dryers upon departure, and some innkeepers are reluctant to provide them.

NORTH SHORE
VERY EXPENSIVE

The Buccaneer ★★★ *(Kids* This large, luxurious, family-owned resort boasts three of the island's best beaches, and the best sports program on St. Croix. The property was once a cattle ranch and a sugar plantation; its first estate house, which dates from the mid–17th century, stands near a freshwater pool. Accommodations are either in the main building or in one of the beachside properties. The baronially arched main building has a lobby opening onto landscaped terraces, with a sea vista on two sides and Christiansted to the west. The rooms are fresh and comfortable, though some of the standard units are a bit small. All have wicker or mahogany furnishings and full bathrooms. The best bathrooms are in the Beachside Doubloons, and come complete with whirlpool tubs. A free Kid's Camp is available year-round.

This resort serves the best cuisine of any hotel on the island—a Caribbean and international repertoire of first-class dishes.

P.O. Box 25200, Gallows Bay (2 miles east of Christiansted on Rte. 82), Christiansted, St. Croix, U.S.V.I. 00824. ℂ **800/255-3881** in the U.S., or 340/773-2100. Fax 340/712-2104. www.thebuccaneer.com. 138 units. Winter $295–$580 double, $525–$840 suite; off season $240–$380 double, $360–$580 suite. Rates include American breakfast. AE, DISC, MC, V. **Amenities:** 4 restaurants; bar; 2 outdoor pools; 18-hole golf course; 8 tennis courts (2 lit); fitness center; spa; children's program; limited room service; massage; babysitting; laundry service, nonsmoking rooms; rooms for those w/limited mobility; kayaks; scuba; snorkeling; Sunfish sailboats. *In room:* A/C, TV, dataport, fridge, beverage maker, hair dryer, iron/ironing board, safe.

Carambola Beach Resort ⚓

This hotel is set on 28 acres above Davis Bay, about a 30-minute drive from Christiansted. It's one of the largest hotels on St. Croix, and it lies adjacent to an outstanding golf course, in a lovely, lush setting on a white-sand beach whose turquoise waters boast fine snorkeling. Despite its spectacular location, this resort doesn't match the Buccaneer's class and style. Originally built as a Rock Resort, it has suffered hurricanes and management changes, and today is hot on the trail of the timeshare market. Guests are housed in red-roofed, two-story buildings, each of which contains six units. The accommodations are furnished in mahogany, with Danish design; each has a balcony partially concealed from outside view, overlooking either the garden or the sea. Rooms have an upscale flair, with louvered doors, tile floors, mahogany trim, and sometimes extras like screened-in porches with rocking chairs. Bathrooms are luxurious and roomy, with oversize showers (with seats) and tiled vanities. If you want the very finest room, ask for the Davis Bay Suite, which was a former Rockefeller private beach home. Its veranda alone is capable of entertaining 50 people, should that many drop in.

The resort is known for its cuisine, especially the Caribbean and international menu at **Mahogany Restaurant**.

Estate Davis Bay (P.O. Box 3031), Kingshill, St. Croix, U.S.V.I. 00851. ℂ **888/ 503-8760** in the U.S., or 340/778-3800. Fax 340/778-1682. www.carambola beach.com. 151 units. Winter $199–$229 suite; off season $179–$209 suite.

Where to Stay in St. Croix

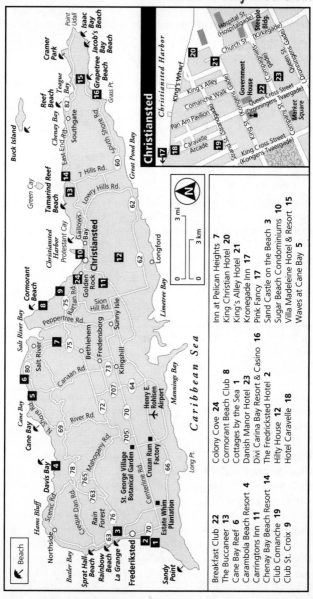

Breakfast Club **22**
The Buccaneer **13**
Cane Bay Reef **6**
Carambola Beach Resort **4**
Carringtons Inn **11**
Chenay Bay Beach Resort **14**
Club Comanche **19**
Club St. Croix **9**

Colony Cove **24**
Cormorant Beach Club **8**
Cottages by the Sea **1**
Danish Manor Hotel **23**
Divi Carina Bay Resort & Casino **16**
The Fredricksted Hotel **2**
Hilty House **12**
Hotel Caravelle **18**

Inn at Pelican Heights **7**
King Christian Hotel **20**
King's Alley Hotel **21**
Kronegade Inn **17**
Pink Fancy **17**
Sand Castle on the Beach **3**
Sugar Beach Condominiums **10**
Villa Madeleine Hotel & Resort **15**
Waves at Cane Bay **5**

AE, DISC, MC, V. **Amenities:** 2 restaurants; bar; outdoor pool; golf course; 4 tennis courts; fitness center; whirlpool; game room; car rental; massage; babysitting; laundry service; dry cleaning; nonsmoking rooms; rooms for those w/limited mobility; dive shop; fishing; library; snorkeling. *In room:* A/C, TV, kitchenette (in some), fridge, beverage maker, hair dryer, iron/ironing board, safe.

Villa Madeleine Hotel & Resort ✺

This deluxe 6½-acre property has some of the island's poshest rooms. When it first opened, the Villa showed great promise of overtaking the Buccaneer. That never happened. The place remains distinguished, but service has fallen off greatly and the Buccaneer is far superior. The Villa is very independent of everything else on St. Croix—guests check in and never leave the grounds. Many of the well-heeled occupants are retirees who live here full-time. The focal point is the great house, whose Chippendale balconies and proportions emulate the Danish colonial era. Inside, a splendidly conceived decor incorporates masses of English chintz and mahogany paneling.

Each stylish one- or two-bedroom villa has its own kitchen, privacy wall, and plunge pool. The marble bathrooms have double dressing areas and oversize tub/shower combinations. The villas within the resort are handled by different management companies; therefore, standards can vary, depending on which one you're assigned. Beach lovers travel ⅓ mile to the nearest beaches, Duggan's Reef. The Villa employs top chefs and is known for its steaks and its rack of lamb.

P.O. Box 26160, Teague Bay (8 miles east of Christiansted), St. Croix, U.S.V.I. 00824. ✆ **800/496-7379** or 340/778-8782. Fax 340/773-2150. www.teaguebayproperties. com. 22 units. Winter $275 1-bedroom villa, $350 2-bedroom villa; off season $200 1-bedroom villa, $275 2-bedroom villa. MC, V. **Amenities:** Restaurant; bar; 22 outdoor pools; golf course nearby; tennis court; car rental; laundry service; nonsmoking rooms; rooms for those w/limited mobility. *In room:* A/C, TV, kitchen, fridge, beverage maker, ceiling fan.

EXPENSIVE

Chenay Bay Beach Resort ✺ *Kids*

These West Indian–style cottages are on a 30-acre beach, with an open-air swimming pool. Home to one of the island's finest beaches for swimming, snorkeling, and windsurfing, Chenay Bay is 3 miles east of Christiansted and is a terrific beach for families. With a quiet and barefoot-casual ambience, each cottage contains a fully equipped kitchenette and bathroom. The 20 original cottages are smaller and more weathered than the newer duplexes numbered 21 to 50. Accommodations are medium in size, with firm mattresses on comfortable beds. Most bathrooms are compact but with adequate shelf space and tubs.

Rte. 82, East End Rd. (P.O. Box 24600), St. Croix, U.S.V.I. 00824. ℂ **800/548-4457** in the U.S., or 340/773-2918. Fax 340/773-6665. www.chenaybay.com. 50 cottages. Winter $272–$594 cottage for 1 or 2; off season $192–$426 cottage for 1 or 2. Extra person $25. Children under age 18 stay free in parent's room. $50 per person extra for all meals and drinks. AE, MC, V. **Amenities:** Restaurant; bar; pool; 2 tennis courts; watersports equipment; children's programs; babysitting. *In room:* A/C, TV, kitchenette, fridge, coffeemaker.

Cormorant Beach Club & Hotel ℛ

This is the poshest gay resort in the Caribbean Basin. About 70% of its clients are gay males, mostly from the eastern United States and California. The 6-acre property is designed in a boxy, modern-looking series of rectangles, with strong horizontal lines and outcroppings of exposed natural stone. It strikes a pleasant balance between seclusion and accessibility. Long Reef lies a few hundred feet offshore from the resort's sandy beachfront. Bedrooms contain a restrained decor of cane and wicker furniture, spacious bathrooms with tubs and showers, and sliding-glass doors that flood the interior with sunlight.

The social life revolves around an open-air clubhouse, with views of the sea. Off the central core is a bar (see "St. Croix After Dark," later in this chapter) and an airy dining room. The restaurant is St. Croix's leading gay eatery (see "Dining," later in this chapter).

4126 La Grande Princesse (about 3 miles northwest of Christiansted, beside Rte. 75), St. Croix, U.S.V.I. 00820. ℂ **800/548-4460** in the U.S., or 340/778-8920. Fax 340/778-9218. www.cormorantbeachclub.com. 40 units. Winter $210 double, $265 suite; off season $110–$160 double, $225 suite. Extra bed $30. AE, MC, V. Dive, golf, scuba, and "commitment ceremony" packages available. **Amenities:** 2 restaurants; bar; outdoor pool; 2 tennis courts; health club; massage; nonsmoking rooms; rooms for those w/limited mobility; Internet cafe; snorkeling. *In room:* A/C, TV, kitchenette (in some), wet bar (in some), fridge, beverage maker, safe, ceiling fan.

Divi Carina Bay Resort and Casino ℛ

Opening onto 1,000 feet of sugar-white beach, this resort brought gambling to the U.S. Virgin Islands. That fact seems to obscure its success as a place of barefoot elegance and a top resort property. The complex was built on the ruins of the Grapetree Shores, which was wiped away by Hurricane Hugo. Accommodations feature oceanfront guest rooms and villa suites with views of the Caribbean. Rooms are good size and well equipped with computer/fax lines, VCRs, a small kitchen, full bathrooms, and balconies. We prefer the accommodations on the ground floor as they are closer to the water's edge. The 20 villas across the street are about a 3-minute walk from the sands.

The kitchen is strong on fresh seafood and serves the island's best Sunday brunch ($25) in its **Starlite Grille.**

25 Estate Turner Hole, Christiansted, St. Croix, U.S.V.I. 00820. ✆ **800/823-9352** in the U.S., or 340/773-9700. Fax 340/773-6802. www.diviresorts.com. 130 units. Winter $195–$263 double, $350–$368 suite; off season $151–$198 double, $277 suite. Children 15 and under stay free in parent's room. AE, MC, V. **Amenities:** 3 restaurants; 2 bars; 2 pools; lit tennis court, health club; spa services; 2 outdoor whirlpools; salon; limited room service; babysitting; massage; laundry service; nonsmoking rooms; rooms for those w/limited mobility; casino; dive center; snorkeling. *In room:* A/C, TV, dataport, kitchen (in some), wet bar, fridge, beverage maker, hair dryer, safe.

CHRISTIANSTED
MODERATE

Danish Manor Hotel ✿   This is a good hotel in the heart of Christiansted. It features hand-painted tropical friezes around the postage-stamp-size swimming pool, plus art and mementos about the courtyard bar. The only drawback is that there's no view of the sea from most rooms. However, some rooms on the top (third) floor overlook the sands of Protestant Cay. An L-shaped three-story addition stands in the rear, with spacious but sterile rooms with air-conditioning and ceiling fans. Bathrooms are small. You can park in a public lot off King Street. The popular Italian/seafood restaurant **Tutto Bene** (p. 135) fronts the hotel. Guests can swim at the beach in Christiansted Harbor, a 5-minute ferry ride from the hotel for $3.

2 Company St., Christiansted, St. Croix, U.S.V.I. 00820. ✆ **800/524-2609** in the U.S., or 340/773-1377. Fax 340/773-1913. 36 units. Winter $121–$138 double, $211 suite; off season $84–$97 double, $146 suite. Rates include continental breakfast. AE, MC, V. **Amenities:** Bar; pool. *In room:* A/C, TV, hair dryer.

Hotel Caravelle ✿ *Value*   The biggest hotel in the historic core of Christiansted, Hotel Caravelle often caters to international business travelers who prefer to be near the center of town. Many sports activities, such as sailing, deep-sea fishing, snorkeling, scuba, golf, and tennis, can be arranged at the reception desk. A swimming pool and sun deck face the water, and shopping and activities in town are close at hand. Reaching the nearest beach requires a ferryboat ride from the harbor. There's an Andalusian-style fountain in the lobby, and the restaurant, Rum Runners Club, is a few steps away.

Accommodations, which are generally spacious and comfortable, are priced according to their views. Bedrooms are a bit small but comfortable. We prefer the rooms on the third floor because they have high ceilings and the best views, although there are no elevators. The least expensive open onto a parking lot. Bathrooms, also small, are neat, with adequate shelf space and shower stalls.

44A Queen Cross St., Christiansted, St. Croix, U.S.V.I. 00820. ℭ **800/524-0410** or 340/773-0687. Fax 340/778-7004. www.hotelcaravelle.com. 44 units. Winter $135–$165 double; $289 suite; off season $110–$130 double, $199 suite. AE, DC, DISC, MC, V. **Amenities:** Restaurant; bar; pool. *In room:* A/C, TV, fridge.

King Christian Hotel   This hotel is on the waterfront, in the heart of everything. All of its front rooms have two double beds and a private balcony overlooking the harbor. No-frills economy rooms have two single beds or one double and no view or balcony. Rooms are either small or medium in size. All have been redone in the past few years, with fresh mattresses on the comfortable beds, new rugs and draperies, and renewed fixtures in the tiny bathrooms. You can relax on the sun deck or on the shaded patio. There's a beach a few hundred yards across the harbor, reached by ferry. Mile Mark Charters watersports center offers daily trips to Buck Island's famous snorkeling trail. In this price category, however, we find King's Alley, a neighbor, far more appealing (see next review).

59 King St. (P.O. Box 3619), Christiansted, St. Croix, U.S.V.I. 00824. ℭ **800/524-2012** in the U.S., or 340/773-6330. Fax 340/773-9411. www.kingchristian.com. 39 units. Winter $100–$135 double; off season $100–$120 double. AE, DC, DISC, MC, V. **Amenities:** Restaurant; freshwater pool; car-rental desk. *In room:* A/C, TV, fridge, safe.

King's Alley Hotel ⭑   This inn is at the water's edge, a 4-minute ferry ride to the nearest beach at Hotel on the Cay. It is furnished with a Mediterranean flair. Many of its rooms—which are small to medium-size—overlook its swimming-pool terrace surrounded by tropical plants. The galleries off the bedrooms are almost spacious enough for entertaining. All rooms have twin or king-size beds with good mattresses; deluxe units have four-poster mahogany beds. The bathrooms are comfortable, with good lighting and concealed vanities.

57 King St., Christiansted, St. Croix, U.S.V.I. 00820. ℭ **800/843-3574** or 340/773-0103. Fax 340/773-4431. 35 units. Winter $149 double; off season $129 double. AE, DC, MC, V. **Amenities:** Pool. *In room:* A/C, TV, coffeemaker.

INEXPENSIVE

Breakfast Club ⭑ *Value*   Here you'll get the best value of any bed-and-breakfast on St. Croix. This comfortable place combines a 1950s compound of efficiency apartments with a traditional-looking stone house rebuilt from a ruin in the 1930s. Each of the units has a kitchenette, a cypress-sheathed ceiling, white walls, a beige tile floor, and simple, summery furniture. The bathrooms are small and adequately maintained. Impromptu parties are likely to develop at random hours of the day or night, and views from the deck stretch as far off as St. John. Toby Chapin, the Ohio-born owner, cooks one of the most appealing breakfasts on the island; try the banana pancakes or the chile rellenos. A three-piece blues band plays twice a month.

18 Queen Cross St., Christiansted, St. Croix, U.S.V.I. 00820. © **340/773-7383.** Fax 340/773-864. www.nav.to/thebreakfastclub. 8 units. Year-round $75 double. Rates include breakfast. AE, V. *In room:* A/C (in some), kitchen, fridge, no phone.

Club Comanche This famous old West Indian inn is right on the Christiansted waterfront. It's based around a 250-year-old Danish-inspired main house, once the home of Alexander Hamilton. Some of its small to medium-size bedrooms have slanted ceilings with carved four-poster beds, old chests, and mahogany mirrors. The public areas have a W. Somerset Maugham aura (or at least Sydney Greenstreet). A more modern addition, reached by a covered bridge, passes over a shopping street to the waterside. Some rooms are at poolside or harborfront buildings. Because accommodations come in such a wide range of styles and sizes, your opinion of this place is likely to be influenced almost entirely by your room assignment. Most of the units face the pool instead of the ocean. The place also features **Comanche Club,** the most popular restaurant in Christiansted (see review in "Where to Dine," later in this chapter). Four minutes by ferry will take you to the beach at Hotel on the Cay.

1 Strand St., Christiansted, St. Croix, U.S.V.I. 00820. © **800/524-2066** or 340/773-0210. Fax 340/713-9145. www.usvi.net/hotel/comanche. 45 units. Winter $100–$175 double, $200 suite; off season $65–$104 double, $150 suite. AE, DC, V. **Amenities:** Restaurant; bar; large saltwater pool. *In room:* A/C, TV, hair dryer.

Kronegade Inn ★ *(Finds)* This small inn offers a certain down-home comfort at reasonable rates. Some guests call it the "best-kept secret in Christiansted." The inn has 12 suites or apartments, each with full kitchen. The decor is in a tropical motif, with white rattan furnishings. The beds are comfortable, and the small bathrooms are tidily maintained. The nearest beach is at the Hotel on the Cay, a 4-minute ferry ride away. The inn doesn't offer food service, but a number of restaurants and cafes are nearby.

1112 Western Suburb, Christiansted, St. Croix, U.S.V.I. 00820. © **340/692-9590.** Fax 340/692-9591. www.kronegadeinn.com. 17 units. Winter $75 double, $85 1 bedroom suite, $107 2-bedroom suite; off season $65 double, $75 1-bedroom suite, $95 2-bedroom suite. AE, MC, V. *In room:* A/C, TV, kitchen, fridge, coffeemaker.

Pink Fancy ★ This unique hotel is a block from the Annapolis Sailing School. You get more atmosphere than anywhere else in town. The oldest part of the four-building complex is a 1780 Danish town house. In the 1950s, the hotel became a mecca for writers and artists, including, among others, Noel Coward. New owners have made major renovations, installing more antiques and fine furnishings. Guest rooms have a bright, tropical feel, with ceiling fans, floral prints, and rattan furnishings. The deluxe rooms are furnished with canopy or iron beds, antiques, and artwork. The medium-size bathrooms have combination tub/showers. A 3-minute launch ride takes guests to the beach on the Cay, the islet in Christiansted's harbor.

27 Prince St., Christiansted, St. Croix, U.S.V.I. 00820. © **800/524-2045** in the U.S., or 340/773-8460. Fax 340/773-6448. www.pinkfancy.com. 11 units. Winter $95–$150 double; off season $85–$150 double. Extra person $20. Ask about packages and weekly rates. AE, DC, MC, V. **Amenities:** Outdoor pool; nonsmoking rooms. *In room:* A/C, TV, dataport, kitchenette, ceiling fan.

FREDERIKSTED
MODERATE
Sand Castle on the Beach   This is the best-known gay and lesbian hotel in Frederiksted. It's a half-mile from the town's shopping and dining. Rooms are comfortably furnished but small; all have good mattresses, tiny private bathrooms, and extras such as VCRs, kitchenettes, and coolers. There are two freshwater swimming pools, a hot tub, and a beachfront patio, where you'll often encounter middle-aged men in G-strings. The resort's restaurant is excellent.

Frederiksted Beach, 127 Smith Field, Frederiksted, St. Croix, U.S.V.I. 00840. © **800/524-2018** or 340/772-1205. Fax 340/772-1757. www.sandcastleonthebeach.com. 23 units. Winter $130–$169 double, $219–$249 suite; $249–$339 villa for up to 4 people; off season $79–$109 double, $129–$179 suite, $159–$249 villa for up to 4 people. Rates include continental breakfast. AE, DISC, MC, V. **Amenities:** Restaurant; 2 freshwater pools; Jacuzzi; watersports equipment rental; coin-op laundry. *In room:* A/C, TV/VCR, kitchenette, fridge, coffeemaker, hair dryer, iron, safe.

INEXPENSIVE
Cottages by the Sea *(Value)*   These isolated cottages are on a wide, sandy beach right outside Frederiksted, about 6 miles from the airport, attracting honeymooners and families. Some cottages are made of cinder blocks, and others are wood. The paneled interiors are a bit worn. The look is a bit spartan, but reasonably comfortable. Most bedrooms have king-size or twin beds, with tight, compact bathrooms. Maintenance is excellent. All cottages have private patios where you can grill your dinners. Watersports have to be arranged elsewhere, but you're welcome to go snorkeling in the waters nearby. If you want to move about, you'll have to depend on taxis or rent a car. On the other hand, you can walk over to the center of Frederiksted for restaurants, bars, and shopping.

127A Smithfield, Frederiksted, St. Croix, U.S.V.I. 00840. © **800/323-7252** or 340/772-1753. Fax 340/772-1753. www.caribbeancottages.com. 17 units. Winter $125–$155 cottage for 2, $150–$190 villa for 4; off season $105–$135 cottage for 2, $135–$155 villa for 4. Extra person $20 in winter, $15 off season. Up to 2 children under age 18 stay free in parent's cottage. AE, DISC, MC, V. **Amenities:** Watersports equipment rental. *In room:* A/C, TV, kitchen, fridge, coffeemaker, iron, no phone.

The Frederiksted Hotel   This contemporary four-story inn is a good choice for the heart of historic Frederiksted. It's in the center of town, about a 10-minute ride from the airport. Much of the activity takes place in the outdoor tiled courtyard, where guests enjoy drinks and listen to live music on Friday and Saturday nights. The cheery rooms are like those of a motel on the mainland, perhaps showing a bit of wear, and with good ventilation but bad lighting. They're done in a tropical motif of pastels. The best (and most expensive) rooms are those with an ocean view; they're subject to street noise but have the best light. Each room comes with a small, tiled bathroom. The nearest beach is Fort Frederik, a 3-minute walk away.

442 Strand St., Frederiksted, St. Croix, U.S.V.I. 00840. © **800/595-9519** in the U.S., or 340/772-0500. Fax 340/772-0500. www.frederikstedhotel.com. 40 units. Winter $100–$110 double; off season $90–$100 double. Extra person $10. AE, DISC, MC, V. **Amenities:** Restaurant; bar; outdoor pool; rooms for those w/limited mobility. *In room:* A/C, TV, fridge, microwave.

BED-&-BREAKFASTS

Carringtons Inn 🐝 *(Finds)*   If you've read all those magazine stories about celebrities, such as screen legend Maureen O'Hara, who own villas on St. Croix, and you wonder what life is like in them, here's your chance to experience one firsthand. This grandly elegant B&B was once the home of a wealthy family who spent winters here. Much evidence of their former lifestyle remains. This is an intimate B&B with personalized attention and five spacious and beautifully furnished guest rooms with first-class private bathrooms. Some have a king-size canopy bed, and wicker furnishings are in tasteful abundance. When guests gather around the pool, a house party atmosphere prevails. Even your breakfast of such delights as rum-flavored French toast can be served poolside. The staff delivers thoughtful touches such as a full concierge service, bathrobes, and even freshly baked cookies in the evening.

4001 Estate Hermon Hill (1 mile west of Christiansted), St. Croix, U.S.V.I. 00820. © **877/658-0508** or 340/713-0508. Fax 340/719-0841. www.carringtonsinn.com. 5 units. Winter $120–$150 double; off season $100–$120 double. Rates include breakfast. AE, MC, V. **Amenities:** Breakfast room; outdoor pool; tennis courts (nearby); health club (nearby); rooms for those w/limited mobility. *In room:* A/C, kitchenette (in some), hair dryer, iron, ceiling fans.

Inn at Pelican Heights ★ *Finds* Opening onto panoramic views of the sea, this B&B is on the north coast between Christiansted and Frederiksted. It's a hideaway, ideal for escapists who shun the resort hotels and want a closer encounter with St. Croix life. Each of the midsize to spacious accommodations are individually decorated and are beautifully maintained, with such personal touches as fruit or flowers provided. Your hosts, Phyllis and Fred Laue, live in the main house, which also offers a large bedroom with a queen-size bed. Below the main house are suites with their own kitchen, plus a cottage with its own kitchen and sitting room as well as a loft. All accommodations come with a bathroom with tub or shower. You can swim in a pool on the grounds or else take a 10-minute walk down to the beach. One of the best breakfasts on the island is offered in the main house, featuring such delights as fruity Finnish pancakes or a breakfast lasagna.

4201 Estate St. John (off Route 751), Christiansted, U.S.V.I. 00820 © 888/445-9458 or 340/713-8526. www.innatpelicanheights.com. 6 units. Winter $110–$140 double, $200 suite; off season $90–$120 double, $150 suite. AE, DISC, MC, V. **Amenities:** Outdoor pool; living room; library. *In room:* TV, ceiling fans, kitchenette in some.

4 Where to Dine

Don't limit yourself to your hotel for dining. St. Croix's many independent restaurants serve some of the best food in the Caribbean.

Most visitors sample diversity in their dining during lunch when, chances are, they are out indulging in beach life, shopping, or visiting attractions. Christiansted is filled with excellent restaurants offering lunch, but lunch in Frederiksted is a bit dicey if cruise ships have arrived. If so, the restaurants here may be packed with your next-door neighbors (the ones you went to St. Croix to avoid).

At night, dining on island becomes more of a problem if you want to venture out. If you're not comfortable with badly lit roads and driving on the left, driving to the restaurant of your choice might present some difficulties. Of course, the easiest way to go is have your hotel call a taxi and let the driver deliver you to a restaurant. Agree upon the hour you're to be picked up, and he'll even return for you, or the restaurant will summon a cab for you if you don't want to lock yourself into a time frame. Most of the resorts are along the north shore, and dining at a different resort every night (unless you're on a meal plan) is easily arranged by taxi.

If you're staying at one of the small hotels or guesthouses in and around Christiansted, you can even walk to your restaurant of choice. If you're at a hotel in Frederiksted, the night is yours, as the cruise-ship crowds have departed and there is a less expensive, earthier, and more laid-back feeling in the small dining rooms here.

NORTH SHORE
EXPENSIVE

The Terrace Restaurant ★★ INTERNATIONAL   This is the island's finest dining room in a hotel. Menu items vary but are likely to include grilled local lobster cakes, served with lemon-caper beurre blanc and accented with fresh tarragon. You might also opt for the poached shrimp with a fresh lime cocktail sauce or a hand-cut New York strip steak in a tamarind dark rum sauce. The delectable pecan-crusted roast pork tenderloin is served sliced over pesto mashed potatoes and red-eye gravy. The roast rack of lamb and the Thai barbecue salmon are classics. The chef prepares a fresh soup nightly, but many patrons begin with a Caesar salad.

At the Buccaneer (p. 119), Gallows Bay. ✆ **340/773-2100.** Reservations recommended. Main courses $18–$35. AE, DC, DISC, MC, V. Daily 7–10:30am and 6–9pm.

MODERATE

Cormorant Beach Club Restaurant ★ INTERNATIONAL   This is the premier gay restaurant on St. Croix. Both the restaurant and its bar are a mecca for gay and gay-friendly people who appreciate its relaxed atmosphere, well-prepared food, and gracefully arched premises overlooking the sea. The menu changes nightly. Lunch specialties may include meal-size salads, club sandwiches, burgers, and fresh fish. To begin, sample the chef's classic Caesar salad. In the evening expect such dishes as roast rack of lamb served with a pecan-and-Parmesan-herb crust or grilled fresh local mahimahi, its flavor enhanced with fresh cilantro and lime-butter sauce. Desserts are sumptuous, especially the Cruzan rum cake with bananas, chocolate, or coconut and the chocolate rum torte with layers of mousse and rum cake sealed in chocolate.

In the Cormorant Beach Club, 4126 La Grande Princesse. ✆ **340/778-8920.** Reservations recommended. Main courses $8–$12 lunch, $18–$26 dinner. AE, DC, DISC, MC, V. Daily 7:30am–9pm.

Duggan's Reef CONTINENTAL/CARIBBEAN   This is one of the most popular restaurants on St. Croix. It's only 10 feet from the still waters of Reef Beach and makes an ideal perch for watching windsurfers and Hobie Cats. At lunch, an array of salads, crepes, and sandwiches is offered. The more elaborate night menu features the popular house specialties: Duggan's Caribbean lobster pasta and Irish whiskey lobster. Begin with fried calamari or conch chowder.

Where to Dine in St. Croix

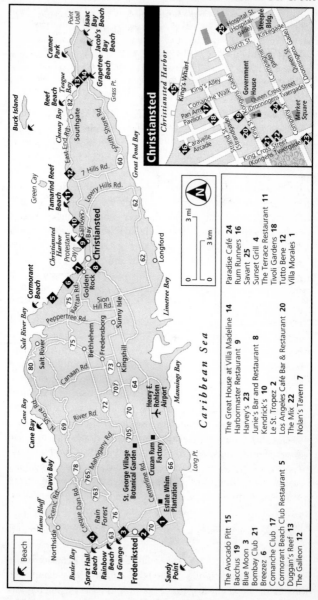

Christiansted

The Avocado Pitt **15**
Bacchus **19**
Blue Moon **3**
Bombay Club **21**
Breezez **6**
Comanche Club **17**
Cormorant Beach Club Restaurant **5**
Duggan's Reef **13**
The Galleon **12**

The Great House at Villa Madeline **14**
Harbormaster Restaurant **9**
Harvey's **23**
Junie's Bar and Restaurant **8**
Kendrick's **10**
Le St. Tropez **2**
Los Angeles Café Bar & Restaurant **20**
The Mix **22**
Nolan's Tavern **7**

Paradise Café **24**
Rum Runners **16**
Savant **25**
Sunset Grill **4**
The Terrace Restaurant **11**
Tivoli Gardens **18**
Tutto Bene **12**
Villa Morales **1**

Main dishes include New York strip steak, fish, and pastas. The local catch of the day can be baked, grilled, blackened Cajun style, or served island style (with tomato, pepper, and onion sauce).

East End Rd., Teague Bay. © **340/773-9800.** Reservations required for dinner in winter. Main courses $17–$32; pastas $16–$23. MC, V. Mon–Fri noon–3pm and 6–9:30pm; Sun brunch 11am–3pm year-round. Closed for lunch in summer. Bar daily noon–11:30pm.

The Galleon FRENCH/NORTHERN ITALIAN   This restaurant, which overlooks the ocean, is a local favorite, and deservedly so. It serves northern Italian and French cuisine, including *osso buco*, as good as that dished up in Milan. Freshly baked bread, two fresh vegetables, and rice or potatoes accompany main dishes. The menu always includes at least one local fish, such as wahoo, tuna, swordfish, mahimahi, or fresh Caribbean lobster. You can order a perfectly done rack of lamb, which will be carved right at your table. There's an extensive wine list, including many sold by the glass. Music from a baby grand accompanies your dinner several nights a week and you can enjoy guitar music on Thursday and Saturday.

East End Rd., Green Cay Marina, 5000 Estate Southgate. © **340/773-9949.** Reservations recommended. Main courses $24–$70; lunch main courses $8–$14. MC, V. Daily 11am–4pm and 6–10pm. Happy hour 4–6pm. Go east on Rte. 82 from Christiansted for 5 min.; after going 1 mile past the Buccaneer, turn left into Green Cay Marina.

CHRISTIANSTED
EXPENSIVE

Bacchus ⚔ STEAKHOUSE/CONTINENTAL   In a restaurant dedicated to the god of wine, the wine *carte* receives as much attention as the regular menu. Their cellar has been praised by both *Spectator* and *Food and Wine.* The decor, service, and presentation of the dishes make for a fine evening out. The kitchen uses first-class ingredients, many imported, to craft a number of dishes that combine flavor and finesse. You're sure to delight in the lobster Bacchus or the rib-eye steak Florentine. One tantalizing dish is the apple-smoked bacon wrapped around a filet mignon. To finish, it doesn't get any better than the rum-infused sourdough bread pudding. Most dishes, except lobster, are at the lower end of the price scale.

Queen Cross St., off King St. © **340/692-9922.** Reservations requested. Main courses $16–$28. AE, MC, V. Tues–Sun 6–10pm.

Kendricks ⚔⚔ FRENCH/CONTINENTAL   Kendricks, the island's toniest restaurant, is in the historic Quin House complex at King Cross and Company streets. Some of its recipes have been featured in *Bon Appétit,* and deservedly so. You'll warm to such specialties as pan-seared Creole shrimp, and grilled filet mignon with a port-wine demi-glace and red-onion confit. The signature appetizer is king-crab cakes with lemon-pepper aioli. Another great choice is the pecan-crusted roast pork loin with ginger mayonnaise.

2132 Company St. ✆ **340/773-9199**. Main courses $23–$33. AE, MC, V. Mon–Sat 6–10pm.

MODERATE

The Bombay Club INTERNATIONAL   This is one of the most enduring restaurants in Christiansted. It's concealed from the street by the brick foundations of an 18th-century planter's town house. You enter through a low stone tunnel and end up near the bar and the courtyard that contains many of its tables. The food, though not overly fancy, is plentiful, full of flavor, and reasonably priced. The best items include the catch of the day, regional dishes such as conch, beef filet, and pasta. The island's best fresh lobster pasta is served here. On our most recent visit, we enjoyed the grilled fish with sun-dried tomatoes and roasted garlic butter.

5A King St. ✆ **340/773-1838**. Reservations recommended. Main courses $12–$19. MC, V. Mon–Fri 11:30am–4pm and 5:30–10pm; Sat–Sun 6–10pm.

Breezez INTERNATIONAL   Sitting poolside at Club Croix, this is one of your best options for a wide selection of dishes. The owners have created a tropical fish theme to go along with the paintings of sunsets and lighthouses that adorn the walls. If you're in the mood for lobster try their lobster thermidor or garlic and herb lobster. Land-lovers should opt for the blackened prime rib with island spices or one of their juicy hamburgers. If you have a sweet tooth, your best bets are the chocolate "oblivion" and chocolate "thunder cakes," or their velvety mango ice cream.

Club St. Croix, 3220 Golden Rock, off Rte. 752, Golden Rock. ✆ **340/773-7077**. Reservations recommended. Main courses $15–$25. AE, MC, DISC, V. Mon–Sat 11:30am–9pm; Sun 9:30am–9pm.

Comanche Club CARIBBEAN/CONTINENTAL   Relaxed yet elegant, Comanche is one of the island's most popular restaurants. It's not the best, but the specialties are eclectic—everything from fish and conch chowder to shark cakes. Each night, a different special and a local dish are featured. Other choices include salads, curries, fish sautéed with lemon butter and capers, and typical West Indian dishes such as conch Creole with *fungi* (a cornmeal and okra dish). There are also standard international dishes like a New York strip.

1 Strand St. ✆ **340/773-0210**. Reservations recommended. Main courses $13–$35; lunch from $7–$12. AE, MC, V. Mon–Sat 11:30am–2:30pm and 5:30–9:30pm.

Los Angeles Café Bar & Restaurant (Kids) AMERICAN   With walls the same color as the ocean just outside your window, this restaurant attracts both locals and visitors. Jean Claude Michelle, known by locals as Bert, was an executive chef in LA, where he grew up, until he left to start a career in St. Croix. "Bert" runs this place, along with another in Christiansted, with a jovial attitude that is contagious. The menu is varied including everything from mozzarella sticks to mahimahi. The lobster with crab meat is grilled to perfection and the fresh fish is always an excellent choice. All the basics and more can be found on the children's menu.

King St. ℂ **340/772-0016.** Reservations recommended. Main courses $12–$40. AE, MC. Daily 7:30–when everyone leaves.

The Mix AMERICAN   In the Holger Danske Hotel, this modern addition to the St. Croix restaurant scene offers both indoor and outdoor dining at the western end of the Christiansted boardwalk. Owners Brett and Amy Fitzgerald try to give diners the sophistication and gourmet taste of a city restaurant without the fuss of a dress code. Their Martini Lounge has become an instant hit with locals and visitors, as has their menu. Choices are creative, including chipotle chicken pasta, lobster bisque, sweet and spicy Thai curry, and a vegetable tower. On Sunday, The Mix hosts a breakfast buffet, for $25. Visitors have their choice of breakfast foods, prime rib, pasta, and seafood, as well as a mimosa or Bloody Mary.

1200 King Cross St. ℂ **340/773-5762.** Main courses $20–$35. AE, MC, V. Daily 11am–4pm and 6–11pm.

Rum Runners (Kids) CARIBBEAN   This open-air restaurant sits on the boardwalk and offers fabulous views to accompany the excellent dining. The ambience reeks of the Caribbean, and the sound of waves in the background can put even the most tense person at ease. Excellent choices include the New York strip steak, the fresh, broiled whole lobster, the Caribbean pork tenderloin served with a grilled banana, and one of the house specials, baby back ribs slow cooked in island spices and Guinness. The younger vacationers can pick from the children's menu.

Hotel Caravelle, on the boardwalk at Queen's Cross St. ℂ **340/773-6585.** Reservations recommended. Main courses $11-$25. AE, MC, V. Mon–Sat 7am–10:30pm, 11:30am–3pm, and 5:30–9:30pm; Sun 8am–2pm and 5:30–9:30pm.

Savant (R) (Finds) CARIBBEAN/THAI/MEXICAN   The spicy cuisines of one region and two nations are combined into a fusion cuisine that is a marvelous burst of flavors to wake up your palate.

The stylish bistro atmosphere is a fun place to dine, but the chefs take the food seriously. Fresh fish is deftly handled to enhance its natural goodness. We gravitate to the tantalizing Thai curries; most of them are mildly spiced for the average diner, but you can request the chef "to go nuclear" if that is your desire. The red coconut curry sauce is one of the best we've ever had on the island. Enchilada lovers will find much happiness here, especially in the enchiladas stuffed with seafood. The maple teriyaki pork tenderloin is one of the chef's specialties and deserves the praise heaped upon it. There are only 20 candlelit tables, so call for a reservation as far in advance as you can.

4C Hospital St. © 340/713-8666. Reservations required. Main courses $14–$30. AE, DC, MC, V. Mon–Sat 6–10pm.

Tivoli Gardens INTERNATIONAL   The large second-floor porch festooned with lights affords the same view of Christiansted Harbor that a sea captain might have. This well-known local gathering spot has white beams, trellises, and hanging plants that evoke its namesake, the pleasure gardens of Copenhagen. Ingredients are fresh and deftly handled. Begin with the house special soup, Tivolienne, made with onions and cabbage in a beef broth, with added flavor from Swiss cheese. There's also a West Indian pea soup made with ham and island spices. Main courses come with garlic bread and include succulent pastas, such as linguine with Italian sausage or penne with chicken and broccoli. Other choices are the Thai seafood curry and the fresh grilled fish of the day—perhaps wahoo, tuna, or dolphin. If you still have room left, opt for the peanut butter pie with chocolate frosting or the local favorite, guava cream pie. The kitchen is also known for its homemade ice creams.

39 Strand St. (upstairs in the Pan Am Pavilion). © 340/773-6782. Reservations recommended after 7pm. Main courses $12–$24. AE, MC, V. Mon–Fri 11am–2:30pm; daily 5:30–9:30pm.

Tutto Bene ITALIAN   In the heart of town, this place seems more like a bistro-cantina than a full-fledged restaurant. The owners, Smokey Odom and Kelly Williams, believe in simple, hearty, uncomplicated *paisano* dishes. You'll dine on wooden tables covered with painted tablecloths, amid warm colors and often lots of hubbub. Menu items are written on a pair of oversize mirrors against one wall. At lunch, you can enjoy bistro-style veggie frittatas, a chicken pesto sandwich, or spinach lasagna. A full range of pastas and well-prepared seafood is offered nightly. You can order a seafood pasta with mussels, clams, and shrimp in a white-wine pesto sauce over linguine. The mahogany bar in back does a brisk business of its own.

2 Company St. ℂ 340/773-5229. Reservations recommended. Main courses $17–$28. AE, MC, V. Daily 6–10pm.

INEXPENSIVE

The Avocado Pitt CARIBBEAN/AMERICAN/VEGETARIAN This is an all-around good choice for breakfast or lunch while you explore the shops and attractions of Christiansted. Paintings by Caribbean artists, which are for sale, create a festive mood. One of the town's best breakfasts is served here, as patronage by locals reveal. Their omelets and pancakes are rib-sticking fare and full of flavor. Lunch options include "Kahuna burgers" and tuna sandwiches, but you can also find more creative offerings, including tofu with sautéed vegetables or fresh yellowfin tuna that is delicately flavored. Vegetarians often frequent the place for its veggie or soy burgers along with freshly made salads and a variety of protein-enriched fruit smoothies. The staff will also pack you a boxed lunch for your tour of the island or an all-day sailing adventure.

Kings Wharf. ℂ 340/773-9843. Main courses $3.50–$8 breakfast, $7.50–$12 lunch. AE, MC, V. Daily 8am–5pm.

Harbormaster Restaurant *(Kids)* AMERICAN This is where guests at the local town inns head for a day at the beach. It's a 4-minute ferry ride across the harbor from Christiansted, at Hotel on the Cay. While here, you don't want to go back into town for lunch, so the hotel has wisely decided to accommodate its many day visitors by offering this quite acceptable restaurant. It offers the usual array of salad platters, sandwiches, omelets, and burgers, but many main dishes are more elaborate and appealing, especially the grilled filet of mahimahi (or swordfish); the conch in a lemon, garlic, and butter sauce; and the barbecued ribs. The excellent Tuesday evening West Indian barbecue costs $23 for all you can eat (kids eat at a 50% discount); steel band music, limbo, fire eating, broken bottle dancing, and the Mocko Jumbie stilt dance accompany the feast.

At the Hotel on the Cay (p. 143), Protestant Cay. ℂ 340/773-2035. Main courses $12–$24; breakfast from $4. AE, DISC, MC, V. Mon–Fri 8am–5pm; Tues 7–9:30pm.

Harvey's CARIBBEAN/CONTINENTAL Forget the plastic and the flowery tablecloths that give this place a 1950s ambience and enjoy the zesty cooking of island matriarch Sarah Harvey, who takes joy in her work and definitely aims to fill your stomach with her basic but hearty fare. Try one of her homemade soups, especially the callaloo or chicken. She'll even serve you conch in butter sauce as an appetizer. For a main dish you might choose from barbecue chicken, barbecue spareribs, boiled filet of snapper, and sometimes even lobster. *Fungi* comes with just about everything. For dessert, try one of the delectable tarts made from guava, pineapple, or coconut.

11B Company St. ℂ **340/773-3433**. Main courses $8–$10. No credit cards. Mon–Sat 11:30am–5pm.

Junie's Bar and Restaurant ℛ *Finds* CARIBBEAN/SEAFOOD

A favorite of local residents, particularly the island's corps of taxi drivers, this restaurant occupies a white-painted cement building about a half-mile south of Christiansted's main core, adjacent to a church and a discount store. Inside, wooden tables, metal chairs, bowls of cut flowers, and a well-scrubbed kind of simplicity add to the appeal. Your hosts, Junie Allen and her daughter Denise, prepare a flavor-filled but basic medley of West Indian staples, including a roster of drinks that you might not have tasted before, such as sea moss (a kind of eggnog flavored with pulverized seaweed), *mauby* (fermented from rain water and tree bark), and ginger beer. Good menu choices include boiled fish, conch, lobster in butter sauce, stewed goat, stewed Creole-style lobster, and pork chops with greens and yams. Desserts include carrot cake and Key lime pie. Because the place has been here for 30 years, it's known by virtually everybody on the island.

132 Peter's Rest. ℂ **340/773-2801**. Main courses $9–$13 lunch, $8–$25 dinner. AE, MC, V. Mon–Sat 10am–10pm; Sun 10am–7pm.

Nolan's Tavern *Value* INTERNATIONAL/CARIBBEAN This

is the best place to go for a warm, cozy tavern with no pretensions. It's across from the capital's most prominent elementary school, the Pearl B. Larsen School. Your host is Nolan Joseph, a Trinidad-born chef who makes a special point of welcoming guests and offering "tasty food and good service." No one will mind if you stop in just for a drink. Mr. Joseph, referred to by some as "King Conch," prepares that mollusk in at least half a dozen ways, including versions with curry, Creole sauce, and garlic-pineapple sauce. He reportedly experimented for 3 months to perfect a means of tenderizing the conch without chemicals. His ribs are also excellent.

5A Estate St. Peter (2 miles east of Christiansted's harbor), Christiansted East. ℂ **340/773-6660**. Reservations recommended only for groups of 6 or more. Burgers $7–$10; main courses $13–$18. AE, MC, V. Kitchen Mon–Sun 3:30–8:30pm. Bar from 3pm.

Paradise Café *Value* DELI/AMERICAN   This neighborhood favorite draws locals seeking good food and great value. Its brick walls and beamed ceiling were originally part of an 18th-century great house. New York–style deli fare is served during the day. Enjoy the savory homemade soups or fresh salads, to which you can add grilled chicken or fish. At breakfast, you can select from an assortment of omelets, or try the steak and eggs. Dinners are more elaborate. The 12-ounce New York strip steak and the pasta specialties are good choices. Appetizers include mango chicken quesadillas and crab cakes.

53B Company St. (at Queen Cross St., across from Government House). (C) 340/ 773-2985. Breakfast $4–$9.50; lunch $5–$10; dinner $14–$21. No credit cards. Mon–Sat 7:30am–9:30pm.

IN & AROUND FREDERIKSTED
MODERATE
Blue Moon INTERNATIONAL/CAJUN   The best little bistro in Frederiksted becomes a hot, hip spot during Sunday brunch and on Friday nights when it offers entertainment. The 200-year-old stone house on the waterfront is a favorite of visiting jazz musicians, and tourists have discovered (but not ruined) it. It's decorated with funky, homemade art from the States, including a trash can–lid restaurant sign. The atmosphere is casual and cafe-like. Begin with the "lunar pie," with feta cheese, cream cheese, onions, mushrooms, and celery in phyllo pastry, or the artichoke-and-spinach dip. Main courses include the catch of the day and, on occasion, Maine lobster. The clams served in garlic sauce are also from Maine. Vegetarians opt for the spinach fettuccine. There's also the usual array of steak and chicken dishes. Save room for the yummy guava pie.

17 Strand St. (C) 340/772-2222. Reservations recommended. Main courses $18–$25. AE, DISC, MC, V. Tues–Fri 11:30am–2pm and 6–9pm (Fri until 2am); Sat 6–9pm; Sun 11am–2pm. Closed Aug.

Le St. Tropez FRENCH/MEDITERRANEAN   This is the most popular bistro in Frederiksted. It's small, so call ahead for a table. If you're visiting for the day, make this bright cafe your lunch stop, and enjoy crepes, quiches, soups, or salads in the courtyard. At night, the atmosphere glows with candlelight, and becomes more festive. Try the Mediterranean cuisine, beginning with mushroom aioli and escargots Provençale, or one of the fresh soups. Main dishes are likely to include medallions of beef with mushrooms, the fish of the day, or a magret of duck. Ingredients are fresh and well prepared.

Limetree Court, 227 King St. (C) 340/772-3000. Reservations recommended. Main courses $16–$36. AE, MC, V. Mon–Fri 11:30am–2:30pm; Mon–Sat 6–10pm.

Villa Morales PUERTO RICAN   This inland spot is the premier Puerto Rican restaurant on St. Croix. You can choose between indoor and outdoor seating. No one will mind if you come here just to drink; a bar is lined with the memorabilia collected by several generations of the family who maintain the place. Look for a broad cross-section of Hispanic tastes here, including many that Puerto Ricans remember from childhood. Savory examples include fried snapper with white rice and beans; stewed conch; roasted or stewed goat; and stewed beef. Meal platters are garnished with beans and rice. Most of the dishes are at the lower end of the price scale. On special occasions, the owners transform the place into a dance hall, bringing in live salsa and merengue bands at no extra charge to patrons.

Plot 82C, Estate Whim (off Rte. 70 about 2 miles from Frederiksted). *(C)* **340/772-0556.** Reservations recommended. Main courses $6–$14 lunch, $8–$15 dinner. MC, V. Thurs–Sat 10am–10pm.

INEXPENSIVE

Sunset Grill *(R)* *(Finds)* CARIBBEAN/AMERICAN   This informal spot is on the west coast, near Sprat Hall Plantation. It's the best place on the island to combine lunch and a swim. The restaurant has been in business since 1948, feeding locals and visitors. Try such local dishes as seafood chowder, tannia soup, and the fried fish of the day. These dishes have authentic island flavor, perhaps more so than any other place on St. Croix. You can also get salads and burgers. The bread is baked fresh daily. The owners allow free use of the showers and changing rooms.

Rte. 63 (1 mile north of Frederiksted). *(C)* **340/772-5855.** Lunch $7–$9; main courses $18–$27. Tues–Sun 11:30am–2:30pm and 5:30–9pm; Sun brunch 11:30am–3pm.

5 Beaches

Beaches are St. Croix's big attraction. The problem is that getting to them from Christiansted isn't always easy. It can also be expensive, especially if you want to go back and forth each day of your stay. Of course, you can always rent a condo right on the water.

The most celebrated beach is offshore **Buck Island,** part of the U.S. National Park Service network. Buck Island is a volcanic islet surrounded by some of the most stunning underwater coral gardens in the Caribbean. The white-sand beaches on the southwest and west coasts are beautiful, but the snorkeling is even better. The islet's interior is filled with such plants as cactus, wild frangipani, and pigeonwood. There are picnic areas for those who want to make a day of it. Boat departures are from Kings Wharf in Christiansted; the ride takes half an hour. For more information, see the section "A Side Trip to Buck Island," later in this chapter.

Your best choice for a beach in Christiansted is the one at the **Hotel on the Cay.** This white-sand strip is on a palm-shaded island. To get here, take the ferry from the fort at Christiansted; it runs daily from 7am to midnight. The 4-minute trip costs $3 round-trip, free for guests of the Hotel on the Cay. Five miles west of Christiansted is the **Cormorant Beach Club,** where some 1,200 feet of white sand shaded by palm trees attracts a gay crowd. Since a reef lies just off the shore, snorkeling conditions are ideal.

We highly recommend **Davis Bay** and **Cane Bay,** with swaying palms, white sand, and good swimming. Because they're on the north shore, these beaches are often windy, and their waters are not always tranquil. The snorkeling at Cane Bay is truly spectacular; you'll see elkhorn and brain corals, all some 750 feet off the "Cane Bay Wall." Cane Bay adjoins Route 80 on the north shore. Davis Beach doesn't have a reef; it's more popular among bodysurfers than snorkelers. There are no changing facilities. It's near Carambola Beach Resort.

On Route 63, a short ride north of Frederiksted, lies **Rainbow Beach,** which has white sand and ideal snorkeling conditions. Nearby, also on Route 63, about 5 minutes north of Frederiksted, is another good beach, called **La Grange.** Lounge chairs can be rented here, and there's a bar nearby.

Sandy Point, directly south of Frederiksted, is the largest beach in all the U.S. Virgin Islands. Its waters are shallow and calm, perfect for swimming. Try to concentrate on the sands and not the unattractive zigzagging fences that line the beach. Continue west from the western terminus of the Melvin Evans Highway (Rte. 66).

There's an array of beaches at the east end of the island; they're somewhat difficult to get to, but much less crowded. The best choice here is **Isaac Bay Beach,** ideal for snorkeling, swimming, or sunbathing. Windsurfers like **Reef Beach,** which opens onto Teague Bay along Route 82, East End Road, a half-hour ride from Christiansted. You can get food at Duggan's Reef (see above). **Cramer Park** is a special public park operated by the Department of Agriculture. It's lined with sea-grape trees and has a picnic area, a restaurant, and a bar. **Grapetree Beach** is off Route 60 (the South Shore Rd.). Watersports are popular here.

6 Fun in the Surf & Sun

WATERSPORTS

FISHING   The fishing grounds at **Lang Bank** are about 10 miles from St. Croix. You'll find kingfish, dolphin fish, and wahoo. Using light-tackle boats to glide along the reef, you'll probably turn up jack or bonefish. At **Clover Crest,** in Frederiksted, local anglers fish right from the rocks.

Serious sportfishers can board the *Fantasy,* a 38-foot Bertram special. It's anchored at King's Alley Hotel at 59 Kings Wharf in Christiansted. Reservations can be made at © **340/773-2628.** The cost for up to six passengers is $450 for 4 hours, $600 for 6 hours, and $800 for 8 hours with bait and tackle, and drinks included.

KAYAKING   The beauty of St. Croix is best seen on a kayak tour offered by **Caribbean Adventure Tours** (© **340/778-1522**). You use stable, sit-on-top ocean kayaks, which are a blast. These enable you to traverse the tranquil waters of Salt River of Columbus landfall fame and enjoy the park's ecology and wildlife. You also go into secluded estuaries and mangrove groves. Some of the land was used as ancient Indian burial grounds. Highlights of the tour are snorkeling on a pristine beach and paddling to where Christopher Columbus and his crew came ashore some 500 years ago. The tour, lasting 3 hours, costs $45 per person and includes water and a light snack.

SNORKELING & SCUBA DIVING 🐾🐾   Sponge life, black coral (the finest in the West Indies), and steep drop-offs near the shoreline make St. Croix a snorkeling and diving paradise. The island is home to the largest living reef in the Caribbean, including the fabled north-shore wall that begins in 25 feet to 30 feet of water and drops to 13,200 feet, sometimes straight down. See "Beaches," above, for information on good snorkeling beaches. The **St. Croix Water Sports Center** (see "Windsurfing," below) rents snorkeling equipment for $20 per day if your hotel doesn't supply it.

Buck Island 🐾🐾 is a major scuba-diving site, with a visibility of some 100 feet. It also has an underwater snorkeling trail. All the outfitters offer scuba and snorkeling tours to Buck Island. See the section "A Side Trip to Buck Island," later in this chapter.

Other favorite dive sites include the historic **Salt River Canyon** (northwest of Christiansted at Salt River Bay), which is for advanced divers. Submerged canyon walls are covered with purple tube sponges, deep-water gorgonians, and black coral saplings. You'll see schools of yellowtail snapper, turtles, and spotted eagle rays. We also like the gorgeous coral gardens of **Scotch Banks** (north of Christiansted), and **Eagle Ray** (also north of Christiansted), the latter so named because of the rays that cruise along the wall there. **Cane Bay** 🐠🐠 is known for its coral canyons.

Davis Bay is the site of the 12,000-foot-deep Puerto Rico Trench. **Northstar Reef,** at the east end of Davis Bay, is a spectacular wall dive, recommended for intermediate or experienced divers only. The wall here is covered with stunning brain corals and staghorn thickets. At some 50 feet down, a sandy shelf leads to a cave where giant green moray eels hang out.

At **Butler Bay,** to the north of the pier on the west shore, three ships were wrecked: the *Suffolk Maid,* the *Northwind,* and the *Rosaomaira,* the latter sitting in 100 feet of water. These wrecks form the major part of an artificial reef system that also contains abandoned trucks and cars. This site is recommended for intermediate or experienced divers.

Anchor Dive, Salt River National Park (✆ **800/523-DIVE** in the U.S., or 340/778-1522), is in the most popular dive destination in St. Croix. It operates three boats. The staff offers complete instruction, from resort courses through full certification, as well as night dives. A resort course is $90, with a two-tank dive going for $80. Dive packages begin at $215 for six dives.

Another recommended outfitter is the **Cane Bay Dive Shop** (✆ **340/773-9913**).

WINDSURFING   Head for the **St. Croix Water Sports Center** (✆ **340/773-7060**), on a small island in Christiansted Harbor and part of the Hotel on the Cay. It's open daily from 11am to 3pm. Windsurfing rentals are $25 per hour. Lessons are available. The center offers parasailing for $65 per person and rents snorkeling equipment for $20 per day and Sea Doos that seat two for $45 per half-hour.

MORE OUTDOOR ADVENTURE

GOLF   St. Croix has the best golf in the U.S. Virgins. Guests staying on St. John and St. Thomas often fly over for a round on one of the island's three courses.

Carambola Golf Course, on the northeast side of St. Croix (✆ **340/778-5638**), was created by Robert Trent Jones, Sr., who called it "the loveliest course I ever designed." It's been likened to a botanical garden. The par-3 holes are known to golfing authorities

> **(Moments** **Going Under Water Without Getting Wet**
>
> St. Croix Water Sports Center (© 340/773-7060), at the Hotel on the Cay, features the *Oceanique,* a semi-submersible vessel that acts as part submarine and part cruiser. It takes visitors on 1-hour excursions through Christiansted Harbor and along Protestant Cay. The inch-thick windows of the vessel's underwater observation room provide views of St. Croix's marine life, in a cool and dry environment. This trip is especially popular with children and non-swimmers. Day and night excursions are available for $45 for adults and $25 for children. Call for reservations.

as the best in the Tropics. The greens fee of $129 in winter, or $90 in summer, allows you to play as many holes as you like. Carts are included.

The Buccaneer, Gallows Bay (© **340/773-2100,** ext. 738), 3 miles east of Christiansted, has a challenging 5,685-yard, 18-hole course with panoramic vistas. Nonguests of this deluxe resort pay $86 in winter or $61 off season, which includes use of a cart.

The **Reef,** on the east end of the island at Teague Bay (© **340/ 773-8844**), is a 3,100-yard, 9-hole course, charging greens fees of $26 including carts. The longest hole here is a 465-yard par 5.

HIKING Scrub-covered hills make up much of St. Croix's landscape. The island's western district, however, includes a dense, 15-acre forest known as the **"Rain Forest"** (though it's not a real one). The network of footpaths here offer some of the best nature walks in the Caribbean. For more details on hiking in this area, see the section, "Exploring the 'Rain Forest,'" later in this chapter. **Buck Island** (see the section "A Side Trip to Buck Island," later in this chapter), just off St. Croix, also offers some wonderful nature trails.

The **St. Croix Environmental Association,** Arawak Building, Suite 3, Gallows Bay (© **340/773-1989;** www.stxenvironmental. org), has regularly scheduled hikes during the weekend from December to March. A minimum of four people are required, costing $30 per person, $15 for children under 12.

HORSEBACK RIDING **Paul and Jill's Equestrian Stables,** 2 Sprat Hall Estate, Route 58 (© **340/772-2880**), the largest equestrian stable in the Virgin Islands, is known throughout the

Caribbean for its horses. It's set on the sprawling grounds of the island's oldest plantation great house. The operators lead trail rides through the forests, along the beach, and past ruins of abandoned 18th-century plantations and sugar mills, to the tops of the hills of St. Croix's western end. Beginners and experienced riders alike are welcome. A 2-hour trail ride costs $60. Tours usually depart daily in winter at 10:30am and 3pm, and in the off season at 4pm, with slight variations according to demand. Reserve at least a day in advance.

TENNIS Some rate the tennis at the **Buccaneer** ☆☆, Gallows Bay ((℃) **340/773-2100,** ext. 736), the best in the Caribbean. The resort offers eight courts, two lit for night play, all open to the public. Non-guests pay $8 daytime, $10 nighttime per person per hour; call to reserve a court at least a day in advance. A tennis pro is available for lessons, and there's also a pro shop.

7 Seeing the Sights

CHRISTIANSTED

The town is easy to explore on foot, with some interesting old buildings, including the **Old Customs House,** and **Fort Christiansvaern,** a well-preserved colonial fortification. You can also visit the **West Indies and Guinea Warehouse,** once the site of slave auctions. You might also take a look at **Government House** and the **Limprecht Gardens and Memorial.**

An additional point of interest in Christiansted is the **St. Croix Archaeological Society Museum,** Company Street ((℃) **340/ 692-2365**), a showcase of many ancient artifacts, some of which date from 4,000 years ago. Look for the 1,000-year-old fertility amulet carved from a shell, and a terra-cotta bowl from the 1400s that was once used to serve up offerings to the gods by the Taíno Indians. Artifacts from archaeological digs, including items from the Ortoiroid, Saladoid, Elenan Ostionoid, and Taíno tribes are displayed. All of these native Indians lived on St. Croix before the Columbus landing at Salt River in 1493. The museum is open on Saturday 10am to 2pm, and admission is free.

FREDERIKSTED ☆

This former Danish settlement at the western end of the island, about 17 miles from Christiansted, is a sleepy port town that comes to life when a cruise ship docks at its pier. Frederiksted was destroyed by a fire in 1879, and the citizens rebuilt it by putting wood frames and clapboards on top of the Danish stone and yellow-brick foundations.

Most visitors begin their tour at russet-colored **Fort Frederik,** at the northern end of Frederiksted next to the cruise-ship pier (© **340/772-2021**). This fort, completed in 1760, is said to have been the first to salute the flag of the new United States. When an American brigantine anchored at port in Frederiksted hoisted a homemade Old Glory, the fort returned the salute with cannon fire, violating the rules of neutrality. Also, on July 3, 1848, Governor-General Peter von Scholten emancipated the slaves in the Danish West Indies, in response to a slave uprising led by Moses "Buddhoe" Gottlieb. In 1998, a bust of Buddhoe was unveiled here. The fort has been restored to its 1840 appearance and is a national historic landmark. You can explore the courtyard and stables. A local history museum has been installed in what was once the Garrison Room. Admission is free. Open Monday through Friday from 8:30am to 4pm.

The Customs House, just east of the fort, is an 18th-century building with a 19th-century two-story gallery. To the south of the fort is **visitor bureau** at Strand Street (© **340/772-0357**), where you can pick up a free map of the town.

EXPLORING THE "RAIN FOREST" ✈

The island's western district contains a dense, 15-acre forest, called the "Rain Forest" (though it's not a real one). The area is thick with mahogany trees, *kapok* (silk-cotton) trees, turpentine (red-birch) trees, *samaan* (rain) trees, and all kinds of ferns and vines. Sweet limes, mangoes, hog plums, and breadfruit trees, all of which have grown in the wild since the days of the plantations, are also interspersed among the larger trees. Crested hummingbirds, pearly eyed thrashers, green-throated caribs, yellow warblers, and perky but drably camouflaged banana quits nest here. The 150-foot-high Creque Dam is the major man-made sight in the area.

The "Rain Forest" is private property, but the owner lets visitors go inside to explore. Some people opt to drive along Route 76 (also known as Mahogany Rd.), stopping beside the footpaths that meander off on either side of the highway into dry riverbeds and glens. Stick to the most worn footpaths. You can also hike along some of the little-traveled four-wheel-drive roads in the area. Three of the best for hiking are the **Creque Dam Road** (Rte. 58/78), the **Scenic Road** (Rte. 78), and the **Western Scenic Road** (Rte. 63/78).

Our favorite trail takes about 2½ hours one-way. From Frederiksted, drive north on Route 63 until you reach Creque Dam Road, where you turn right, park the car, and start walking. About a mile past the Creque Dam, you'll be deep within the forest's magnificent flora and fauna. Continue until you come to the Western Scenic Road. Eventually, you reach Mahogany Road (Rte. 76), near St. Croix Leap Project. Hikers rate this trail moderate in difficulty.

You could also begin near the junction of Creque Dam Road and Scenic Road. From here, your trek will cover a broad triangular swath, heading north and then west along Scenic Road. First, the road will rise, and then descend toward the lighthouse on the island's extreme northwestern tip, **Hams Bluff.** Most trekkers decide to retrace their steps after about 45 minutes of northwesterly hiking. Real die-hards will continue all the way to the coastline, then head south along the coastal road (Butler Bay Rd.), and head east along Creque Dam Road to their starting point at the junction of Creque Dam Road and Scenic Road. Embark on this longer expedition only if you're really prepared for a hike lasting about 5 hours.

AROUND THE ISLAND

North of Frederiksted, you can drop in at **Sprat Hall,** the island's oldest plantation, or continue along to the "Rain Forest" (see above). Most visitors come to the area to see the jagged estuary of the northern coastline's **Salt River.** The Salt River was where Columbus landed on November 14, 1493. Marking the 500th anniversary of Columbus's arrival, former President George H. W. Bush signed a bill creating the 912-acre **Salt River Bay National Historical Park and Ecological Preserve.** The park contains the site of the original Carib village explored by Columbus and his men, including the only ceremonial ball court ever discovered in the Lesser Antilles. Also within the park is the largest mangrove forest in the Virgin Islands, sheltering many endangered animals and plants, plus an underwater canyon attracting divers from around the world.

Carl and Marie Lawaetz Museum The home of one of the island's oldest and most prestigious families can be visited for a glimpse into plantation life. This 1750 farmstead has been owned by the Lawaetz family since 1899. Set in a valley at La Grange, the estate can be toured, as you're shown around by a member of the family. Originally a sugar plantation, the estate was later turned into a cattle ranch. On the grounds are the reminders of a bygone era, including a decaying sugar mill on a nearby hill. The 19 acres of land are filled with beautiful flowers and tropical trees and bushes.

The St. Croix Heritage Trail

A trail that leads into the past, **St. Croix Heritage Trail,** launched at the millennium, helps visitors relive the Danish colonial past of the island. All you need are a brochure and map, available at the tourist office in Christiansted (p. 114). This 72-mile itinerary includes a combination of asphalt-covered roadway, suitable for driving, and woodland trails which must be navigated on foot. Many aficionados opt to drive along the route whenever practical, descending onto the footpaths wherever indicated, then returning to their cars for the continuation of the tour. En route, you'll be exposed to one of the Caribbean's densest concentrations of historical and cultural sites.

The route connects the towns of Christiansted and Frederiksted, going past the sites of former sugar plantations. The trail traverses the entire 28-mile length of St. Croix, passing cattle farms, suburban communities, even industrial complexes and resorts. It's not all manicured and pretty, but much is scenic and worth the drive. Allow at least a day for this trail, with stops along the way.

Nearly everyone gets out of the car at **Point Udall,** the easternmost point under the U.S. flag in the Caribbean. You'll pass an eclectic mix of churches and even a prison. The route consists mainly of existing roadways; the brochure will identify everything you're seeing.

The highlight of the trail is the **Estate Mount Washington** (p. 148), a well-preserved sugar plantation. Another highlight is **Estate Whim Plantation** (p. 148), one of the best of the restored great houses with a museum and gift shop. Another stop is along **Salt River Bay,** which cuts into the northern shoreline. This is the site of Columbus's landfall in 1493.

Of course, you'll want to stop and get to know the locals. We recommend a refreshment break at **Smithens Market.** You'll find it off Queen Mary Highway. Vendors offer fresh-squeezed sugar-cane juice and sell local fruits and homemade chutneys.

Inside you can inspect the family heirlooms, many brought over from Denmark. Marie decorated the home with her paintings, still hanging in almost every room. You're even shown the mahogany four-poster bed in which all seven of the Lawaetz family were born.

Mahogany Rd., Rte. 76, Estate Little La Grange. ② 340/772-1539. www.stcroix landmarks.com. Admission $8 adults, $5 students and seniors, $4 ages 6–12, free for ages 5 and under. May–Oct Tues, Thurs, and Sat 10am–2pm; Nov–Apr Wed–Sat 10am–4pm.

Cruzan Rum Factory　This factory distills the famous Virgin Islands rum, which some consider the finest in the world. Guided tours (including a mixed drink) depart from the visitor's pavilion; call for reservations and information.

Estate Diamond 3, W. Airport Rd., Rte. 64. ② 340/692-2280. Admission $4. Tours given Mon–Fri 9–11:30am and 1–4:15pm.

Estate Mount Washington Plantation　This is the island's best-preserved sugar plantation and a highlight along the St. Croix Heritage Trail. It flourished from 1780 to 1820 when St. Croix was the second largest producer of sugar in the West Indies. The on-site private residence is closed to the public, but you can go on a self-guided tour of the 13 acres at any time of the day (there is no admission charge, although donations are appreciated). You'll see what is the best antiques store on St. Croix, but it can only be visited by calling ② **340/772-1026** and asking for an appointment (see "Shopping," below).

At the very southwestern tip of the island, off Rte. 63, a mile inland from the highway that runs along the Frederiksted coast. Free admission.

Estate Whim Plantation Museum　This restored great house is unique among those of the many sugar plantations whose ruins dot the island. It's composed of only three rooms. With 3-foot-thick walls made of stone, coral, and molasses, the house resembles a luxurious European château. A division of Baker Furniture Company used the Whim Plantation's collection of models for one of its most successful reproductions, the "Whim Museum–West Indies Collection." Upscale reproductions of some of the furniture on display within the Whim Plantation, plus others from the Caribbean, are for sale on-site. Slightly different inventories are available from an associated store in downtown Christiansted: **The St. Croix Landmarks Museum Store,** 58 Queen St. (② **340/713-8102**). For more information, refer to "Shopping," later in this chapter.

The ruins of the plantation's sugar-processing plant, complete with a restored windmill, also remain.

Centerline Rd. (2 miles east of Frederiksted). ✆ **340/772-0598**. Admission $8 adults, $4 children. Mon–Sat 10am–4pm.

Little Princess Estate   This estate, established in 1749 as a sugar plantation, might be called the *Gone With the Wind* of St. Croix. Today, the decaying site occupies 25 acres and has been turned into a Nature Preserve. The centerpiece of the property is the Great House, built in the 1730s by Fredrik Moth, the first Danish governor of St. Croix. Walking paths have been cut through the grounds, taking you by the ruins of a hospital, old windmill, sugar and rum factory, and workers' village, and through a garden.

Signposted north at Five Corners traffic light along Rte. 75. ✆ **340/773-5575**. $5 donations recommended. Daily 9am–4pm.

St. George Village Botanical Garden   This is a 16-acre Eden of tropical trees, shrubs, vines, and flowers. The garden is a feast for the eye and the camera, from the entrance drive bordered by royal palms and bougainvillea to the towering kapok and tamarind trees. It was built around the ruins of a 19th-century sugar-cane workers' village. Self-guided walking-tour maps are available at the entrance to the garden's great hall. Facilities include restrooms and a gift shop.

127 Estate St., 1 St. George, Frederiksted (just north of Centerline Rd., 4 miles east of Frederiksted). ✆ **340/692-2874**. Admission $6 adults, $1 children 12 and under; donations welcome. Daily 9am–5pm.

ORGANIZED TOURS

BUS TOURS   Organized tours operate according to demand. Many are conducted at least three times a week during the winter, with fewer departures in summer. A typical 4-hour tour costs $25 per person. Tours usually go through Christiansted and include visits to the botanical garden, Whim Estate House, the rum distillery, the Rain Forest, the St. Croix LEAP mahogany workshop (see "Shopping," below), and the site of Columbus's landing at Salt River. Check with your hotel desk, or call **Travellers' Tours,** Henry E. Rohlsen Airport (✆ **340/778-1636**), for more information.

TAXI TOURS   Many visitors explore St. Croix on a taxi tour (✆ **340/778-1088**), which for a party of two costs $75 for 2 hours or $100 for 3 hours. The fare should be negotiated in advance. Extra fees are charged for the following sights: $10 for the botanical gardens, $10 for the Whim Estate House, and $8 for the rum distillery. Taxi tours are far more personalized than bus tours. You can get on and off where you want and stay as long or as little as you wish at a destination.

WALKING TOURS   For a guided walking tour of either Christiansted or Frederiksted, contact **St. Croix Heritage Tours** (© 340/ 778-6997). The tour of Christiansted is available upon request, leaves at 9:30am, and costs $12 per person or $8 for children 12 and under. The Frederiksted tour leaves on Wednesday at 9:30am, and costs $10 per person or $6 for children 12 and under. Call for details and to arrange meeting places. This company also does Safari tours departing from Christiansted, with stops to the botanical garden and the Heritage Museum.

8 Shopping

Christiansted is the shopping hub of St. Croix. The emphasis here is on hole-in-the-wall boutiques selling handmade goods. Most of the shops are compressed into a half-mile or so. There's also the **King's Alley Complex** (© 340/778-8135), a pink-sided compound filled with the densest concentration of shops on St. Croix.

In recent years, **Frederiksted** has also become a popular shopping destination. Its urban mall appeals to cruise-ship passengers arriving at Frederiksted Pier. The mall is on a 50-foot strip of land

SHOPPING A TO Z IN CHRISTIANSTED
ANTIQUES
Estate Mount Washington Antiques 𝑅𝑅   The owners are always there and you'll be able to browse through the best treasure trove of colonial West Indian furniture and "flotsam" in the Virgin Islands. Afterward, you can walk around the grounds of an 18th-century sugar plantation. Call for an appointment. 4 Estate Mount Washington. © 340/772-1026.

ARTS & CRAFTS
Folk Art Traders 𝑅 *(Finds)*   The operators of this store travel throughout the Caribbean ("in the bush") to add to their unique collection of local art and folk-art treasures—carnival masks, pottery, ceramics, original paintings, and hand-wrought jewelry. The assortment also includes batiks from Barbados and high-quality iron sculpture from Haiti. There's nothing else like it in the Virgin Islands. Strand St. © 340/773-1900.

CLOTHES

The Coconut Vine   This is one of the most colorful and popular little boutiques on the island. Hand-painted batiks for both men and women are the specialty. Kings Alley. ✆ 340/773-1991.

From the Gecko   At this hip, eclectic outlet, you can find anything from hand-painted local cottons and silks to the old West Indian staple, batiks. We found the Indonesian collection here among the most imaginative in the U.S. Virgin Islands—everything from glass jewelry to banana-leaf knapsacks. 1233 Queen Cross St. ✆ 340/778-9433.

Gone Tropical   About 60% of the merchandise in this unique shop is made in Indonesia (usually Bali). Prices of new, semi-antique, or antique sofas, beds, chests, tables, mirrors, and carvings are the same as (and sometimes less than) those of new furniture in conventional stores. Gone Tropical also sells art objects, jewelry, batiks, candles, and baskets. 5 Company St. ✆ 340/773-4696.

Urban Threadz   This is the most comprehensive clothing store in Christiansted's historic core, with a two-story, big-city scale and appeal. It's the store where island residents prefer to shop because of the hip, urban styles. Men's items are on the street level, women's upstairs. The inventory includes everything from Bermuda shorts to summer blazers and men's suits. The store carries Calvin Klein, Polo, and Oakley, among others. 52C Company St. ✆ 340/773-2883.

GIFTS

Many Hands   The merchandise here includes pottery and handmade jewelry. The collection of local paintings is also intriguing, as is the year-round "Christmas tree." In the Pan Am Pavilion, Strand St. ✆ 340/773-1990.

Purple Papaya   This is the best place to go for inexpensive island gifts. It has the biggest array of embroidered T-shirts and sweatshirts on island. Although you're in the Caribbean and not Hawaii, there is a large selection of Hawaiian shirts and dresses, along with beachwear for the whole family, plus island souvenirs. 39 Strand St., Pan Am Pavilion. ✆ 340/713-9412.

Royal Poinciana 𝒜   This is the most interesting gift shop on St. Croix, looking like an antique apothecary. You'll find such items as hot sauces, seasoning blends for gumbos, island herbal teas, Antillean coffees, and a scented array of soaps, toiletries, lotions, and shampoos. There's also a selection of museum-reproduction greeting cards and calendars. Also featured are educational but fun gifts for children. 1111 Strand St. ℂ **340/773-9892.**

Textile with a Story   All in tropical colors and designs, this souklike store sells unusual gift items and home furnishings. Its Oriental carpets are some of the best on island and you can also purchase rugs made from jute and cotton along with hammocks. The pillows come in various designs and colors, and there is an array of exotic soaps, candles, and tablecloth sets. The handcrafted batik sarongs evoke Dorothy Lamour in all those 40s Road movies made with Crosby and Hope. 52 King St. ℂ **340/692-9867.**

JEWELRY

Colombian Emeralds   Stunning emeralds, as well as rubies and diamonds, will dazzle you here. The staff will also show you the wide range of 14-karat gold jewelry, along with the best buys in watches, including Seiko quartz. Fake jewelry is peddled throughout the Caribbean, but Colombian Emeralds sells the genuine thing. 43 Queen Cross St. ℂ **340/773-1928.**

Crucian Gold ⚑ *Finds*   This West Indian cottage holds the gold and silver creations of island-born Brian Bishop. His most popular item is the Crucian bracelet, which contains a "True Lovers' Knot" in its design. The outlet also sells hand-tied knots (bound in gold wire), rings, pendants, and earrings. 59 Kings Wharf. ℂ **340/773-5241.**

Elegant Illusions Copy Jewelry   This branch of a hugely successful chain based in California sells convincing fake jewelry. The look-alikes range in price from $20 to $1,000 and include credible copies of the baroque and antique jewelry your great-grandmother might have worn. If you want the real thing, you can go next door to **King Alley Jewelry** (ℂ **340/773-4746**), which is owned by the same company and specializes in fine designer jewelry, including Tiffany and Cartier. 55 King St. ℂ **340/773-2727.**

Sonya Ltd.   Sonya Hough is the matriarch of a cult of local residents who wouldn't leave home without wearing one of her bracelets. She's famous for her sterling silver or gold (from 14- to 24-karat) versions of her original design, the C-clasp bracelet. Locals say that if the cup of the "C" is turned toward your heart, it means you're emotionally committed; if the cup is turned outward, it means you're available. Prices range from $30 to $2,000. She also sells rings, earrings, and necklaces. 1 Company St. ℂ **340/778-8605.**

Waterfront Larimar Mines   Everything sold in this shop is produced by the largest manufacturer of gold settings for larimar in the world. Discovered in the 1970s, larimar is a pale-blue pectolyte prized for its color. It comes from mines located in only one mountain in the world, on the southwestern edge of the Dominican Republic, near the Haitian border. Objects range from $25 to $1,000. Although other shops sell the stone as well, this emporium has the widest selection. The Boardwalk/King's Walk. © 340/692-9180.

PERFUME

Violette Boutique   This is a small department store, with many boutique areas carrying famous lines. Here you can get many famous and exclusive fragrances and hard-to-find toiletry items, as well as the latest in Cartier, Fendi, Pequignet, and Gucci. There's also a selection of gifts for children. Mont Blanc pens are sold here, as well. Many famous brand names sold here are found nowhere else on the island, but are certainly found elsewhere in the Caribbean. In the Caravelle Arcade, 38 Strand St. © 340/773-2148.

AROUND THE ISLAND

If you're touring western St. Croix in or around Frederiksted, you might want to stop off at the following offbeat shops.

Island WeBe   This is a one-of-a-kind shop that sells aromatic coffees along with West Indian spices, teas, and jams, each one a product of the Caribbean. The artistic owner also makes and sells *mocko jumbie* dolls whose roots go back to Africa but were carried over to the New World by slaves. These dolls, or so it is said, evoke the souls of the ancestors of these slaves uprooted from their homeland. 210 Stand St., Frederiksted. © 340/772-2555.

St. Croix LEAP ✪ *(Finds*   If you're on western St. Croix, near Frederiksted, come here for an offbeat adventure. In this open-air shop, you can see stacks of rare and beautiful wood being fashioned into tasteful objects. This is a St. Croix Life and Environmental Arts Project, dedicated to manual work, environmental conservation, and self-development. The end result is a collection of mahogany serving boards, tables, hangings, and clocks. Sections of unusual pieces are crafted into functional, artistic objects.

St. Croix LEAP is 15 miles from Christiansted, 2 miles up Mahogany Road from the beach north of Frederiksted. Large mahogany signs and sculptures flank the driveway. Visitors should bear to the right to reach the woodworking area and gift shop. The site is open daily from 9am to 5pm. Mahogany Road, Rte. 76. ⓒ 340/772-0421.

Whim Museum Store This unique store offers a wide selection of gifts, both imported and local. They also carry historical books, local art, and West Indian furniture. And if you buy something, your money goes to a worthy cause: the upkeep of the museum and the grounds (p. 148). 52 Estate Whim Plantation Museum, east of Frederiksted on Centerline Rd. ⓒ 340/772-0598.

9 St. Croix After Dark

St. Croix doesn't have the nightlife of St. Thomas. To find the action, consult the publication *St. Croix This Week,* which is distributed free to cruise-ship and air passengers and is available at the tourist office.

Try to catch a performance of the **Quadrille Dancers** 𝔊𝔊𝔊, a real cultural treat. Their dances have changed little since plantation days. The women wear long dresses, white gloves, and turbans, and the men wear flamboyant shirts, sashes, and tight black trousers. When you've learned their steps, you're invited to join the dancers on the floor. Ask at your hotel if and where they're performing.

Note: Women entering bars alone at night in Christiansted or Frederiksted should expect some advances from men. It is generally assumed here that when a women enters a bar alone, she is seeking companionship. Nonetheless, women are fairly safe in bars providing they know how to deal with some leering. It is not wise to leave the bar alone and walk the lonely streets. Take a taxi back to your hotel—it's worth the investment.

THE CLUB & MUSIC SCENE

Blue Moon 𝔊 This hip little dive, which is also a good bistro, is the hottest spot in Frederiksted on Friday, when a five-piece ensemble entertains. On Sunday, a jazz trio performs. 17 Strand St. ⓒ 340/772-2222. No cover.

The Terrace Lounge This lounge off the main dining room of one of St. Croix's most upscale hotels welcomes some of the Caribbean's finest entertainers every night, often including a full band. In the Buccaneer (p. 119). ⓒ 340/773-2100. Cover $6.

2 Plus 2 Disco This is a real Caribbean disco. It features the regional sounds of the islands, not only calypso and reggae but also salsa and soca (a hybrid of calypso and reggae). Usually there's a DJ, except on weekends when local bands are brought in. The place isn't fancy or large; it has a black-tile dance floor with a simple lighting system. Come here for Saturday Night Fever. Hours are Thursday and Sunday 11am to 2am and Friday and Saturday 10pm to either 4 or 5am. 17 La Grande Princesse. ℭ 340/773-3710. Cover $15 when there's a live band.

THE BAR SCENE

Cormorant Beach Club Bar   This romantic bar lies within a predominantly gay resort about 3 miles northwest of Christiansted (p. 123). It caters both to clients of the resort and to gay men and women from other parts of the island. You can sit at tables overlooking the ocean or around an open-centered mahogany bar, adjacent to a gazebo. The chairs are comfortable and the lighting is soft. Excellent tropical drinks are mixed here, including the house specialty, a Cormorant Cooler, made with champagne, pineapple juice, and triple sec. 4126 La Grande Princesse. ℭ 340/778-8920. No cover.

THE CASINO

Divi Carina Bay Casino   After much protest and controversy, this casino introduced gambling to St. Croix in 2000. Many visitors who heretofore went to such islands as Aruba for gambling now stay within the realm of U.S. possessions. The 10,000-square-foot casino boasts 20 gaming tables and 300 slot machines. No passport is needed to enter, but you do need some form of ID. In lieu of a nightclub, the casino offers nightly live music on an open stage on the casino floor. There are two bars, a main bar plus a smaller cafe-style bar where you can order light meals. Open Monday to Thursday noon to 4am and Friday to Sunday 24 hours a day. In the Divi Carina Bay Resort (p. 123). ℭ 340/773-9700. No cover.

10 A Side Trip to Buck Island ★★★

The crystal-clear water and white coral-sand of **Buck Island,** a satellite of St. Croix, are legendary. Some call it the single most important attraction of the Caribbean. Only about ½ mile wide and a mile long, Buck Island lies 1½ miles off the northeastern coast of St. Croix. A barrier reef here shelters many reef fish, including queen angelfish and smooth trunkfish. In years past the island was frequented by the swashbuckling likes of Morgan, LaFitte, Blackbeard, and even Captain Kidd.

Buck Island's greatest attraction is its underwater snorkeling trails, which ring part of the island. Equipped with a face mask, swim fins, and a snorkel, you'll be treated to some of the most beautiful underwater views in the Caribbean. Plan on spending at least two-thirds of a day at this famous ecological site, which is maintained by the National Park Service. There are also many labyrinths and grottoes for scuba divers. The sandy beach has picnic tables and barbecue pits, as well as restrooms and a small changing room.

You can also take hiking trails through the tropical vegetation that covers the island. Circumnavigating the island on foot will take about 2 hours. Buck Island's trails meander from several points along its coastline to its sun-flooded summit, affording views over nearby St. Croix. *A couple of warnings, though:* Bring protection from the sun's merciless rays; even more important, don't rush to touch every plant you see. The island's western edge has groves of poisonous machineel trees, whose leaves, bark, and fruit cause extreme irritation when they come into contact with human skin.

Sometimes small boat operators trying to make an extra buck might run people over for a negotiated fee from Christiansted Harbor. These services are unscheduled and likely to be available in winter only. It's best to stick to the charter companies we recommend, as they are more reliable. Nearly all charters provide snorkeling equipment and allow for 1½ hours of snorkeling and swimming. See "Fun in the Surf & Sun," earlier in this chapter, for companies in addition to the two discussed below.

Mile Mark Watersports, in the King Christian Hotel, 59 King's Wharf, Christiansted (© **340/773-2628**), conducts two different types of tours. The first option is a half-day tour aboard a glass-bottom boat departing from the King Christian Hotel, daily from 9:30am to 1pm and 1:30 to 5pm; it costs $40 per person. The second is a full-day tour, offered daily from 10am to 4pm on a 40-foot trimaran for $70. Included in this excursion is a box lunch.

Captain Heinz (© **340/773-3161** or 340/773-4041) is an Austrian-born skipper with more than 25 years of sailing experience. His trimaran, *Teroro II,* leaves the Green Cay Marina "H" Dock at 9am and 2pm, never filled with more than 23 passengers. This snorkeling trip costs $50 for adults, $30 for children 10 and under. The captain is not only a skilled sailor but also a considerate host. He will even take you around the outer reef, which the other guides do not, for an unforgettable underwater experience.

5

The British Virgin Islands

The British Virgin Islands embrace 40-odd islands, some no more than just rocks or spits of land in the sea. Only three of the islands are of any significant size: Virgin Gorda (Fat Virgin), Tortola (Dove of Peace), and Jost Van Dyke. These craggy volcanic islands are just 15 minutes by air from St. Thomas; there is also regularly scheduled ferry service between St. Thomas and Tortola.

With its small bays and hidden coves, once havens for pirates, the British Virgin Islands are among the world's loveliest cruising areas. The islands attract those who like to sail, although landlubbers will delight in the beaches. Despite predictions that mass tourism will invade, the islands are still an escapist's paradise. Norman Island is said to have been the prototype for Robert Louis Stevenson's novel *Treasure Island.* On Deadman Bay, Blackbeard reputedly marooned 15 pirates and a bottle of rum, giving rise to the well-known ditty.

Even though they lie right near each other and are part of the same archipelago, the British Virgin Islands and the U.S. Virgin Islands are as different as Julia Roberts and Dame Judi Dench. U.S. islands like St. Thomas are deep into mega-resort tourism, but in the B.V.I., the pace is much slower and laid-back, and the people seem more welcoming and friendlier. Even the capital, Tortola, seems to exist in a bit of a time capsule.

Most of the resorts on Virgin Gorda are so isolated from each other that you'll feel your hotel has the island to itself. For those who want to be truly remote, there is a scattering of minor hotels on a handful of the smaller islands. Peter Island has the poshest lodgings, and there are modest inns on Jost Van Dyke and Anegada. Some places are so small that you basically get to know all the locals after about a week. With no casinos, no nightlife, no splashy entertainment, and often no TV, what does one do at night? Jost Van Dyke has only 150 souls but six bars. Question answered.

1 Essentials

VISITOR INFORMATION

Before you go, contact the **British Virgin Islands Tourist Board,** 1270 Broadway, Suite 705, New York, NY 10017 (© **212/696-0400**). Other branches of the **British Virgin Islands Information Office** are located at 3450 Wilshire Blvd., Suite 1202, Los Angeles, CA 90010 (© **213/736-8931**), and at 3400 Peachtree Rd. NE, Suite 1735, Lenox Towers, Atlanta, GA 30326 (© **404/467-4741**). In the United Kingdom, contact the **B.V.I. Information Office,** 15 Upper Grosvenor St., London W1K 7PS (© **020/355-9585**).

The tourist board's official website is **www.bvitouristboard.com**.

GETTING THERE

Your gateway to the B.V.I. will most likely be either Tortola or Virgin Gorda. Supplies and services on the other islands are extremely limited.

BY PLANE   There are no direct flights from North America to Tortola or the other British Virgin Islands, but you can make easy connections from St. Thomas, St. Croix, or San Juan in Puerto Rico. Beef Island, the site of the major airport serving the British Virgin Islands, is connected to Tortola by the Queen Elizabeth Bridge.

American Eagle (© **800/433-7300** in the U.S.; www.aa.com) has four daily flights from San Juan, Puerto Rico, to Beef Island. San Juan is serviced by dozens of daily nonstop flights from cities in North America, including Boston, Toronto, New York, Chicago, Miami, and Raleigh-Durham. You can fly **American Airlines** (© **800/433-7300;** www.aa.com) to St. Thomas, then hop on an American Eagle flight to Tortola. **Air Sunshine** (© **800/327-8900** or 284/495-8900; www. airsunshine.com) flies from San Juan or St. Thomas to Beef Island and on to Virgin Gorda.

Another choice, if you're on one of Tortola's neighboring islands, is the less reliable **LIAT** (© **888/844-5428** within the Caribbean, or 868/624-4727; www.liatairline.com). This Caribbean carrier makes short hops to Tortola from St. Kitts, Antigua, St. Martin, St. Thomas, and San Juan in small planes not known for their careful scheduling.

Tips Currency Note

The British Virgin Islands use the U.S. dollar as their form of currency. British pounds are not accepted.

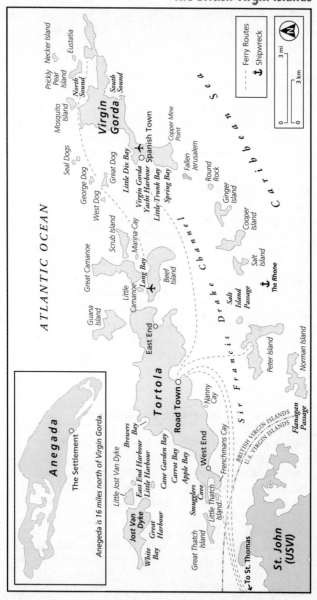

The British Virgin Islands

ATLANTIC OCEAN

Necker Island
Eustatia
Prickly Pear Island
North Sound
Mosquito Island
South Sound
Virgin Gorda
Seal Dogs
George Dog
West Dog
Great Dog
Little Dix Bay
Spanish Town
Copper Mine Point
Virgin Gorda Yacht Harbour
Little-Trunk Bay
Spring Bay
Fallen Jerusalem
Round Rock
Ginger Island

Scrub Island
Marina Cay
Long Bay
Beef Island
Great Camanoe
Little Camanoe
Guana Island
Cooper Island
Salt Island
The Rhone
Salt Island Passage

East End

Tortola
Road Town
Nanny Cay
Peter Island
Norman Island
Sir Francis Drake Channel

Brewers Bay
Little Jost Van Dyke
East End Harbour
Little Harbour
Cane Garden Bay
Carrot Bay
Apple Bay
West End
Frenchmans Cay
Smugglers Cove
Little Thatch Island
Great Thatch Island
Jost Van Dyke
Great Harbour
White Bay

Flanagan Passage

BRITISH VIRGIN ISLANDS
U.S. VIRGIN ISLANDS

St. John (USVI)
←To St. Thomas

Caribbean Sea

— — — Ferry Routes
⚓ Shipwreck

3 mi
3 km

Anegada

Anegada
The Settlement

Anegada is 16 miles north of Virgin Gorda.

Flying time to Tortola from San Juan is 30 minutes; from St. Thomas, 15 minutes; and from the most distant of the LIAT hubs (Antigua), 60 minutes. There's also a small airport on Virgin Gorda; see "Essentials," in section 3, "Virgin Gorda," for details.

BY FERRY You can travel from Charlotte Amalie (St. Thomas) by public ferry to West End and Road Town on Tortola, a 45-minute voyage. Boats making this run include **Native Son** (© 284/495-4617), **Smith's Ferry Service** (© 284/495-4495), and **Inter-Island Boat Services** (© 284/495-4166). The latter specializes in a somewhat obscure routing—that is, from St. John to the West End on Tortola. One-way and round-trip fares range from $20 to $40.

GETTING AROUND

BY BOAT On Tortola, **Smith's Ferry** (© 284/495-4495) and **Speedy's Fantasy** (© 284/495-5240) operate ferry links to the Virgin Gorda Yacht Club (the trip lasts 30 min.). The **North Sound Express** (© 284/495-2138), near the airport on Beef Island, has daily connections to the Bitter End Yacht Club on Virgin Gorda. **Peter Island Boat** (© 284/495-2000) also shuttles passengers between Road Town on Tortola and Peter Island at least seven times a day. The ferry cost for both round-trip and one-way is $15.

BY CAR, BUS, OR TAXI There are car-rental agencies on Virgin Gorda and Tortola; taxis also operate on these islands, as well as on some of the smaller ones. Bus service is available on Tortola and Virgin Gorda only.

FAST FACTS: The British Virgin Islands

Banks Banks are generally open Monday to Thursday 9am to 3pm, Friday 9am to 5pm. Most banks have ATMs.

Business Hours Most offices are open Monday to Friday 9am to 5pm. Government offices are open Monday to Friday 8:30am to 4:30pm. Shops are generally open Monday to Friday 9am to 5pm and Saturday 9am to 1pm.

Emergencies If you have a medical emergency, call **Peebles Hospital**, Porter Road, Road Town (© 284/494-3497), which has X-ray and laboratory facilities. Your hotel can also put you in touch with the local medical staff. For police and fire emergencies, call © **999**.

Internet Access Internet access is limited in the B.V.I. If your hotel or resort doesn't provide service, there are some options, mostly in Tortola and Virgin Gorda (see the Fast Facts boxes for these islands).

Liquor Laws The legal minimum age for purchasing liquor or drinking alcohol in bars or restaurants is 21. Alcoholic beverages can be sold any day of the week, including Sunday. You can have an open container on the beach, but be careful not to litter or you might be fined.

Lost Property Go to the local police station. Sometimes they'll broadcast a notice on the local radio station.

Mail Postal rates in the British Virgin Islands are 35¢ for a postcard (airmail) to the United States or Canada, 55¢ for a first-class airmail letter (½ oz.) to the United States or Canada.

Maps The best map of the B.V.I. is published by Vigilate and is sold at most bookstores in Road Town on Tortola.

Newspapers & Magazines The B.V.I. has no daily newspaper, but the *Island Sun,* published Wednesday and Friday, is a good source of information on local entertainment, as is the *BVI Beacon,* published on Thursday. *Standpoint* is another helpful publication that comes out on Monday and Saturday.

Police The main police headquarters is on Waterfront Drive near the ferry docks on Sir Olva Georges Plaza (✆ 284/494-3822) in Tortola. There are also police stations on Virgin Gorda (✆ 284/495-9828) and on Jost Van Dyke (✆ 284/495-9345).

Safety Crime barely occurs on many of the remote islands of the B.V.I. chain. The most crime, usually minor robberies, occurs in Tortola, with less theft reported on Virgin Gorda. The usual precautions that a careful person would follow anywhere are advised, of course.

Taxes There is no sales tax. A government tax of 7% is imposed on all hotel rooms. A $20 departure tax is collected from everyone leaving by air, $5 for those departing by ferry, and $7 for those departing by cruise ship.

Telephone You can call the British Virgins from the U.S. by dialing **1,** the area code **284,** and the number. From all public phones and from some hotels, you can access **MCI** by dialing ✆ 800/888-8000. You can reach **Sprint** at ✆ 800/877-4646 and **AT&T** at ✆ 800/225-5288.

Tipping & Service Charges Most hotels add on a 5% to 15% service charge; ask if it's included when you're initially quoted a price. A 10% service charge is often (but not always) added to restaurant bills; you can leave another 5% if you thought the service was unusually good. You usually don't need to tip taxi drivers, since most own their own cabs, but you can tip 10% if they've been unusually helpful.

Tourist Office The headquarters of the B.V.I. Tourist Board is in the center of Road Town, close to the ferry dock, south of Wickhams Cay I (© 284/494-3134).

2 Tortola ★★

Road Town, on Tortola's southern shore, is the capital of the British Virgin Islands and the site of the Government House and other administrative buildings. Wickhams Cay, a 28-hectare (70-acre) town center project, has brought in a large yacht-chartering business and has transformed the sleepy village into more of a bustling center.

The southern coast of this 62-sq.-km (24-sq.-mile) island, including Road Town, is characterized by rugged mountain peaks. On the northern coast are white-sand beaches, banana and mango trees, and clusters of palms.

ESSENTIALS
GETTING THERE
Close to Tortola's eastern end is **Beef Island,** the site of the main airport for all the British Virgin Islands. This tiny island is connected to Tortola by the one-lane Queen Elizabeth Bridge.

Taxis meet every arriving flight. Government regulations prohibit anyone from renting a car at the airport—visitors must take a taxi to their hotels. The fare from the Beef Island airport to Road Town is $18 for one to three passengers.

GETTING AROUND
BY TAXI   The best driver we've found on Tortola is O'Dean "Mr. Quick" Chalwell. What he doesn't know about his island isn't worth knowing. Call **Quick's Taxi Service** at © 284/496-7127. For other options in Road Town, dial © 284/494-2322; on Beef Island, © 284/495-1982. Your hotel can also call a taxi for you.

Tortola

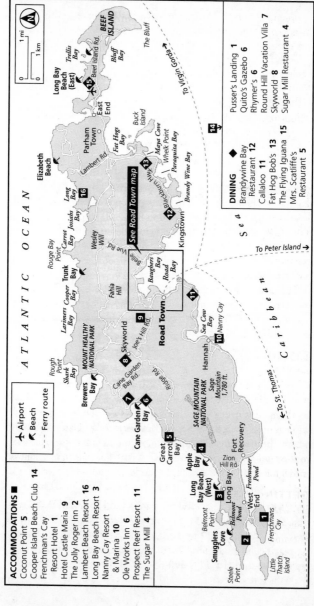

ACCOMMODATIONS ■

Coconut Point **5**
Cooper Island Beach Club **14**
Frenchman's Cay
  Resort Hotel **1**
Hotel Castle Maria **9**
The Jolly Roger Inn **2**
Lambert Beach Resort **16**
Long Bay Beach Resort **3**
Nanny Cay Resort
  & Marina **10**
Ole Works Inn **6**
Prospect Reef Resort **11**
The Sugar Mill **4**

✈ Airport
⚓ Beach
‑ ‑ ‑ Ferry route

Pusser's Landing **1**
Quito's Gazebo **6**
Rhymer's **6**
Round Hill Vacation Villa **7**
Skyworld **8**
Sugar Mill Restaurant **4**

DINING ◆

Brandywine Bay
  Restaurant **12**
Callaloo **11**
Fat Hog Bob's **13**
The Flying Iguana **15**
Mrs. Scatliffe's
  Restaurant **5**

163

Road Town

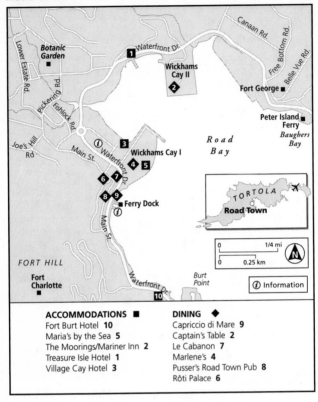

BY BUS It's better to use taxis unless your budget is limited. If wish to travel by bus, try **Scato's Bus Service** (© **284/494-2365**), which operates from the north end of the island to the west end, picking up passengers who hail it down. The bus runs Monday through Friday from 7:30am to dusk; it's most crowded in the morning when the school kids are picked up. Fares are $1 to $3.

BY CAR A handful of local companies and U.S.-based chains rent cars. **Itgo** (© **284/494-5150**) is at 1 Wickhams Cay, Road Town; **Avis** (© **800/331-1212** in the U.S., or 284/494-2193 on Tortola; www.avis.com) maintains offices opposite police headquarters in Road Town; and **Hertz** (© **800/654-3131** in the U.S., or 284/495-4405 on Tortola; www.hertz.com) has offices outside Road Town, on the island's West End, near the ferry landing dock. Rental companies will usually deliver your car to your hotel. All three companies require a valid driver's license and a temporary B.V.I. driver's license, which the car-rental agency can sell to you for $10; it's valid for 3 months. Because of the volume of tourism to Tortola, you should reserve a car in advance, especially in winter.

Remember: Drive on the left. Roads are pretty well paved, but they're often narrow, windy, and poorly lit, and they have few, if any, lines, so driving at night can be tricky. It's a good idea to rent a taxi to take you to that difficult-to-find beach, restaurant, or bar.

FAST FACTS: Tortola

American Express The local representative is **Travel Plan, Ltd.,** located at Waterfront Drive (✆ **284/494-2347**), in Road Town.

Banks Local bank branches include the **Bank of Nova Scotia** (Scotia Bank), Wickhams Cay (✆ **284/494-2526**), and **First Caribbean National Bank,** Wickhams Cay (✆ **284/494-2171**), both in Road Town. There's also a branch of **First Bank** on Wickhams Cay in Road Town (✆ **284/494-2662**). Each has its own ATM.

Bookstores The best bookstore is the **National Educational Services Bookstore,** Wickhams Cay, in Road Town (✆ **284/494-3921**).

Cameras & Film The best place for supplies and film developing is **Bolo's Brothers,** Wickhams Cay, in Road Town (✆ **284/494-2867**).

Dentists For dental emergencies, contact **Dental Surgery** (✆ **284/494-3474**), which is in Road Town behind the police station, off Waterfront Drive.

Doctors Go to **Peebles Hospital,** Road Town, Porter Road (✆ **284/494-3497**).

Drugstores The best pharmacy is **Medicure Pharmacy,** Hodge Building near Road Town Roundabout, Road Town (✆ **284/494-6189**).

Emergencies Call ✆ **911.**

Hospitals In Road Town, you can go to **Peebles Hospital,** Porter Road (✆ **284/494-3497**), which has X-ray and laboratory facilities.

Information The **B.V.I. Tourist Board Office** (© **284/494-3134**) is in the center of Road Town near the ferry dock, south of Wickhams Cay I. Here you'll find information about hotels, restaurants, tours, and more. Pick up *The Welcome Tourist Guide,* which has a map of the island.

Internet Access If there's no Web access at your hotel, here are two places to go for Internet access on Tortola: **Data Pro,** Road Town (© **284/494-6633**); and **Copyright Systems,** Palmgrove House, behind First Caribbean International Bank (© **284/494-5030**).

Laundry One of the best places is **Freeman's Laundry & Dry Cleaning,** Purcell Estate, Road Town (© **284/494-2285**).

Police The main police headquarters is on Waterfront Drive near the ferry dock on Sir Olva Georges Plaza (© **284/494-2945**).

WHERE TO STAY

Many of the island's hotels are small, informal, family-run guesthouses offering the basic amenities. Other lodgings are more elaborate, boasting a full range of resort-related facilities. None of them, however, are as big, splashy, and all-encompassing as the mega-resorts in the U.S. Virgin Islands, and many of the island's repeat visitors like that just fine. Remember all of Tortola's beaches are on the northern shore, so guests staying elsewhere (at Road Town, for example) will have to drive or take a taxi to reach them.

Note: All rates given within this chapter are subject to a 10% service charge and a 7% government tax. Rates are usually discounted significantly in summer. The term "MAP" stands for "Modified American Plan"; this means that the hotel provides breakfast and dinner (or lunch if you prefer) for an extra charge.

IN ROAD TOWN

If you want to be near the center of all the activity (such as there is), opt for a hotel in or around Road Town. You might also want to combine a night or two in Road Town with a few other nights in a more secluded part of the island.

Expensive

The Moorings/Mariner Inn ⟨ Right in Road Town, close to restaurants, shops, and bars, the Caribbean's most complete yachting resort is outfitted with at least 180 sailing yachts, some worth $2 million or more. This is an excellent place to rent your own yacht. Situated on a 3 hectare (8-acre) property, the inn was obviously designed with the yachting crowd in mind, offering not only support facilities and services but also shoreside accommodations. This lively spot is the place to go if you want to sample town life rather than tropical seclusion. The rooms are spacious; all suites have kitchenettes, and most of them open onto the water. Obviously, the boaties get more attention here than the landlubbers do. The nearest beach is Cane Garden Bay, about 15 minutes away by car; you'll either have to drive there in a rental car or take a taxi.

Wickhams Cay II (P.O. Box 216), Road Town, Tortola, B.V.I. ℂ **800/535-7289** in the U.S., or 284/494-2332. Fax 284/494-1638. 40 units. Winter $170 double, $230 suite; off season $95 double, $125 suite. Extra person $15. MC, V. **Amenities:** Restaurant; 2 bars; outdoor pool; tennis court; watersports equipment rental (including yacht rental); limited room service. *In room:* A/C, kitchenette, fridge, hair dryer.

Treasure Isle Hotel ⓐ
This centrally located resort is at the edge of the capital on 6 hectares (15 acres) of hillside overlooking a marina (not on the beach). The core of this attractive hotel is a splashy and colorful open-air bar boasting lovely views. The motel-like, midsize rooms are on two levels along the hillside terraces; a third level is occupied by more elegantly decorated suites at the crest of a hill. Details like local art, tile floors, stucco walls, floral upholstery, and rattan make for an inviting atmosphere in the rooms. Bathrooms are small; only one has a tub; the rest have showers. Adjoining the lounge and pool is an open-air dining room overlooking the harbor. The cuisine is well-respected. The hotel offers a barbecue Saturday nights and full a la carte menu at dinner.

Pasea Estate (P.O. Box 68), Road Town, Tortola, B.V.I. ℂ **284/494-2501.** Fax 284/494-2507. www.treasureislehotel.net. 43 units. Winter $170 double, $253 suite; off season $104–$143 double, $137–$209 suite. MAP (breakfast and dinner) $41 per person extra. Extra person $25. AE, DISC, MC, V. **Amenities:** Restaurant; bar; outdoor pool; watersports equipment rental; limited room service; laundry service; dry cleaning; nonsmoking rooms. *In room:* A/C, TV, dataport (in some), kitchenette (in suites), beverage maker (in suites).

Moderate

Fort Burt Hotel
The staff at this inn devote much of their energy to the property's popular pub and restaurant, which is run by the New England Culinary Institute, but they also rent some very pleasant rooms. The hotel was built in 1960 on the ruins of a 17th-century Dutch fort, and is covered with flowering vines. The rooms are set at a higher elevation than any others in Road Town, offering

excellent views from private terraces to the waterfront below. Simple, sun-flooded, and cozy, rooms have a colonial charm and a feeling of relaxed warmth. The suite rentals are a bit expensive, but the regular doubles are spacious enough and have recently been refurbished. There's a pool on the grounds, and guests can walk to Garden Bay Beach or Smuggler's Cove Beach in just 3 minutes.

Fort Burt (P.O. Box 3380), Road Town, Tortola, B.V.I. ✆ 284/494-2587. Fax 284/494-2002. 18 units. Year-round $135–$165 double; $155–$185 suite with kitchen; $225–$370 suite with private pool but no kitchen. AE, MC, V. **Amenities:** Restaurant; bar; outdoor pool. *In room:* A/C, TV, coffeemaker, hair dryer.

Maria's by the Sea   In the heart of Road Town, this hotel has a Caribbean charm, boasting little balconies that open onto the sound of lapping waves in the harbor. At night, you can enjoy the harbor lights from your balcony perch. The staff is friendly and helpful. Bedrooms, though fairly minimalist, depend for their allure on the sea breezes that seem to blow constantly. All units include a kitchenette, a balcony, and a small bathroom. It's a 10- to 15-minute drive to the nearest beach. Maria, the owner and manager, serves excellent Caribbean cuisine. From her famous conch chowder to her home-baked rolls, dining here in the evening is a delight.

Road Town (P.O. Box 206), Tortola, B.V.I. ✆ 284/494-2595. Fax 284/494-2420. www.islandsonline.com/mariasbythesea. 40 units. Winter $130–$170 double; off season $110–$150 double. AE, MC, V. **Amenities:** Restaurant; bar; pool; watersports equipment rental; car-rental desk. *In room:* A/C, TV, kitchenette.

Village Cay Hotel ✿   Set in the heart of Road Town, this is the most centrally located full-service lodging in the British Virgin Islands. Yachties are often drawn here. The most expensive rooms (called "A" rooms) overlook a marina filled with yachts from around the world; if you're seeking a beachfront location you'll have to look elsewhere. All the rooms are medium-size to spacious and have been recently refurbished, and some have balconies and patios. "A" rooms are better furnished than "B" units, which are smaller but are a good value if you're on a budget. Anything you need is within a 5-minute walk, including ferry service to other islands, secretarial services for business clients, or taxi service to anywhere on Tortola. Sailing and motoring cruises can be booked directly through the hotel.

Wickhams Cay I, Road Town, Tortola, B.V.I. ✆ 284/494-2771. Fax 284/494-2773. www.villagecay.com. 21 units. Winter $125–$190 double, $225–$350 suite; off season $100–$150 double, $185–$285 suite. AE, MC, V. **Amenities:** Restaurant; bar; outdoor pool; limited room service; laundry service; dry cleaning; coin-op laundry; boat trips. *In room:* A/C, TV, dataport, fridge, coffeemaker, hair dryer, safe.

AROUND THE REST OF THE ISLAND
Very Expensive

Long Bay Beach Resort & Villas ⟨⟩   A favorite of travelers since the 1960s, this resort is on a 2km-long (1¼-mile) sandy beach on the north shore, about 10 minutes from West End. It's the only full-service resort on the island, a low-rise complex set in a 21-hectare (52-acre) estate. Complaints about overbuilding and problems with maintenance have marred its once-stellar reputation, but there is still much to enjoy. Accommodations include hillside rooms and studios, plus two- and three-bedroom villas complete with a kitchen, a living area, and a large deck with a gas grill. The smallest and most basic units have simple furnishings, while the deluxe beachfront rooms and cabanas have either balconies or patios that overlook the ocean. All units have ocean views, one four-poster king-size or two queen-size beds, and large bathrooms with tiled showers.

The **Beach Café** is in the ruins of an old sugar mill. The alfresco **Garden Restaurant** offers dinner by reservation only, serving a variety of local and international dishes in a more elegant setting. The cuisine, especially the fresh fish, is among the finest at any hotel on the island, and the wine list is extensive.

P.O. Box 433, Road Town, Tortola, B.V.I. ℂ 800/345-0356 in the U.S. and Canada, or 284/495-4252. Fax 284/495-4677. www.longbay.com. 152 units. Winter $316–$470 double, $420–$605 suite, $875 2-bedroom villa; off-season $225–$255 double, $300–$355 suite, $490 2-bedroom villa. MAP (breakfast and dinner) $48 per person extra. AE, MC, V. **Amenities:** 2 restaurants; 3 bars; outdoor pool; 2 tennis courts; health club; spa; sauna; watersports equipment rental; car-rental desk; babysitting; laundry service; dry cleaning; nonsmoking rooms; horseback riding; snorkeling. *In room:* A/C, TV, dataport, kitchen (in villas), wet bar, beverage maker, hair dryer, safe.

The Sugar Mill ⟨⟩   In a lush tropical garden on the site of a 300-year-old sugar mill on the north side of Tortola, this secluded cottage colony sweeps down the hillside to its own beach, with flowers and fruits brightening the grounds. The accommodations are contemporary and well designed, ranging from suites and cottages to studios, all with kitchenettes. The latest addition, the Plantation House suites, evokes traditional Caribbean architecture with fine stonework, breezy porches, and lacy gingerbread detailing. All rooms have twin or king-size beds, private terraces with views, and well-maintained private bathrooms with showers. Four of the units are suitable for families of four. Just steps from the beach, two-bedroom air-conditioned suites have tropical decor and sea views.

Lunch is served down by the beach at Islands, which features Caribbean specialties such as jerk ribs and stuffed crab, plus burgers and salads. Dinner is offered at the **Sugar Mill Restaurant** (p. 178).

Apple Bay (P.O. Box 425), Road Town, Tortola, B.V.I. © **800/462-8834** in the U.S., or 284/495-4355. Fax 284/495-4696. www.sugarmillhotel.com. 23 units. Winter $325 double, $340 triple, $355 quad, $665 2-bedroom villa; off season $240–$260 double, $255–$275 triple, $270–$290 quad, $520–$560 2-bedroom villa. MAP available for $65 per person. AE, MC, V. Closed Aug–Sept. From Road Town, drive west 11km (6¾ miles), turn right (north) over Zion Hill, and turn right at the T-junction opposite Sebastians; Sugar Mill is .8km (½ mile) down the road. Children 11 and under not accepted in winter. **Amenities:** 2 restaurants; 2 bars; outdoor pool; car rental; babysitting; laundry service; dry cleaning; 1 room for those w/limited mobility; scuba diving; snorkeling; windsurfing. *In room:* A/C, TV (in villa and master suite), dataport, kitchenette (in some), fridge, hair dryer, iron.

Expensive

Frenchman's Cay Resort Hotel ⊛ This intimate resort is tucked away at the windward side of Frenchman's Cay, a little island connected by bridge to Tortola. The 5-hectare (12-acre) estate enjoys year-round breezes and views of Sir Francis Drake Channel and the outer Virgins. The individual one- and two-bedroom villas (actually a cluster of condos) are well furnished, each with a shady terrace, full kitchen, dining room, and sitting room. Each two-bedroom villa has two full bathrooms—a vacation in and of itself for families looking to escape the morning bathroom line. Pastel colors and tropical styling make for an inviting aesthetic, and each unit has good linen and a tub/shower combination. A small beach with rocks offshore is best for snorkeling. The Clubhouse Restaurant and lounge bar are in the main pavilion, offering a good Continental and Caribbean menu.

West End (P.O. Box 1054), Tortola, B.V.I. (U.S. address: Box 11156, St. Thomas, VI 00801). © **800/235-4077** in the U.S., 800/463-0199 in Canada, or 284/495-4844. Fax 284/495-4056. www.frenchmans.com. 9 units. Winter $200–$285 1-bedroom villa, $230–$325 2-bedroom villa; off season $145–$230 1-bedroom villa, $165–$260 2-bedroom villa. MAP (breakfast and dinner) $50 per person extra. AE, DISC, MC, V. Closed Sept. From Tortola, cross the bridge to Frenchman's Cay, turn left, and follow the road to the eastern tip of the cay. **Amenities:** Restaurant; bar; outdoor pool; tennis court; car rental; babysitting; horseback riding; island tours; kayaks; sailing; snorkeling; windsurfing. *In room:* Dataport, kitchen, beverage maker.

Lambert Beach Resort ⊛ *Finds* On the remote northeastern section of the island, this is the place for escapists who want isolation. Perched in an amphitheater sloping to the water, the resort opens onto a .8km (½-mile) beach of white sand set against a backdrop of palm trees. To reach the resort, you'll need to rent a car or take a taxi; it's about a 15-minute car ride from Road Town. Once here, you'll find some of the B.V.I's best white-sand cove beaches, along with a large swimming pool. Playground facilities for children make this a family favorite.

The cottage cluster is designed in the Mediterranean style, with accommodations spread across eight one-floor structures under red tile roofing. The preferred rooms open onto the beach, while the others front tropical gardens. Bedrooms are spacious and feature sand-hued walls, stained wood, ceramic tiled floors, and tropical motifs. Each comes with a private bathroom with tub or shower. The cottages are a combination of suites with a living room, veranda, and bedrooms. The food here is Caribbean cuisine with Italian, French, and international overtones. Dishes, boasting market-fresh ingredients, are well-made.

Lambert Bay, East End, Tortola, B.V.I. ℭ **284/495-2877.** Fax 284/495-2876. www.lambertbeachresort.com. 40 units. Winter $160–$245 double, $410 condo; off season $115–$195 double, $350 condo. AE, DC, MC, V. **Amenities:** Restaurant; bar; outdoor pool; tennis court; watersports equipment; limited room service; reef fishing. *In room:* A/C, minibar.

Prospect Reef Resort ℛ

This is the largest resort in the British Virgin Islands. It rises above a small, private harbor in a sprawling series of two-story concrete buildings scattered over 18 hectares (44 acres) of steeply sloping, landscaped terrain. The panoramic view of Sir Francis Drake Channel from the bedrooms is one of the best anywhere, though there's no beach to speak of.

Each of the resort's buildings contains up to 10 individual accommodations. Initially designed as condominiums, units include studios, town houses, and villas, in addition to guest rooms. All have private balconies or patios; larger units, which are perfect for families, have kitchenettes, living and dining areas, and separate bedrooms or sleeping lofts. Eighty percent of the rooms are air-conditioned; ceiling fans and the trade winds cool the rest of the rooms. Bathrooms are well maintained, and come with showers.

The food at the hotel's **Callaloo** restaurant (p. 177), a combination of Continental specialties and island favorites, was praised by *Gourmet* magazine.

Drake's Hwy. (P.O. Box 104), Road Town, Tortola, B.V.I. ℭ **800/356-8937** in the U.S., 800/463-3608 in Canada, or 284/494-3311. Fax 284/494-5595. www.prospectreef. com. 137 units. Winter $155–$315 double, $480 2-bedroom villa for 4; off season $109–$250 double, $320 2-bedroom villa for 4. Ask about packages. AE, MC, V. **Amenities:** 2 restaurants; bar; 2 outdoor pools; 5 tennis courts; fitness center; spa; Jacuzzi; car rental; limited room service; massage; babysitting; laundry service; dry cleaning; nonsmoking rooms; 1 room for those w/limited mobility; dive shop; kayaks; sailing; scuba diving; shuttle to beaches; snorkeling; sport-fishing. *In room:* A/C, TV, dataport, kitchenette (in villas), beverage maker, iron, safe.

Moderate

Coconut Point ⟨ (*Finds*)   Opening onto Carrot Bay, these vacation apartments are light and breezy, with real Caribbean style. All of the comfortable one- or two-bedroom units have a king- or queen-size bed, ceiling fans (a few units also offer air-conditioning), and over-size porches with dining tables. For guests who'd like to barbecue their own meals, some accommodations offer an outdoor grill fueled by gas. The Orchid unit, with its whirlpool, is perfect for honeymooners. The Hibiscus, Bougainvillea, and Frangipani units come with two bedrooms each, making them suitable for families. The property is a 3-minute walk from a small beach.

Carrot Bay (P.O. Box 441), Road Town, Tortola, B.V.I. © **284/495-4892.** Fax 284/495-4466. www.go-bvi.com/coconut_point. 5 units. Winter $1,100–$1,750 per week; off season $700–$1,400 per week. MC, V. **Amenities:** Outdoor pool; babysitting. *In room:* A/C in some units, TV, kitchen, coffeemaker.

Cooper Island Beach Club ⟨ (*Finds*)   This ultimate escapist's retreat is far from luxurious, but is the perfect place for those who want to experience simplicity. This one-of-a-kind hotel lies on a hilly island on the southern tier of the Sir Francis Drake Channel, about 8km (5 miles) south of Tortola. Snorkelers come here to plunge into the waters at the southern end of Manchioneel Bay, and charter boaters often stop off to eat at the casual beachfront restaurant, which serves marvelous grilled fish and makes a mean conch Creole. Outside of the occasional visits, the island slumbers in the past, with no roads and no electricity.

The midsize units come with a bedroom, a living room, and a kitchen, plus a balcony and a bathroom with a shower that is almost outdoors. Lighting and ceiling fans are powered by 12-volt DC, and there is one 110-volt outlet in each room which can be used to recharge batteries for razors. A freshwater supply is stored in a cistern under each room, and a solar hot water heater is used. All toilets are flushed with seawater. The on-site Sail Caribbean Divers offers snorkeling, kayaks, dinghy rentals, and full scuba services.

Machioneel Bay, Road Town, Tortola, B.V.I. © **800/542-4624** or 413/863-3162. www.cooper-island.com/hoteld.html. 12 units. Year-round $100–$180 double. AE, MC, V. **Amenities:** 2 restaurants; bar; watersports equipment rental and dive shop. *In room:* Kitchenettes, no phone.

Nanny Cay Resort & Marina ⟨   Few other resorts cater as aggressively to yacht owners as Nanny Cay, a sprawling, somewhat disorganized resort where great wealth (in the form of hyper-expensive yachts) lies cheek by jowl with more modest fishing craft. This place competes with Village Cay for the boat owner or sailor; we think Village Cay is superior. Accommodations are in a two-story motel-style building, where windows overlook open-air hallways. Each unit contains a kitchen and comfortable (albeit bland) furniture. The heart and soul of the resort is the 180-slip marina, headquarters to at least three yacht-chartering companies and permanent home to many fishing and pleasure boats. The resort sprawls over 10 hectares (25 acres) of steamy flatlands, adjacent to a saltwater inlet that's favored because of the protection it offers to boats during storms and hurricanes. Don't expect the spit-and-polish of a resort catering to the conventional resort trade. This place is artfully and deliberately raffish, which seems to be the way folks here want to keep it.

Road Town (P.O. Box 281), Tortola, B.V.I. © 800/74-CHARMS in the U.S., or 284/494-4895. Fax 284/494-0555. www.nannycay.com. 38 studios. Winter $160–$195 double, $245 suite, $185–$220 triple; off season $100–$145 double, $195 suite, $125–$170 triple. MC, V. **Amenities:** Restaurant; bar; outdoor pool; tennis court; watersports equipment rental; laundry service; sailing trips. *In room:* A/C, TV, kitchenette, hair dryer, coffeemaker.

Inexpensive

Hotel Castle Maria This inn sits on a hill overlooking Road Town Harbour, just a few minutes' walk from the center of Road Town. The lush, tropical garden out front is one of the most beautiful in the British Virgin Islands. An orchard produces avocados, mangoes, and bananas, which guests can enjoy. Rooms are basic, but offer reasonable comfort, with balconies, patios, and kitchenettes. The hotel is a 10- to 15-minute taxi ride away from the nearest sands.

Road Town (P.O. Box 206), Tortola, B.V.I. © 284/494-2553. Fax 284/494-2111. www.islandsonline.com/hotelcastlemaria. 33 units. Winter $90–$95 double, $115–$130 triple, $130–$140 quad; off season $85–$90 double, $105–$115 triple, $120–$130 quad. MC, V. **Amenities:** Bar; outdoor pool; car-rental desk; babysitting. *In room:* A/C, TV, kitchenette in some units, fridge, coffeemaker.

The Jolly Roger Inn This small harborfront hotel is located at Soper's Hole, only 91m (300 ft.) from the dock for the ferry to St. Thomas and St. John. The accommodations are clean and very simple. The small rooms are comfortably and pleasantly decorated with color-coordinated draperies and bedspreads, but only two have a private bathroom. There's no air-conditioning, but the rooms are breezy. The atmosphere is fun, casual, and definitely laid-back. The beach at Smuggler's Cove is a 20- to 30-minute walk over the hill.

West End, Tortola, B.V.I. © **284/495-4559.** Fax 284/495-4184. www.jollyrogerbvi. com. 5 units, 2 with private bathroom. Winter $67–$77 double without bathroom, $86 double with bathroom, $78–$88 triple without bathroom, $97 triple with bathroom; off season $50–$60 double without bathroom, $60 double with bathroom, $70–$80 triple without bathroom, $80 triple with bathroom. AE, MC, V. Closed early Aug–Oct 1. **Amenities:** Restaurant; watersports equipment rental. *In room:* A/C in some, no phone.

Ole Works Inn *Finds*   This hotel occupies the historic premises of a 300-year-old sugar refinery. It is a far less expensive alternative to the island's other Sugar Mill, although it doesn't have the cuisine or the facilities of the more famed property. Still, it puts you right on the beach. It's inland from Cane Garden Bay, across the road from a beautiful white-sand beach, and has the best musical venue on Tortola—a rustic indoor/outdoor bar called Quito's Gazebo. The rooms are cramped but cozy, outfitted with angular furniture and pastel colors; many have water views, and some are built as hillside units. The bathrooms are all a bit too small. The most romantic unit is the honeymoon suite in the beautiful tower. On the premises is a boutique-style art gallery showing watercolors by local artists and selling souvenirs. There are seven restaurants on the beach. The in-house bar is a magnet for fans of modern calypso music, because it's supervised by the hotel owner Quito (Enriquito) Rymer, who's the most famous recording star ever on Tortola. Quito himself performs Tuesday, Thursday, Saturday, and Sunday.

Cane Garden Bay (P.O. Box 560), Tortola, B.V.I. © **284/495-4837.** Fax 284/495-9618. www.quitorymer.com. 18 units. Winter $95–$145 double; $165–$200 suite; off season $70–$120 double; $140–$175 suite. Extra person $35. Children age 11 and under stay free in parent's room. Rates include continental breakfast. AE, MC, V. **Amenities:** Bar; outdoor pool. *In room:* A/C, TV, fridge, hair dryer, coffeemaker.

WHERE TO DINE

Most guests dine at their hotels, but if you want to venture out, try one of the suggestions below. *Note:* Many of the less expensive restaurants on the island serve rotis, Indian-style turnovers stuffed with such treats as potatoes and peas or curried chicken.

IN ROAD TOWN

Road Town offers the largest concentration of cheap and authentic Caribbean eateries in the B.V.I.

Expensive

Le Cabanon FRENCH   How about a touch of Gaul in the tropics? Islanders and visitors gather at this restaurant and bar to enjoy good

French food and an outdoor patio. Delicious appetizers include Mediterranean fish soup with *rouille,* herring and potato salad, and Camembert flambé with Calvados. Much of the menu is classically inclined, including dishes such as snapper meuniére. Especially tasty options include the almond curried Madras chicken, the Chilean sea bass with wasabi sauce, and the yellowfin tuna in a soy and basil sauce. For dessert, finish off with a crème brûlée or the chocolate mousse accurately billed as "heavenly" on the menu.

Waterfront Dr. © 284/494-8660. Reservations recommended. Main courses $19–$33. MC, V. Mon–Fri noon–3pm and 7–10pm; Sat 5–10pm.

Moderate

Captain's Table CONTINENTAL   Amid a cluster of palm trees on the marina, the Captain's Table offers outdoor dining in an inviting atmosphere. For appetizers, you can enjoy selections from gazpacho to escargot. One of the best items is honey-dipped chicken, which is lightly coated with flour and deep-fried to a golden brown, then served with french fries on the side. For a lighter meal, you may want to try the Cajun chicken over a Caesar salad. For more substantial appetites, the menu offers dolphin (not Flipper, but a species of fish), sautéed or grilled, grilled salmon, and lobster. For something unusual, try filet of Jamaican jerk duck.

Wickhams Cay II, Road Town. © 284/494-3885. Reservations recommended. Main courses $16–$30. AE, DC, MC, V. Mon–Fri 11am–3pm and 5–10pm; Sat–Sun 5–9pm.

Inexpensive

Capriccio di Mare ⋒ ITALIAN   Created in a moment of whimsy by the owners of the more upscale Brandywine Bay Restaurant (p. 176), this local favorite is small, casual, and laid-back. It's the most authentic-looking Italian cafe in the Virgin Islands. At breakfast time, many locals stop in for an Italian pastry along with a cup of cappuccino, or a full breakfast. If it's evening, you might try the mango Bellini, a variation of the champagne-based cocktail served at Harry's Bar in Venice. Begin with such appetizers as *piedini* (flour tortillas with various toppings), then move on to a selection from the fresh pastas with succulent sauces, the best pizzas on the island, or the well-stuffed sandwiches. If you arrive on the right night, you might be treated to stuffed Cornish hen with scalloped potatoes. The fresh salads are delicious; we favor the *insalata mista* with large, leafy greens and slices of fresh Parmesan.

Waterfront Dr., Road Town. © **284/494-5369.** Main courses $9–$16. MC, V. Mon–Sat 8am–9:30pm.

Marlene's CARIBBEAN   This centrally located restaurant provides takeout as well as indoor dining. Try the Caribbean pâtés—conch, swordfish, chicken, or beef wrapped in pastry dough, then baked or fried. Other examples of local fare include rotis and curries. You can also order baked chicken, steak, or seafood, including lobster and other shellfish. The desserts are made from scratch.

Wickhams Cay I, Road Town. ☎ **284/494-4634**. Breakfast $2.50–$5; pâtés $1.50–$2.50; main courses $7–$12. AE, MC, V. Mon–Sat 10am–10pm.

Pusser's Road Town Pub CARIBBEAN/ENGLISH PUB   On the waterfront across from the ferry dock, the original Pusser's serves Caribbean fare, English pub grub, and good pizzas. This place is not as fancy as Pusser's Landing in the West End (p. 179), nor is the food as good, but it's a lot more convenient and has faster service. The complete lunch and dinner menu includes savory English pies (*Gourmet* magazine asked for the recipe for the chicken-and-asparagus pie), and deli-style sandwiches. John Courage ale is on draft, but the drink to order here is the famous Pusser's Rum, the same blend of five West Indian rums that the Royal Navy has served to its men for more than 300 years. Thursday is nickel beer night.

Waterfront Dr. and Main St., Road Town. ☎ **284/494-3897**. Reservations recommended. Main courses $6–$20. AE, DISC, MC, V. Daily 10am–midnight.

Rôti Palace CARIBBEAN   The best rotis in the British Virgin Islands are served here, on the old main street of the island's capital— they're as good as those in Port-of-Spain, Trinidad. This is primarily a lunch stop, although it's a good choice for an affordable dinner or a standard breakfast. Choices (other than the famed rotis) include a wide selection of tasty vegetable, local conch, lobster, beef, and chicken dishes, many of which are spicy. Sea snails are a specialty; they're mixed with onions, garlic, and celery, spiced with curry, and served in a butter sauce. Ginger beer, juices, and wines serve as accompaniments to your meal.

Main St., Road Town. ☎ **284/494-4196**. Main courses $8–$16. No credit cards. Mon–Sat 7am–9:30pm.

AROUND THE REST OF THE ISLAND
Expensive
Brandywine Bay Restaurant ☆☆ ITALIAN/INTERNATIONAL   On a cobblestone garden terrace along the south shore, overlooking Sir Francis Drake Channel, this is one of Tortola's most elegant and romantic restaurants. Davide Pugliese, the chef, and his wife, Cele, have earned a reputation for their outstanding Florentine fare. The

skillful cooking produces dishes that range from classic to inspired. Davide changes his menu daily, based on the availability of fresh produce. The best dishes include beef carpaccio, roast duck, homemade pasta, his own special calves'-liver dish (the recipe is a secret), and homemade mozzarella with fresh basil and tomatoes. Appropriate dress is required.

Brandywine Estate, Sir Francis Drake Hwy. ℰ **284/495-2301.** Reservations required. Main courses $25–$30. AE, MC, V. Mon–Sat 6:30–9:30pm. Closed Aug–Oct. Drive 5km (3 miles) east of Road Town (toward the airport) on South Shore Rd.

Callaloo ℛ INTERNATIONAL   One of the best hotel restaurants on Tortola, this place is romantic at night, especially if it's a balmy evening and the tropical breezes are blowing. It's the kind of cliché Caribbean setting that always works, and the food is quite good, too. The menu is hardly imaginative, but the chefs do well with their limited repertoire. Begin with the coconut prawns or steamed mussels, and don't pass on the house salad, which has a zesty papaya dressing. The best dishes are fresh lobster when available (not as good as the Maine variety, though), pan-fried duck breast with a citrus-flavored spinach sauce, and fresh fish such as tuna, swordfish, or mahimahi. One heavenly special dish is Virgin Gorda swordfish with a tropical fruit salsa and red-pepper essence. For dessert, make it the coconut bread pudding or the Key lime pie. Downstairs is the less expensive **Scuttlebutt Pub,** open for lunch and dinner daily.

In Prospect Reef Resort, Drake's Hwy., Road Town. ℰ **284/494-3311.** Reservations recommended. Main courses $13–$30. AE, MC, V. Daily 7am–3pm; Thurs–Sun 6–10pm.

Mrs. Scatliffe's Restaurant ℛ *Finds* WEST INDIAN   This Tortola mama offers home-cooked meals on the deck of her island home. Some of the vegetables come right from her garden, although others might be from a can. You'll enjoy excellent authentic West Indian dishes: perhaps spicy conch soup followed by curried goat, "old wife" fish (triggerfish, in this case filleted, boiled, and served with onion sauce), or chicken in a coconut shell. Service, usually from an inexperienced teenager, is not exactly efficient.

You may be exposed to Mrs. Scatliffe's gentle preaching of her Christian faith. A Bible reading and a heartfelt rendition of a gospel song sometimes accompany a soft custard dessert.

Carrot Bay. ℰ **284/495-4556.** Reservations required by 5pm. Fixed-price meal $28–$35. No credit cards. One seating daily begins 7–8pm.

Round Hill Vacation Villa ☆ *Finds* CARIBBEAN One of your most memorable meals in Tortola is likely to be eaten with Joycelyn and Allan Rhymer, who will dazzle you with a home-cooked five-course dinner. You'll get good food, made with fresh ingredients, and a warm welcome from the Rhymers. (Mr. Rhymer may even regale you with stories about Jimmy Carter and other luminaries he's met during his hospitality career.) The villa opens onto a panoramic vista over Cane Garden Bay Beach. This is one of the best vantage points for enjoying the sinking sun, so you may want to arrive early to enjoy the view of the sunset.

The menu changes every night based on market availability. Sample dishes include Cornish game hen in a fruit-flavored tropical sauce, poached mahimahi in a delectable garlic-laced lemon-butter sauce, and tender and perfectly roasted prime rib.

You must call for a reservation as early as possible, since this is a small and special place. If you're interested, there is a one-bedroom apartment here that goes for $750 a week in winter, reduced to $450 a week off season. The apartment offers a handsomely furnished bedroom with a queen-size bed, along with a sizeable eat-in kitchen and a living room with a TV.

P.O. Box 602, West End, Tortola, B.V.I. ✆ 284/495-9353. Fax 284/495-4281. www.islandsonline.com/roundhill. Reservations required. Fixed-price 5-course dinner $40 per person. No credit cards. Mon–Tues and Thurs–Sat at 7pm.

Skyworld ☆☆ INTERNATIONAL Skyworld, one of the best restaurants on the island, continues to be all the rage. On one of Tortola's loftiest peaks, at a breezy 400m (1,312 ft.), it offers views of both the U.S. Virgin Islands and the British Virgin Islands. The restaurant is divided into two sections—a main dining room and a bar. Both sections offer the same menu.

The fresh fish chowder is an island favorite, as are other, oft-changing soups, including one with peaches and coconuts, and another of champagne, coconut, and melons. The fresh fish of the day is your best bet. Recently we enjoyed the oven-baked yellowfin tuna with a tantalizing pistachio-and-sesame-seed crust. Try the island's best Key lime pie or the heavenly cheesecake for dessert.

Ridge Rd., Road Town. ✆ 284/494-3567. Reservations recommended. Main courses $24–$30. AE, MC, V. Daily 10am–2:30pm and 5–11pm. Closed Christmas Day.

Sugar Mill Restaurant ☆ CALIFORNIA/CARIBBEAN This transformed 3-century-old sugar mill is a romantic spot for dining. Colorful works by Haitian painters hang on the stone walls, and copper basins have been planted with flowers. Before going to the dining room, once part of the old boiling house, visit the open-air bar on a deck that overlooks the sea. Your hosts, the Morgans, know a lot about food and wine. Some of their recipes have been printed in *Gourmet.* One of their most popular creations, published in *Bon Appétit,* is curried banana soup. You might begin with the roasted pepper salad or the especially tasty wild mushroom soup. For a main course, we recommend such dishes as the pan-roasted duck breast served with Asian coleslaw and soba noodles, or the grilled fresh fish with a pineapple pepper salsa. This place also offers accommodations (p. 169).

Apple Bay. ℂ 284/495-4355. Reservations required. Main courses $22–$35. AE, MC, V. Daily 7–8:30pm. Closed Aug–Sept. From Road Town, drive west 11km (6¾ miles), turn right (north) over Zion Hill, and turn right at the T-junction opposite Sebastians; Sugar Mill is .8km (½ mile) down the road.

Moderate

Fat Hog Bob's CARIBBEAN/BARBECUE   Behind a protective reef at Maya Cove, you can enjoy the best ribs in the B.V.I., at least the equal of some of those served in Georgia and the Carolinas. This place has the look of an American sports bar, except for the covered porch that is sprawled 30m (100 ft.) over the water. You can order from a selection of appetizers such as salt fish cakes and soups (including West Indian pumpkin). The famed barbecued Danish baby back ribs, served at both lunch and dinner, are marinated in Guinness and then perfectly grilled with the chef's secret sauce. They're so tender that the meat literally falls off the bone. If you don't want ribs, there are fat sandwiches at lunch; main courses at night include great catches from Anegada, not only lobster but also game fish, and steaks (including a juicy porterhouse) that will delight the Texan in you. For dessert, the pumpkin cheesecake is an unexpected delight.

Maya Cove, East End. ℂ 284/495-1010. www.fathogbobs.com. Reservations recommended. Main courses $11–$19 lunch, $20–$45 dinner. AE, MC, V. Daily 11am–11pm (later if business warrants it).

Pusser's Landing CARIBBEAN   This Pusser's location, opening onto the water in West End, is better located than the original Pusser's Road Town Pub, which is on the waterfront across from the ferry dock. In this nautical setting, you can enjoy fresh grilled fish of the day cooked to order. Begin with a hearty soup, perhaps pumpkin or freshly-made seafood chowder. Many of the main courses have real island flavor, the most justifiably popular being the jerk chicken Jamaican-style and the grilled chicken breast with fresh pineapple salsa. A classic is the curried shrimp over rice. Mud pie remains the choice dessert here, but the Key lime pie and mango soufflé beckon as well. Happy hour is daily from 5 to 7pm.

Frenchman's Cay, West End. ⒸⒹ 284/495-4554. Reservations required. Main courses $15–$45. AE, DISC, MC, V. Daily 11am–10pm.

Quito's Gazebo ⒻⓘⓝⓓⓈ *Finds* CARIBBEAN/INTERNATIONAL This restaurant, owned by Quito Rymer, the island's most acclaimed musician, is the most popular of those along the shore of Cane Bay. Quito performs after dinner several nights a week. The restaurant, which is designed like an enlarged gazebo, is set directly on the sands of the beach. Frothy rum-based drinks are the order of the day here (ask for the piña colada or the Bushwacker, made with four different kinds of rum). The food has a true island flavor and a lot of zest. Lunch includes sandwiches, salads, and platters. Evening meals are more elaborate, and might feature dishes such as conch or pumpkin fritters, mahimahi with a wine-butter sauce, a conch dinner with (Callwood) rum sauce, chicken roti, and steamed local mutton served with a sauce of island tomatoes and pepper. On Wednesday night, for only $15, you can enjoy barbecue ribs, chicken, roti, corn on the cob, and johnnycakes.

Cane Garden Bay. ⒸⒹ 284/495-4837. www.quitorymer.com. Main courses $18–$40; lunch platters, sandwiches, and salads $6–$12. AE, MC, V. Mon–Fri 7am–6pm; Sat 7am–4pm; bar Tues–Sun 11am–midnight.

BEACHES

Beaches are rarely crowded on Tortola unless a cruise ship is in port. To get to the sands, rent a car or a jeep, or take a taxi (and don't forget to arrange a time to be picked up).

Tortola's finest beach is **Cane Garden Bay** Ⓕ, on Cane Garden Bay Road, directly west of Road Town. You'll have to navigate some roller-coaster hills to get there, but these fine white sands, with sheltering palm trees, are among the most popular in the B.V.I., and the lovely bay is many Yachties' favorite. Outfitters here rent Hobie Cats, kayaks, and sailboards. Windsurfing is possible as well. There are some seven places to eat along the beach, plus a handful of bars. Be prepared for crowds in the high season.

Surfers like **Apple Bay,** west of Cane Garden Bay along North Shore Road. The beach isn't big, but that doesn't diminish activity when the surf's up. Conditions are best in January and February. After enjoying the white sands, you can have a drink at the Bomba's Surfside Shack, a classic dive of a beach bar at the water's edge (p. 185).

Smugglers Cove ⋒, known for its tranquillity and for the beauty of its sands, is at the extreme western end of Tortola, opposite the offshore island of Great Thatch, and just north of St. John. It's a lovely crescent of white sand with calm turquoise waters. A favorite with locals, Smugglers Cove is also popular with snorkelers, who explore a world of sea fans, sponges, parrot fish, and elkhorn and brain corals. Beginning snorkelers in particular appreciate the fact that the reef is close to shore. The beach, sometimes called "Lower Belmont Bay," is at the end of bumpy Belmont Road. Once you get here, even if you're a little worse for wear, you'll think the crystal-clear water and the beautiful palm trees are worth the effort.

East of Cane Garden Bay, **Brewers Bay,** accessible via the long, steep Brewers Bay Road, is ideal for snorkelers and surfers. This clean, white-sand beach is a great place to enjoy walks in the early morning or at sunset. Or just sip a rum punch from the beach bar and watch the world go by. There is a campground here if you want to spend the night.

The 2km-long (1¼-mile) white-sand beach at **Long Bay West,** reached along Long Bay Road, is one of the most beautiful in the B.V.I. Joggers run along the water's edge, and spectacular sunsets make this spot perfect for romantic strolls. The Long Bay Beach Resort stands on the northeast side of the beach; many visitors like to book a table at the resort's restaurant overlooking the water.

If you'd like to escape from the crowds at Cane Garden Bay and Brewers Bay, head east along Ridge Road until you come to **Josiah's Bay Beach** on the north coast. This beach lies in the foreground of Buta Mountain. On most occasions we have found it either empty or with only a handful of bathers. The area is ideal for a picnic. If you visit in winter, beware: On many days there's a strong undertow, and there are no lifeguards.

At the very east end of the island, **Long Bay East,** reached along Beef Island Road, is a great spot for swimming. Cross Queen Elizabeth Bridge to reach this 2km-long (1¼-mile) beach with great views and white sands.

EXPLORING THE ISLAND

Travel Plan Tours, Romasco Place, Harbour House (P.O. Box 437), Road Town (② **284/494-2872**), offers a 3½-hour tour that touches on the natural highlights of Tortola (a minimum of four participants is required). The cost is $35 per person, with a supplement of $10 per person if you want to extend the tour with hill climbing in the rainforest. The company also offers 2½-hour **snorkeling tours** for

$61 per person (with snacks included). A full-day **sailing tour** aboard a catamaran that goes from Tortola to either Peter Island or Norman Island costs $86 per person; a full-day tour, which goes as far afield as the Baths at Virgin Gorda and includes lunch, costs $120 per person. And if **deep-sea fishing** appeals to you, you can go for a half-day excursion, with equipment, for four fishermen and up to two "nonfishing observers" for $783, or for a full-day excursion for $1,083.

A **taxi tour** of the island costs $45 for two passengers for 2 hours, or $60 for 3 hours. To call a taxi in Road Town, dial *②* **284/494-2322;** on Beef Island, *②* **284/495-1982.**

The Wreck of the *Rhone* & Other Dive Sites

The site in the British Virgin Islands that lures divers over from St. Thomas is **the wreck of the HMS *Rhone* 🐠🐠**, which sank in 1867 near the western point of Salt Island. *Skin Diver* magazine called it "the world's most fantastic ship-wreck dive." The wreck teems with marine life and coral formations, and was featured in the 1977 movie *The Deep*.

Although it's no *Rhone*, *Chikuzen* is another intriguing site off Tortola. It's an 81m (266-ft.) steel-hulled refrigerator ship, which sank off the island's east end in 1981. The hull, still intact under about 24m (79 ft.) of water, is now home to a vast array of tropical fish, including yellowtail, barracuda, black-tip sharks, octopus, and drum fish.

South of Ginger Island, **Alice in Wonderland** is a deep-dive site with a wall that begins at around 3.6m (12 ft.) and slopes gently to 30m (98 ft.). It abounds with marine life such as lobsters, crabs, rainbow-hued fan coral, and mammoth mushroom-shaped coral. **Spyglass Wall** is another offshore dive site dropping to a sandy bottom and filled with seafans and large coral heads. The drop is from 3m (10 ft.) to 18m (60 ft.). Divers here should keep an eye out for tarpon, eagle rays, and stingrays.

Blue Waters Divers, Road Town (*②* **284/494-2847**), is a PADI outfitter that offers various dive packages, including one to the wreck of the *Rhone*. A resort course costs $95; a PADI open-water certification is $360.

No visit to Tortola is complete without a trip to **Sage Mountain National Park** 𝒜, rising to an elevation of 534m (1,751 ft.). Here, you'll find traces of a primeval rainforest, and you can enjoy a picnic while overlooking neighboring islets and cays. Covering 37 hectares (91 acres), the park protects the remnants of Tortola's original forests (those that were not burned or cleared during the island's plantation era). Go west from Road Town to reach the mountain. Before you head out, stop by the tourist office and pick up the brochure *Sage Mountain National Park.* It has a location map, directions to the forest and parking, and an outline of the main trails through the park. From the parking lot, a trail leads to the main park entrance. The two main trails are the Rainforest Trail and the Mahogany Forest Trail.

Shadow's Ranch, Todman's Estate (𝒞 **284/494-2262**), offers horseback rides through the national park or down to the shores of Cane Garden Bay. Call for details daily from 9am to 4pm. The cost is from $60 per hour.

OUTDOOR ACTIVITIES

SNORKELING A good beach for snorkeling is **Brewers Bay** (p. 181). Snorkelers should also consider heading to the islet of **Marina Cay,** or taking an excursion to **Cooper Island,** across the Sir Francis Drake Channel. **Underwater Safaris** leads expeditions to both sites.

The best choice for a snorkeling trip is one with **High Sea Adventures** (𝒞 **284/495-1300**), led by one of Tortola's best charter captains, Captain Roy. The excursions are designed to make any level of swimmer feel comfortable. Capt. Roy patiently spends his time in the water pointing out the fascinating underwater plants, coral, and countless species of colorful marine life. Make sure to ask him about the parrotfish "poop" (it's how coral is made). Equipment rental is included, or you can bring your own. Capt. Roy even throws in his special tropical punch on the way home. The company expanded this year to include day trips to Anegada (p. 24).

YACHT CHARTERS Tortola boasts the largest fleet of bareboat sailing charters in the world. The best place to get outfitted is the **Moorings,** Wickhams Cay (𝒞 **888/535-7289** or 888/952-8420 in the U.S. and Canada, or 284/494-2332 in the British Virgin Islands; www.moorings.com). This outfit, along with a handful of others, makes the British Virgins the cruising capital of the world. You can choose from a fleet of sailing yachts, which can accommodate up to five couples in comfort and style. Depending on your nautical knowledge and skills, you can arrange a bareboat rental (with no crew) or a fully crewed rental with a skipper, a staff, and a cook. Boats come equipped with a portable barbecue, snorkeling gear, a dinghy, linens, and galley equipment. The Moorings has an experienced staff of mechanics, electricians, riggers, and cleaners. If you're going out on your own, you'll get a thorough briefing session on Virgin Island waters and anchorages.

If you'd like sailing lessons, consider **Steve Colgate's Offshore Sailing School** (© **800/221-4326**), which offer courses in seamanship year-round.

SHOPPING

Most of Tortola's shops are on Road Town's Main Street. Unfortunately, the British Virgins have no duty-free shopping. British goods are imported without duty, though, and you can find some good buys among these items, especially in English china. In general, store hours are Monday to Saturday from 9am to 4pm.

You might start your shopping expedition at **Crafts Alive,** an open-air market lying in the center of Road Town and impossible to miss. It consists of a series of old-fashioned West Indian–style buildings that are stocked with local crafts and locally made goods, ranging from Caribbean dolls to straw hats, and from crocheted doilies to pottery to the inevitable B.V.I. T-shirts.

Sunny Caribbee Herb and Spice Company, Main Street, Road Town (© **284/494-2178**), in an old West Indian building, was the first hotel on Tortola. It's now a shop specializing in Caribbean spices, seasonings, teas, condiments, and handicrafts. With an aroma of spices permeating the air, this factory is an attraction in itself. You can buy two famous specialties here: the West Indian hangover cure, and the Arawak love potion. A Caribbean cosmetics collection, Sunsations, includes herbal bath gels, island perfume, and sunscreens. There's a daily sampling of island products—perhaps tea, coffee, sauces, or dips.

Caribbean Fine Arts Ltd., Main Street, Road Town (© **284/494-4240**), sells original watercolors and oils, limited-edition serigraphs and sepia photographs, and pottery and primitives.

Samarkand, Main Street, Road Town (© **284/494-6415**), is an unusually good bet for jewelry and other items. Look for an intriguing selection of bracelets, pins, pendants in both silver and gold, and pierced earrings. Caribbean motifs such as palms and sea birds often appear in the designs of the jewelry.

Bargain hunters gravitate to **Sea Urchin,** Mill Mall, Road Town (℃ 284/494-4108), for print shirts and shorts, T-shirts, bathing suits, and sandals.

Pusser's Company Store, Main Street and Waterfront Road, Road Town (℃ 284/494-2467), has gourmet food items including meats, spices, fish, and a nice selection of wines. Pusser's Rum is one of the best-selling items here.

Arawak, on the dock at Nanny Cay (℃ 284/494-5240), is known for its household furnishings, such as placemats and candleholders, but also sells sporty clothing for adults and kids, along with a selection of gifts and souvenirs.

Flamboyance, Waterfront Drive (℃ 284/494-4099), is the best place to shop for perfume and upscale cosmetics.

If you've rented a villa or condo, or even if your accommodations have a kitchenette, consider a visit to **Ample Hamper,** Villa Cay Marina, Wickham's Cay I, Road Town (℃ 284/494-2494). This outlet stocks some of the best packaged food and bottled wines on the island. It also offers fresh fruit and a tasty selection of cheeses.

Philatelists from all over flock to the **British Virgin Islands Post office,** Main Street, Road Town (℃ 284/494-3701, ext. 4996), for its exquisite, unusual stamps in beautiful designs. Though the stamps carry U.S. monetary designations, they can only be used in the B.V.I.

TORTOLA AFTER DARK

Ask around to find out which hotel might have entertainment on any given evening. Steel bands and fungi or scratch bands (African Caribbean musicians who improvise on locally available instruments) appear regularly, and nonresidents are usually welcome. Pick up a copy of *Limin' Times,* an entertainment magazine that lists what's happening locally; it's usually available at hotels.

Bomba's Surfside Shack, Cappoon's Bay (℃ 284/495-4148) is the island's oldest, most memorable hangout, on the beach near the West End. It attracts an uninhibited crowd. It's covered with Day-Glo graffiti, and odds and ends of plywood, driftwood, and old tires. Despite its makeshift appearance, the shack has the sound system to create a really great party. Every month (dates vary), Bomba's stages a full-moon party, with free house tea spiked with hallucinogenic mushrooms. (The tea is free because it's illegal to sell it.) This place is also wild on Wednesday and Sunday nights, when there's live music and an $8 all-you-can-eat barbecue. It's open daily from 10am to midnight (or later, depending on business).

The bar at the **Moorings/Mariner Inn,** Wickhams Cay (© **888/ 535-7289** or 888/952-8420 in the U.S. and Canada, or 284/494-2332 in the British Virgin Islands), is the preferred watering hole for upscale yacht owners. Interestingly, drink prices are low. Open to a view of its own marina, and bathed in a dim and flattering light, this place has a relaxed atmosphere. Another popular choice is the **Spyglass Bar,** in the Treasure Isle Hotel, Road Town (© **284/494-2501**), where a sunken bar on a terrace overlooks the pool and faraway marina facilities of this popular hotel.

Other places worth a stop on a bar-hopping jaunt include the **Jolly Roger,** West End (© **284/495-4559**), where you can hear local or sometimes American bands playing everything from reggae to blues. In the same area, visit **Stanley's Welcome Bar,** Cane Garden Bay (© **284/495-9424**), where a rowdy frat-boy crowd gathers to drink, talk, and drink some more. Finally, check out **Sebastians,** Apple Bay (© **284/495-4212**), especially on Sunday, when you can dance to live music under the stars, at least in winter.

Rhymer's, on the popular stretch of beach at Cane Garden Bay (© **284/495-4639**), serves up cold beer or tropical rum concoctions, along with a casual menu of ribs, conch chowder, and more. The beach bar and restaurant is open daily 8am to 9pm.

The joint is jumping at the **Road House,** West End (© **284/494-1667**), on Friday to Sunday nights. This place is usually packed with locals and a smattering of visitors who come to listen to a DJ or to live salsa and reggae.

3 Virgin Gorda ✶✶✶

The second-largest island in the British cluster, Virgin Gorda is 16km (10 miles) long and 3.2km (2 miles) wide, with a population of some 1,400 people. It's 19km (12 miles) east of Tortola and 41km (26 miles) east of St. Thomas.

In 1493, on his second voyage to the New World, Columbus named the island Virgin Gorda, or "Fat Virgin," because the mountain on it looked (in his opinion) like a protruding stomach.

Virgin Gorda was a fairly desolate agricultural community until Laurance Rockefeller established the resort of Little Dix in the early 1960s. He envisioned a "wilderness beach," where privacy and solitude reigned. Other major hotels followed in the wake of Little Dix, but privacy and solitude still reign supreme.

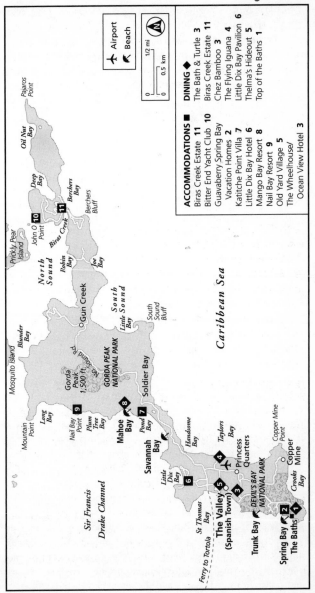

DINING ◆

The Bath & Turtle **3**
Biras Creek Estate **11**
Chez Bamboo **3**
The Flying Iguana **4**
Little Dix Bay Pavilion **6**
Thelma's Hideout **5**
Top of the Baths **1**

ACCOMMODATIONS ■

Biras Creek Estate **11**
Bitter End Yacht Club **10**
Guavaberry Spring Bay
Vacation Homes **2**
Katitche Point Villa **7**
Little Dix Bay Hotel **6**
Mango Bay Resort **8**
Nail Bay Resort **9**
Old Yard Village **5**
The Wheelhouse/
Ocean View Hotel **3**

ESSENTIALS
GETTING THERE

BY PLANE   You can get to Virgin Gorda by air via St. Thomas in the U.S. Virgin Islands. **Air St. Thomas** (📞 **800/522-3084** or 340/776-2722) flies to Virgin Gorda Monday to Saturday from St. Thomas. A one-way trip (40 min.) costs $83.

BY BOAT   Speedy's Fantasy (📞 **284/495-5240**) operates a ferry service between Road Town, on Tortola, and Virgin Gorda. Monday through Saturday, four ferries a day leave from Road Town; three ferries make the trip on Sunday. The cost is $15 one-way or $20 round-trip. There is also service from St. Thomas to Virgin Gorda three times a week (on Tues, Thurs, and Sat), costing $35 one-way or $60 round-trip.

You'll also find that the more luxurious resorts have their own boats to take you from the airport on Beef Island to Virgin Gorda.

GETTING AROUND

BY BUS   Independently operated open-sided **safari buses** run along the main road. Holding up to 14 passengers, these buses charge upwards from $3 to $4 per person to transport a passenger, say, from the Valley to the Baths.

BY CAR   If you'd like to rent a car, try one of the local firms, including **Mahogany Rentals,** The Valley, Spanish Town (📞 **284/495-5469**), across from the yacht harbor. This company has the least expensive rentals on the island, beginning at around $55 daily for a Suzuki Sidekick. Road conditions on Virgin Gorda range from good to extremely poor. *Remember:* Drive on the left.

An aerial view of the island shows what looks like three bulky masses connected by two very narrow isthmuses. The most northeasterly of these three masses (which contains two of the most interesting hotels) is not even accessible by road at all, requiring ferryboat transit from the more accessible parts of the island.

One possibility for exploring Virgin Gorda by car is to drive from the southwest to the northeast along the island's rocky and meandering spine. This route will take you to the **Baths** (in the extreme southeast), **Spanish Harbour** (near the middle), and eventually, after skirting the mountainous edges of **Gorda Peak,** to the most northwesterly tip of the island's road system, near **North Sound.** Here, a mini-armada of infrequently scheduled ferryboats departs and arrives from Biras Creek and the Bitter End Yacht Club.

FAST FACTS: Virgin Gorda

American Express The local American Express representative is **Travel Plan,** Virgin Gorda Yacht Harbour (✆ **284/494-5586**).

Banks **First Caribbean Bank** (✆ **284/495-5217**) is located in Spanish Town at the Virgin Gorda Shopping Centre. It has the only ATM on the island.

Cameras & Film Try **Kysk Tropix,** Virgin Gorda Yacht Harbour (✆ **284/495-5636**), open daily 9:30am to 6pm.

Dentists & Doctors Contact **Medicure Health Center** at Spanish Town (✆ **284/495-5479**).

Drugstore Go to **Island Drug Centre** at Spanish Town (✆ **284/495-5449**).

Internet Access Go to the **Chandlery,** Yacht Harbour Marina (✆ **284/495-5628**), where the cost is $5 for the first 10 minutes, 50¢ per minute thereafter. You can also pay a flat fee of $20 per hour.

Laundry **Stevens Laundry & Dry Cleaning,** near the Virgin Gorda Yacht Harbour (✆ **284/495-5525**), is open daily 8am to noon and 1 to 9pm.

Police There is a station in the Valley at Spanish Town (✆ **284/495-7584**).

Tourist Information The tourist office is in Virgin Gorda Yacht Harbor, Spanish Town (✆ **284/495-5182**).

WHERE TO STAY

The best agency for a villa rental is **Virgin Gorda Villa Rentals Ltd.,** P.O. Box 63, Leverick Bay, Virgin Gorda, B.V.I. (✆ **284/495-7421;** www.virgingordabvi.com). They manage villas throughout the island, most of which are quite expensive. A 5-night minimum stay is required in the off season, and a 7-night minimum is requested in winter. The cheapest weekly rentals in winter are around $833 per week, dropping to $714 per week during off season.

Remember that all accommodations rates given within this chapter are subject to a 12% service charge and a 7% government tax.

VERY EXPENSIVE

Biras Creek Estate ✦✦✦   Stay at this sophisticated, relaxing hideaway if you want to retreat from the world. This private, romantic resort is the classiest place on the island—Bitter End is more family-oriented, and Little Dix Bay more of a conventional resort. It stands at the northern end of Virgin Gorda like a hilltop fortress, opening onto the ocean. On a 60-hectare (148-acre) estate with its own marina, it occupies a narrow neck of land flanked by the sea on three sides. All the attractive, tropically decorated units have well-furnished bedrooms and private patios. Some have king-size beds, plus spacious bathrooms with inviting garden showers. There are no TVs in the rooms, but you do get such luxuries as oceanview verandas. Guests get their own bikes for their stay, and there are lots of hiking trails near the property. The hotel restaurant and open-air bar are quietly elegant, and there's always a table with a view. The food has won high praise, and the wine list is excellent. A barbecued lunch is often served on the beach.

North Sound (P.O. Box 54), Virgin Gorda, B.V.I. © **800/223-1108** in the U.S., or 284/494-3555. Fax 284/494-3557. www.biras.com. 31 units. Winter $810–$1,100 double, $1,710 suite for 4; off season $585–$885 double, $1,185 suite for 4. Rates include all meals. Ask about packages. AE, MC, V. Take the private motor launch from the Beef Island airport, $160 per person round-trip. No children under age 8. **Amenities:** Restaurant; 2 bars; outdoor pool; 2 lit tennis courts; fitness center; massage; babysitting; laundry service; dry cleaning; bikes; free beach trips; Hobie Cats; kayaks; snorkeling; Sunfish sailboats; taxi service to launch. *In room:* A/C, dataport, fridge, beverage maker, hair dryer, iron, safe.

Bitter End Yacht Club ✦✦✦   This place is the liveliest of the B.V.I. resorts, and is better equipped than the more exclusive Biras Creek. It's the best sailing and diving complex in the British chain, opening onto one of the most unspoiled, secluded deep-water harbors in the Caribbean. Guests have unlimited use of the resort's million-dollar fleet and a complimentary introductory course at the Nick Trotter Sailing and Windsurfing School. The Bitter End offers an informal yet elegant experience in either a hillside chalet or a well-appointed beachfront or hillside villa overlooking the sound. Most units have varnished hardwood floors, sliding-glass doors, and wicker furnishings. All villas have two twins, two queen-size, or a king-size bed, plus a large dressing area and a shower with sea views.

For something novel, you can stay aboard one of the 9m (30-ft.) yachts, yours to sail, complete with dockage and daily maid service, meals in the Yacht Club dining room, and overnight provisions. Each yacht has a shower and can accommodate four comfortably.

First-rate meals are available in the Clubhouse Steak and Seafood Grille, the English Carvery, and the Pub, and a steel drum or reggae band often provides entertainment.

John O Point, North Sound (P.O. Box 46), Virgin Gorda, B.V.I. © 800/872-2392 in the U.S. for reservations, or 284/494-2746. Fax 284/494-4756. www.beyc.com. 85 units, 4 yachts. Winter (double occupancy) $630–$760 beachfront villa, suite, yacht, or hillside villa; off season (double occupancy) $465–$490 all units. Rates include all meals. AE, MC, V. Take the private ferry from the Beef Island airport, $25 per person one-way. **Amenities:** 3 restaurants; pub; outdoor pool; fitness center; babysitting; laundry service; dry cleaning; boat trips to nearby cays; Boston whalers; scuba diving; snorkeling; sport-fishing; Sunfish sailing; windsurfing. *In room:* A/C (in some), TV (available upon request), fridge, beverage maker.

Katitche Point Greathouse ★★★ (Finds)

Designed by British architect Michael Helm, this luxurious, spacious "greathouse" serves the needs of the most discerning travelers. Affording total privacy, it can only be rented as a complete villa for up to 13 people, with more than 185 sq. m (2,000 sq. ft.) of living space. Sometimes 6 couples or one family or even two families share the villa like a first-class commune. This luxury vacation spot comprises a pool, four suites, and one master bedroom, all lying just above the panoramic sweep of Mahoe Bay and its beach. The main structure of the villa is shaped like a pyramid, rising three floors. Each bedroom comes with its own bathroom with shower plus a private veranda opening onto sweeping views. All four suites are identical in size and furnishings, while the master bedroom is decorated differently. All the beds are made of handcrafted teak, and are furnished with a king-size, anti-allergic mattress. A steel ladder leads to the tallest point of the villa, a "Crow's Nest" at the top of the pyramid on the third level.

Plum Bay Rd., The Valley, Virgin Gorda, B.V.I. © 284/495-5672. Fax 284/495-5674. www.katitchepoint.com. 5 units. Winter 4 suites $10,925 weekly, 4 villas and master suite $14,950 weekly; off season 4 villas $12,400 weekly, 4 villas and master suite $17,500 weekly. Additional supplement for those who wish to also rent the master bedroom. MC, V. **Amenities:** Bar; outdoor pool; watersports equipment; laundry service. *In room:* A/C, TV, hair dryer.

Little Dix Bay Hotel ★★ (Kids)

This palace of low-key luxury is scattered along a .8km (½-mile) crescent-shaped, white-sand beach and private bay, on a 200-hectare (494-acre) preserve. Many guests find this resort too pricey and stuffy; we ourselves prefer the more casual elegance of Biras Creek Estate and the Bitter End Yacht Club, though Little Dix Bay does have an undeniably lovely setting, fine service, and a quiet elegance.

All rooms are surrounded by forest, and boast private terraces with views of the sea or gardens. Trade winds come through louvers and screens, and units have ceiling fans and air-conditioning. Some units are two-story rondavels (like Tiki huts) raised on stilts to form their own breezeways. Accommodations are roomy, airy, and decorated with tropical flair; each has a smart private bathroom with shower stall. All guest rooms have been renovated. The new furnishings and fabrics evoke Southeast Asia—beautiful wicker or reed furniture, bamboo beds, Balinese boxes and baskets, and ceramic objets d'art. The hotel has added two villas on an isolated stretch of white beach, each with dazzling white interiors and alfresco dining pavilions.

1km (⅔ mile) north of Spanish Town (P.O. Box 70), Virgin Gorda, B.V.I. ⓒ 888/ 767-3966 in the U.S., or 284/495-5555. Fax 284/495-5661. www.littledixbay.com. 100 units. Winter $625–$825 double, $1,800 suite; off season $325–$595 double, from $900 suite. MAP (breakfast and dinner) $90 per person extra. Extra person $75. AE, DC, MC, V. Take the private ferry from the Beef Island airport, $75 per person round-trip. **Amenities:** 3 restaurants; 2 bars; 7 tennis courts; fitness center; sauna; children's programs; limited room service; massage; babysitting; laundry service; deep-sea fishing; island tours; jeep rental; kayaks; scuba diving; snorkeling; Sunfish sailboats; water-skiing. *In room:* A/C, fridge, iron, safe.

EXPENSIVE

Nail Bay Resort ⓡ   Near Gorda Peak National Park, and a short walk from a trio of usually-deserted beaches, this resort enjoys an idyllic position. You can enjoy some of the best sunset views of Sir Francis Drake Channel and the Dog Islands from this 59-hectare (146-acre) site. All the units are comfortable and tastefully furnished, and each has a bathroom containing a shower stall. Accommodations options are wide ranging, from deluxe bedrooms to suites to apartments to villas. The villa community has a core of a dozen units in two structures on a hillside, with sitting areas amid old sugar mill ruins. The most modest units are hotel-style bedrooms in the main building. The best accommodations are the four estate villas—Sunset Watch, Mystic Water, Island Spice, and Island Dream.

At night, Nail Bay evokes a luxury property in Asia, its landscaping highlighted by meandering stone walkways. One devotee told us that when she found the resort, it had the "terra-ultima exclusivity of Mustique, without that island's elitism."

Nail Bay (P.O. Box 69), Virgin Gorda, B.V.I. ⓒ 800/871-3551 in the U.S., 800/487-1839 in Canada, or 284/494-8000. Fax 284/495-5875. www.nailbay.com. Winter $125–$250 double; off season $99–$175 double. AE, DISC, MC, V. **Amenities:** Restaurant; swim-up bar; outdoor pool; lit tennis court; Jacuzzi; babysitting; laundry service; dry cleaning; nonsmoking rooms; kayaks; scuba diving; snorkeling; water skiing; windsurfing. *In room:* A/C, TV, dataport, kitchen, beverage maker, hair dryer, iron, safe.

Old Yard Village 🐀🐀 Under the name of Olde Yard Inn, this was the coziest and most intimate B&B in the B.V.I. But the Olde Yard Inn is no longer. Owner Carol Kaufman has entered the 21st century with some of the most up-to-date accommodations on the island—a choice of luxury studios, one-, two-, and three-bedroom apartments, and two-bedroom town houses ranging from small to spacious. (All accommodations are non-smoking). Every bedroom comes with a private bathroom with tub or shower. The top-floor units have the most expansive ocean views. Wide, breezy porches on each unit are another allure. Surrounded by foliage, the complex faces the ocean. The nearest and best beach is at Savannah Bay, a 1.6km (1-mile) drive away. On-site is **La Brasserie,** serving Continental meals, and a commissary where you can buy groceries.

The Valley, Virgin Gorda, B.V.I. ℭ 284/495-5544. Fax 284/495-5986. www.oldeyard village.com. 26 units. Winter (minimum 3 nights): $266 studio, $295 1-bedroom, $328–$358 2-bedroom, $410 3-bedroom; off season (2 night minimum stay): $210 studio, $240 1-bedroom, $270–$300 2-bedroom, $350 3-bedroom. **Amenities:** Restaurant; bar; outdoor pool; 2 tennis courts; fitness center; in-room massage; babysitting; coin-operated laundry; 1 room for those w/limited mobility room; playground; sailing; scuba diving; snorkeling. *In room:* A/C, TV, dataport, kitchen, hair dryer, iron, safe.

MODERATE

Guavaberry Spring Bay Vacation Homes 🐀 Staying in one of these hexagonal, white-roofed redwood houses, all of which are built on stilts, is like living in a tree house. Screened and louvered walls let in sea breezes. Each unique home, available for daily or weekly rental, has one or two bedrooms; all have full kitchens, dining areas, and private bathrooms with showers. Each also has an elevated sun deck overlooking Sir Francis Drake Passage. Within a few minutes of the cottage colony is the beach at Spring Bay, and the Baths, with its excellent sandy beach, is also nearby. The Yacht Harbour Shopping Centre is 2km (1¼ miles) away.

Spring Bay (P.O. Box 20), Virgin Gorda, B.V.I. ℭ 284/495-5227. Fax 284/495-5283. www.guavaberryspringbay.com. 18 units. Winter $195 1-bedroom house, $265 2-bedroom house; off season $130 1-bedroom house, $185 2-bedroom house. Extra person $17–$22. No credit cards. **Amenities:** Babysitting; fishing; sailing; scuba diving; snorkeling; boats; jeep rental; shop. *In room:* Kitchen, fridge, beverage maker, no phone.

Mango Bay Resort 🐀 *Value* This well-designed compound of eight white-sided villas is on lushly landscaped grounds overlooking the scattered islets of Drake's Channel, on the island's western shore. You get good value for your money here. The accommodations are the most adaptable on the island—doors can be locked or unlocked to divide each villa into as many as four independent units. Costs vary with the proximity of your unit to the nearby beach. Interiors are stylish yet simple, often dominated by the same turquoise as the seascape in front of you. Daily maid service is included. You can cook in, or dine on-site at **Giorgio's Table** (see "Where to Dine," below), which is quite good and serves three meals a day.

Mahoe Bay (P.O. Box 1062), Virgin Gorda, B.V.I. ℂ **800/223-6510** in the U.S., 800/424-5500 in Canada, or 284/495-5672. Fax 284/495-5674. www.mangobayresort.com. 15 units. Winter $132–$187 studio, $275 1-bedroom unit, $363 2-bedroom unit, $275 beachfront suite, $700 2-bedroom beachfront villa; off season $109–$143 studio, $197 1-bedroom unit, $259 2-bedroom unit, $197 beachfront suite, $510 2-bedroom beachfront villa. MC, V. **Amenities:** Restaurant; bar; nonsmoking rooms; kayaks; sailing; snorkeling. *In room:* A/C, kitchen.

INEXPENSIVE
The Wheelhouse/Ocean View Hotel
This cinder-block building is definitely no-frills, although it is conveniently located near a shopping center and the Virgin Gorda Marina, and only a 15-minute walk from the beach. The rooms are clean and simply furnished, often done in pastels with two single beds or a double bed. All are equipped with a small bathroom. Children are welcome, and babysitting can be arranged. The rooms are on the second floor, with a long porch front and back, and downstairs is an inexpensive restaurant. There's also a garden in back.

Spanish Town, across from the marina. ℂ **284/495-5230.** 12 units. Winter $85 double; off season $70 double. AE, MC, V. **Amenities:** Restaurant; bar; babysitting. *In room:* A/C, TV.

WHERE TO DINE
EXPENSIVE
Biras Creek Estate 𝓰𝓰 INTERNATIONAL   With even better cuisine than that of Little Dix Bay Pavilion (see below), this hilltop restaurant is our longtime favorite, and for good reason. The resort hires the island's finest chefs, who turn out superb cuisine based on quality ingredients. The menu changes every night, but the panoramic view of North Sound doesn't. A recent sampling of the appetizers turned up five-spice duck salad for starters, followed by such main courses as pan-seared salmon wrapped in Parma ham in a lentil-cream sauce. The chef makes grilled lobster daily. Desserts are prepared fresh, and are likely to range from a chilled green-apple parfait to a choice of sorbets served with a chilled cantaloupe soup.

In Biras Creek, North Sound. ℂ **284/494-3555.** Reservations required. Fixed-price dinner $65. AE, MC, V. Seatings daily 7–8:30pm.

Little Dix Bay Pavilion ✿ INTERNATIONAL The most romantic of the dining spots on Virgin Gorda, this pavilion is our preferred choice at this deluxe resort, which also operates Sugar Mill Restaurant. Guests (most middle-aged and well-heeled) sit under a large thatched roof as trade winds breeze in through open doors. The chefs change the menu daily. Although many of the ingredients are shipped in frozen, especially meats, there is much that is fresh and good. The seafood keeps us returning again and again. Most dishes are at the lower end of the price range.

In the Little Dix Bay Hotel, 1km (²⁄₃ mile) north of Spanish Town. ✆ **284/495-5555.** Reservations recommended. Main courses $25–$45. AE, MC, V. Daily 9–10am, 12:30–2:30pm, and 6–9pm.

MODERATE

Chez Bamboo ✿ *Finds* CAJUN/CREOLE This is the closest approximation to a New Orleans supper club in Virgin Gorda. Located within a 5-minute walk north of the yacht club, the building features a big veranda. Inside, there's a wraparound mural showing a jazz band playing within a forest of bamboo; bamboo artifacts continue the theme. Owner Rose Giacinto and chef Joyce Rodriguez concoct superb dishes, including conch gumbo and Nassau grouper *en papillote*. Desserts such as apple *crostini* and crème brûlée are among the very best on the island. Live music, usually blues or jazz, is presented every Friday night on the terrace.

Next to the Virgin Gorda Yacht Harbour, Spanish Town. ✆ **284/495-5752.** Reservations recommended. Main courses $20–$40. AE, MC, V. Daily 3–10pm.

The Flying Iguana MEDITERRANEAN/FRENCH/WEST INDIAN The owner of this place, Puck (aka Orlington Baptiste), studied his craft in Kansas City, with the Hilton Group, before setting up this amiable restaurant overlooking the airport's landing strip and the sea. Potted hibiscus and lots of effigies of iguanas, stuffed and carved, ornament a room that's a celebration of West Indian mystique. The house drink is the Iguana Sunset, a concoction whose ingredients change according to the whim of the bartender. Whatever the recipe, it usually produces a lightheaded effect that goes well with the cuisine. The finest examples include fresh fish and all kinds of shellfish, often served in combination. You'll also find steak, chicken, and lamb, seasoned in a way that evokes both the Caribbean and the Mediterranean. Happy hour is from 4 to 6pm daily.

The Valley, at the airport. ✆ **284/495-5277.** Reservations recommended. Main courses $6–$15 lunch, $15–$40 dinner. MC, V. Daily 7am–9pm (last order).

Giorgio's Table 🅡 Finds ITALIAN   This is the only authentic Italian restaurant on the island, with chefs flown in for the season from Venice, Milan, and Florence. A 15-minute drive north of Spanish Town, the restaurant opens onto a covered terrace. We like to sit out here at night, gazing up at the heavens with the sounds of the surf nearby. The varnished interior evokes a yacht. The chef says he cooks Italian instead of "American Italian," and the food is good, despite its reliance on a lot of imported ingredients. Fresh local fish is generally the best bet. You can also order an array of pastas and such standard Italian staples as veal scaloppine. Pizzas and sandwiches fill you at lunch. We decided that the restaurant's owner, Giorgio, has an appropriate last name—Paradisio.

Mahoe Bay. 🕿 **284/495-5684.** Reservations recommended. Main courses $15–$20 lunch, $30–$40 dinner. AE, MC, V. Daily noon–3pm and 6:30–9pm.

INEXPENSIVE

The Bath & Turtle INTERNATIONAL   At the end of the waterfront shopping plaza in Spanish Town sits the most popular pub on Virgin Gorda, packed with locals during happy hour, from 4 to 6pm. There are indoor and courtyard tables. You might want to join the regulars over midmorning mango coladas or peach daiquiris. If you're hungry, you can order fried fish fingers, tamarind-ginger wings, spicy chili, pizzas, fresh pasta, barbecued chicken, steak, lobster, or daily seafood specials. There's live music every Wednesday and Friday night, at 8:30 pm, during the summer.

Virgin Gorda Yacht Harbour, Spanish Town. 🕿 **284/495-5239.** Reservations recommended. Breakfast $4–$10; main courses $10–$15 lunch, $10–$32 dinner. AE, MC, V. Daily 7:30am–11pm.

Thelma's Hideout 🅡 Finds CARIBBEAN   Mrs. Thelma King, one of the grande dames of Virgin Gorda (who worked in Manhattan for many years before returning to her native B.V.I.), runs this convivial gathering place for the island's locals. It's in a concrete house with angles softened by ascending tiers of verandas. Food choices include steamed and grilled fish, fish filets, and West Indian stews containing pork, mutton, goat, or chicken. Limeade or mauby are available, but many stick to rum or beer. Live music is presented on Saturday nights in winter, and every other Saturday off season.

The Valley. 🕿 **284/495-5646.** Reservations required prior to 3pm for dinner. Main courses $9–$12 lunch, $18–$25 dinner. No credit cards. Daily 8–10am, 11:30am–2:30pm, and 6–9pm; bar daily 8am–9pm.

Top of The Baths CARIBBEAN This aptly-named green-and-white restaurant overlooks the famous Baths (see below), and has a patio with a swimming pool. Locals gather to enjoy the food they grew up on. At lunch, you can order an array of appetizers, sandwiches, and salad plates. At night, the kitchen turns out good home-style cookery, including fresh fish, lobster, chicken, steaks, and West Indian dishes. Save room for a piece of that rum cake. Steel bands perform on Sunday, and you're invited to swim in the pool before or after dining.

The Valley. ✆ 284/495-5497. Dinner $16–$31; sandwiches and salads $6.50–$10. AE, MC, V. Daily 8am–10pm.

EXPLORING THE ISLAND

The northern side of Virgin Gorda is mountainous, with Gorda Peak reaching 417m (1,370 ft.). In contrast, the southern half of the island is flat, with large boulders at every turn.

If you're over for a day trip, the best way to see the island is to call **Andy Flax** at the Fischer's Cove Beach Hotel. He runs the **Virgin Gorda Tours Association** (✆ 284/495-5252), which will give you a tour of the island for $20 per person. The tour leaves twice daily, or more often based on demand. You can be picked up at the ferry dock if you give 24-hour notice.

SURF & SAND

HITTING THE BEACH The best beaches are at **the Baths** ⋆⋆, where giant boulders form a series of tranquil pools and grottoes flooded with seawater (nearby snorkeling is excellent, and you can rent gear on the beach). Scientists think the boulders were brought to the surface eons ago by volcanic activity. The Baths and surrounding areas are part of a proposed system of parks and protected areas in the B.V.I. The protected area encompasses 273 hectares (684 acres) of land, including sites at Little Fort, Spring Bay, the Baths, and Devil's Bay on the east coast.

Devil's Bay National Park can be reached by a trail from the Baths. The walk to the secluded coral-sand beach takes about 15 minutes through boulders and dry coastal vegetation. Neighboring the Baths is **Spring Bay,** one of the best of the island's beaches, with white sand, clear water, and good snorkeling. **Trunk Bay** is a wide, sandy beach reachable by boat or along a rough path from Spring Bay. **Savannah Bay** is a sandy beach north of the yacht harbor, and **Mahoe Bay,** at the Mango Bay Resort, has a gently curving beach with neon-blue water.

DIVING   **Kilbrides Sunchaser Scuba** is at the Bitter End Resort at North Sound (© **800/932-4286** in the U.S., or 284/495-9638). Kilbrides offers the best diving in the British Virgin Islands, at 15 to 20 dive sites including the wreck of the ill-fated HMS *Rhone*. Prices range from $80 to $95 for a two-tank dive on one of the coral reefs. A one-tank dive in the afternoon costs $65. Equipment, except wet suits, is supplied at no charge. Hours are 7:45am to 5pm daily.

HIKING   Consider a trek up the stairs and hiking paths that criss-cross Virgin Gorda's largest stretch of undeveloped land, the **Gorda Peak National Park.** To reach the best departure point for your uphill trek, drive north of the Valley on the only road leading to North Sound for about 15 minutes of very hilly driving (using a four-wheel-drive vehicle is a very good idea). Stop at the base of the stairway leading steeply uphill. There's a sign pointing to the Gorda Peak National Park.

It will take between 25 and 40 minutes to reach the summit of Gorda Peak, the highest point on the island, where views out over many islets of the Virgin Islands archipelago await you. There's a tower at the summit, which you can climb for even better views. Admire the flora and the fauna (birds, lizards, and nonvenomous snakes) en route. Because the vegetation you'll encounter is not particularly lush, wear protection against the sun. Consider bringing a picnic—tables are scattered along the hiking trails.

SHOPPING

There isn't much here. Your best bet is the **Virgin Gorda Craft Shop** at Yacht Harbour (© **284/495-5137**), which has some good arts and crafts, especially straw items. Some of the more upscale hotels have boutiques, notably the Bitter End Yacht Club's **Reeftique** (© **284/494-2745**), with its selection of sports clothing, including sundresses and logo wear. You can also purchase a hat here for protection from the sun. You might also check out **Island Silhouette in Flax Plaza** (no phone), located in Flax Plaza near Fischer's Cove Beach Hotel, which has a good selection of resort-style clothing that's been hand-painted by local artists. **Pusser's Company Store,** Leverick Bay (© **284/495-7369**), sells rum products, sportswear, and gift and souvenir items. **Tropical Gift Collections,** the Baths (© **284/495-5380**), is a good place to shop for local crafts. Here you'll find island spices, bags, T-shirts, wraps, jewelry, maps, and pottery on sale at good prices.

VIRGIN GORDA AFTER DARK

There isn't a lot of action at night, unless you want to make some of your own. **The Bath & Turtle** pub, at Yacht Harbour (© 284/495-5239), brings in local bands for dancing in the summer on Wednesday and Friday at 8:30pm. The **Bitter End Yacht Club** (© 284/494-2746) has live music on Fridays. Accessible only by boat, this is the best bar on the island. With its dark wood, it evokes an English pub and serves British brews. Call to see what's happening at the time of your visit, and see p. 190 for more on the establishment.

Andy's **Chateau de Pirate,** at the Fischer's Cove Beach Hotel, The Valley (© 284/495-5252), is a sprawling, sparsely furnished local hangout. It has a simple stage, a very long bar, and huge oceanfront windows, which almost never close.

4 Peter Island ⓕ

Half of this island, boasting a marina and docking facilities, is devoted to the yacht club. The other part is deserted. A gorgeous beach is at palm-fringed Deadman's Bay, which faces the Atlantic but is protected by a reef. All goods and services are at the one resort (see below). The island is so sparsely populated that about the only company you'll encounter will be an iguana or a feral cat whose ancestors were abandoned generations ago by shippers (the cats are said to have eliminated the island's rodents).

A complimentary, hotel-operated ferry, **Peter Island Boat** (© 284/495-1288), departs Tortola from the pier at Trellis Bay, near the airport. Other boats depart six or seven times a day from Baugher's Bay in Road Town, on Tortola. Passengers must notify the hotel 2 weeks before their arrival so transportation can be arranged.

WHERE TO STAY & DINE

Peter Island Resort ⓕⓕⓕ   This 720-hectare (1,778-acre) tropical island is dedicated to Peter Island Resort guests and to yacht owners who moor their crafts here. The island's tropical gardens and hillside are bordered by five gorgeous private beaches, including Deadman's Beach (often voted one of the world's most romantic beaches in travel-magazine reader polls). The resort contains 32 rooms facing Sprat Bay and Sir Francis Drake Channel (oceanview or garden rooms) and 20 larger rooms on Deadman's Bay Beach (beachfront rooms). Designed with a casual elegance, each has a balcony or terrace. The least desirable rooms are also the smallest, housed in two-story,

A-frame structures next to the harbor. Bathrooms with tub/shower combinations range from standard motel-unit types to luxurious offerings, depending on your room assignment. The Crow's Nest, a four-bedroom villa, overlooks the harbor and Deadman Bay, and features a private swimming pool. The Hawk's Nest villas are three-bedroom villas on a hillside.

Peter Island (P.O. Box 211), Road Town, Tortola, B.V.I. © **800/346-4451** in the U.S., or 284/495-2000. Fax 284/495-2500. www.peterisland.com. 54 units. Winter $865–$1,015 double, $4,000 3-bedroom villa, $8,000 4-bedroom villa; off season $550–$650 double, $2,850–$3,200 3-bedroom villa, $5,700-$7,900 4-bedroom villa. Rates include all meals and transportation from the Tortola airport. AE, MC, V. **Amenities:** 2 restaurants; 2 bars; outdoor pool; 4 tennis courts; fitness center; spa; limited room service; massage; babysitting; laundry service; dry cleaning; nonsmoking rooms; bikes; deep-sea fishing; sea kayaks; scuba diving; snorkeling gear; Sunfish sailboats; water-skiing; windsurfing. *In room:* A/C, minibar, hair dryer, iron, safe.

5 Guana Island ⟨★

This 340-hectare (840-acre) island, a nature preserve and wildlife sanctuary, is one of the most private hideaways in the Caribbean. Consider vacationing here if you want to retreat from the world. This small island, off the coast of Tortola, offers seven virgin beaches, plus nature trails ideal for hiking. Unusual species of plant and animal life abound, and Arawak relics have been found here. You can climb 242m (794-ft.) Sugarloaf Mountain for a panoramic view. It's said that the name of the island comes from a jutting rock that resembles the head of an iguana.

The Guana Island Club will send a boat to meet arriving guests at the Beef Island airport (trip time is 10 min.).

WHERE TO STAY & DINE

Guana Island Club ⟨★★   Guana Island was bought in 1974 by Henry and Gloria Jarecki, dedicated conservationists who run the resort as a nature preserve and wildlife sanctuary. Upon your arrival on the island, a Land Rover will meet you and transport you up one of the most scenic hills in the region, in the northeast of Guana.

The cluster of white cottages was built as a private club in the 1930s. The stone cottages never hold more than 30 guests (and have only two phones), and because the dwellings are staggered along a flower-dotted ridge overlooking the Caribbean and the Atlantic, the sense of privacy is almost absolute. The entire island can be rented by groups of up to 30. Although water is scarce, each of the airy accommodations has a shower. The decor is rattan and wicker, and each unit has a ceiling fan. Renting North Beach cottage, the most luxurious, is like renting a private home complete with a freshwater pool. The panoramic sweep from the terraces is spectacular, particularly at sunset. There are seven beaches, some of which require a boat to reach. Guests will find a convivial atmosphere at the rattan-furnished clubhouse. Casually elegant dinners are served by candlelight on the veranda, with menus that include homegrown vegetables and Continental and U.S. specialties.

P.O. Box 32, Road Town, Tortola, B.V.I. ℭ 800/544-8262 in the U.S., or 284/494-2354. Fax 284/495-2900 or 284/499-2080. (For reservations, write or call the Guana Island Club Reservations Office, 10 Timber Trail, Rye, NY 10580; ℭ 800/544-8262 in the U.S., or 914/967-6050; fax 914/967-8048.) www.guana.com. 15 units. Winter $895 double, $1,850 cottage; off season $595–$650 double, $1,250–$1,350 cottage. Rent the island for $12,500–$16,500. Rates include all meals and drinks served with meals. MC, V. Closed Sept–Oct. **Amenities:** Restaurant; self-service bar; 2 tennis courts; massage; babysitting; laundry service; dry cleaning; complimentary transport; fishing; kayaks; sailboats; snorkeling; nature trails; waterskiing; windsurfing. *In room:* Dataport, no phone.

Index

THE NEW TRAVELOCITY GUARANTEE

EVERYTHING YOU BOOK WILL BE RIGHT, OR WE'LL WORK WITH OUR TRAVEL PARTNERS TO MAKE IT RIGHT, RIGHT AWAY.

*To drive home the point,
we're going to use the word "right" in every single sentence.*

Let's get right to it. Right to the meat! Only Travelocity guarantees everything about your booking will be right, or we'll work with our travel partners to make it right, right away. Right on!

Here's a picture taken smack dab right in the middle of Antigua, where the guarantee also covers you.

The guarantee covers all but one of the items pictured to the right.

For example, what if the ocean view you booked actually looks out at a downright ugly parking lot? You'd be right to call – we're there for you. And no one in their right mind would be pleased to learn the rental car place has closed and left them stranded. Call Travelocity and we'll help get you back on the right track.

Now, you may be thinking, "Yeah, right, I'm so sure." That's OK; you have the right to remain skeptical. That is until we mention help is always right around the corner. Call us right off the bat, knowing that our customer service reps are there for you 24/7. Righting wrongs. Left and right.

Now if you're guessing there are some things we can't control, like the weather, well you're right. But we can help you with most things – to get all the details in righting,* visit **travelocity.com/guarantee**.

*Sorry, spelling things right is one of the few things not covered under the guarantee.

I'd give my right arm for a guarantee like this, although I'm glad I don't have to.

travelocity
You'll never roam alone.